Books by Thomas H. Ormsbee

Early American Furniture Makers

The Story of American Furniture

If You're Going to Live in the Country
(with Richmond Huntley)

Collecting Antiques in America

Staffordshire Pottery
(with Josiah Wedgwood)

Antique Furniture of the Walnut Period
(with R. W. Symonds)

A Storehouse of Antiques

Prime Antiques and Their Current Prices

Care and Repair of Antiques

Field Guide to Early American Furniture

Field Guide to American Victorian Furniture

Know Your Heirlooms

English China and Its Marks

The Windsor Chair

Field Guide
TO
AMERICAN
Victorian Furniture

A VICTORIAN ORIGINAL

Parlor of the Theodore Roosevelt birthplace, New York City. The furniture is in the Louis XV Victorian substyle (1850 to 1865).

Field Guide

TO

AMERICAN
Victorian Furniture

by

Thomas H. Ormsbee

DRAWINGS BY ERNST HALBERSTADT

Bonanza Books · New York

This edition published by Bonanza Books,
a division of Crown Publishers, Inc.,
by arrangement with Little, Brown and Company

I

To

N. B.

who piloted the stream

Code Symbols
and Table of Comparative Values

A		*Under* $ 15	
AA	$ 15	to	$ 40
AAA	$ 40	to	$ 75
B	$ 75	to	$ 125
BB	$ 125	to	$ 175
BBB	$ 175	to	$ 250
C	$ 250	to	$ 400
CC	$ 400	to	$ 600
CCC	$ 600	to	$ 900
#	*Over* $ 900		

Note:

Fine, authentic Belter armchairs, side chairs, sofas, etc., in original unrepaired condition have a comparative value approaching double that indicated for Belter furniture in general.

Acknowledgments

THE AUTHOR is indebted to many Victorian furniture enthusiasts for information in this book. For their patience in answering his many questions and their kindness in putting their knowledge at his disposal, he wishes to express his deep appreciation.

For the loan of pictures and furniture manufacturers' catalogues he especially wishes to thank Walter Baker & Co., Dorchester, Mass.; S. A. Beckwith, Litchfield, Conn.; Miss Beverly Bender, Pound Ridge, N. Y.; Albert Brinkman, Jr., Buffalo, N. Y.; John V. Bronk, Wilton, Conn.; Leo Albert Busky, Utica, N. Y.; Gifford A. Cochran, North Salem, N. Y.; Dr. George P. Coopernail, Bedford Village, N. Y.; Chester County Historical Society, West Chester, Pa.; Mr. and Mrs. Robert Curry, Lewisboro, N. Y.; Jack Daniel, Centralia, Ill.; Philip Dunn, Long Ridge, Stamford, Conn.; the Edison Institute, Dearborn, Mich.; Frederick M. Feiker, Washington, D. C.; Mrs. Edward M. Foote, Cornwall, Conn.; W. J. French, Camden, Me.; French & Company, New York City; Miss Helen C. Frick, New York City; Rockwell Gardner, Long Ridge, Stamford, Conn.

Also O. Rundle Gilbert, Garrison-on-Hudson, N. Y.; Mrs. Dolle Gorin, Norwalk, Conn.; Robert G. Hall, Dover-Foxcroft, Me.; Robert Harpin, West Warwick, R. I.; the Home Insurance Company, New York City; Index of American Design, National Gallery of Art,

Washington, D. C.; C. Albert Jacob, Jr., Scarsdale, N. Y.;
Mrs. Samuel Joseph, Cincinnati, Ohio; Chauncey H.
Jordan, Wilton, Conn.; Raymond Krotz, Ridgefield,
Conn.; Mrs. Florine Maine, Ridgefield, Conn.; Mr. and
Mrs. John Meinke, Westport, Conn.; the Metropolitan
Museum of Art, New York City; Munson-Williams-
Proctor Institute, Utica, N. Y.; the Museum of Arts and
Decorations, Cooper Union, New York City; the
Museum of the City of New York; Barry Oliver, Wilton,
Conn.; Miss Helen Ormsbee, Brooklyn, N. Y.; Martha
Jane Parkinson, Philadelphia, Pa.; the Philadelphia
Museum of Art; Mrs. Harris K. Prior, Utica, N. Y.; the
Roosevelt Memorial Association, New York City; Miss
Pearl Ann Reeder, Editor, *Hobbies;* Mr. and Mrs. Walter
S. Sands, Essex, Conn.; Herman A. Schindler, Charles-
ton, S. C.; the Sheldon Art Museum, Middlebury,
Vermont; Harriet Sherry, New York City; Miss Marjorie
M. Smith, Editor, *Spinning Wheel;* the Smithsonian In-
stitution, Washington, D. C.; Rena Walker Thayer, Sun-
cook, N. H.; the Valentine Museum, Richmond, Va.;
H. D. Wall, Nashville, Tenn.; Mrs. William H. Whitton,
Pound Ridge, N. Y.; Miss Alice Winchester, Editor,
Antiques; H. Ogden Wintermute, Editor, *American
Antiques Journal;* the Wisconsin State Historical Society,
Madison, Wisconsin and G. Arthur Cook, Boylston, Ala.

Contents

Furniture Makers' Language

ACORN FINIAL. End ornament acorn-shaped.

ACANTHUS LEAF. A conventionalized carved detail.

APPLIED CRESTING. Carved piece, done separately, and attached to the top rail of a chair or sofa as a crest.

APPLIED ORNAMENT. A detail that is shaped or carved separately, and later attached to the surface of a piece. Also called "Applied work."

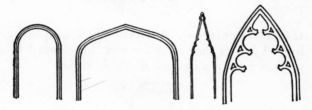

ARCHES. Those used on Victorian furniture include the Roman or semicircular, the Gothic or pointed, the very slender or lancet, and the flat (or cusp) arch.

ARCADED. A series of low-relief arches used to decorate cornice or frieze.

ARCHED MOLDING. Plain, half-round convex molding used singly or in pairs.

ARCHITECTURAL FURNITURE. Large piece in which the design includes architectural features or matches the trim of a room.

ARM PAD. A stuffed upholstered pad on a chair arm.

ARM STUMP. The front support of a chair arm that replaces the upward extension of a front leg. Sometimes called an "Arm support."

ASTRAGAL. A convex molding chiefly used to overlap the joining of double doors in secretaries, cupboards and bookcases.

BAIL HANDLE. A brass pendent half-loop, with ends anchored in the attached posts, serving as a drawer pull.

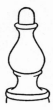

BALL-AND-STEEPLE FINIAL. A turned finial with a well-formed ball as the lowest element, surmounted by a series of ring turnings that diminish in size.

BALL FOOT. Boldly turned in the shape of a ball, small or of ample proportions.

BALL LEG TIP. A small brass ball-shaped foot with cup above, which fits over the end of a table or chair leg.

BALLOON BACK. A chair back shaped like the outline of a spherical balloon.

BALUSTER-TURNED. Originally one of the small columns supporting a railing. In furniture, a turning that resembles such a column.

BANDING. A narrow border framing a drawer front, a band of contrasting inlay or a border of veneer framing the textile or leather panel on the writing surface of a desk.

BAROQUE FURNITURE. Characterized by conspicuous curves, scrolls and highly ornate decoration. Of Italian origin. In Victorian furniture, typical of the Louis XV substyle.

BASE. The element on a piece of case furniture (*see* Case Piece) immediately above the feet. Also the lower section of any two-part piece.

BATTENS. Projecting strips of wood fastened across one or more boards as cleats.

BEAD MOLDING. *See* Cock-Bead Molding.

BEARER STRIP. A narrow piece of wood, at the bottom of a drawer opening, on which the front rests when drawer is closed.

BEVEL. A slanting cutting-away of the edge of a board or sheet of glass to reduce thickness.

BLACKAMOOR. A carved wooden figure of a Negro in Arabic or Turkish dress. Originally copied from the slaves owned by wealthy early Venetians. Generally made in pairs.

BOBBIN-TURNED. The bulging element of turned lengths, so called from resemblance to a wound bobbin.

BODY-CONFORMING. Shaped to the human form. Used with seats of Windsor chairs and wooden settees.

BOSS. A small circular or oval applied ornament.

BOW FRONT. The front of a case piece (*see* Case Piece) with a continuous outcurve.

BOX STRETCHER. One where the square or turned members are so placed as to form a square or rectangle.

BRACKET. A shaped support that reinforces the joining of a leg to the seat rail of a chair, or to a table bed.

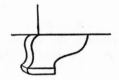

BRACKET FOOT. A simple case support running two ways from a mitered or rounded corner, with inner edges cut in silhouette. Is of two types, plain or scrolled.

BREAK FRONT. A type of front on a case piece, having a projecting central section.

BROKEN PEDIMENT. A pediment where the cyma-curved or straight slanting elements do not meet at the apex.

BURL VENEER. Figured, mottled or speckled veneer, cut from an excrescence on a tree trunk.

BUTT HINGE. Hinge with plain rectangular leaves. Is attached on doors so that only rounded pin point shows.

BUTT JOINT. A joining of squared edges of two members at right angles.

CABRIOLE LEG. A curved leg with outcurved knee and incurved ankle. Originated in Italy and is a conventionalized representation of the rear leg of a leaping goat.

CANE. Long, narrow strips of rattan bark used for weaving seats and backs of chairs and settees.

CANOPY. The framework, frequently textile-covered, that surmounts the tall posts of a bed. Also called a "tester."

CANTED. Slanting or sloping. Part of a piece of furniture that slants or slopes, such as a canted corner or leg.

CARCASE. The body of a case piece of furniture.

CARTOUCHE. Ornamental feature, carved or inlaid; usual form an unrolled scroll or an oval tablet.

CASE PIECE. Any piece of furniture of boxlike structure.

CLEAT. A strip of wood attached to a flat surface for strength, bracing or to prevent warping.

CLEATED ENDS. The strips of wood nailed or mortise-and-tenoned to the ends of some table tops.

CLUSTERED COLUMN. Three or more columns clustered together, generally done in medium relief to form a single support. Used for tall bedposts.

COCK-BEAD MOLDING. A small, half-round projecting molding.

COLONETTE. A miniature column, most frequently used in groups of four as a table pedestal.

COIL SPRING. A circular expansion spring formed of heavy wire. Used mostly for upholstered seats.

COMMODE. From French meaning "commodious," "convenient," and also a low ornamental chest of drawers. In the United States during Victorian Period, used to designate a washstand with enclosed cupboard.

CONVERSATION CHAIR. A double chair with separate seats placed vis-à-vis.

COMPOSITION. A molded substitute for carving, made of plaster of Paris, rosin and size mixed with water. Also called "Compo."

CONSOLE. From the French meaning "bracket." A table having only front legs and attached, bracketlike, to a wall.

CORNER BLOCK. A shaped or triangular block used to brace the joinings of legs and seat rails of chairs or sofas.

CORNER CHAIR. Seat is set on diagonal, fits into the corner of a room; hence the name.

CORNER STILES. The vertical members at the corner of a piece of furniture.

CORNICE. The top horizontal molding or group of moldings of a piece of furniture.

COUCH. A sofa with raised headrest and half back or none.

COVE MOLDING. Large, concave molding chiefly in cornices.

CREST RAIL. The top rail of a chair back, particularly when shaped or carved.

CRESTING. The ornamental top member of a chair, settee sofa back, or top of a pediment.

CROSS MEMBER. A structural horizontal part of a piece of furniture joined to sides or uprights.

CROSS RAIL. A horizontal member in a chair back.

CROTCH-GRAIN VENEER. Veneer generally cut from the main crotch of a mahogany tree.

CROTCHET. A small rounded and carved detail, occurring at regular intervals on the slanting edges of chair-back tops and pediments of furniture in the Gothic substyle.

CUP CASTER. A brass furniture roller with cup above that fits over the end of a chair or table leg.

CURULE CHAIR. Originally the Roman chair of office. In the Victorian Period, either an armchair or a rocker where legs are replaced by semicircular segments.

CUSP ARCH. *See* Arches.

CUSP FINIAL. A Gothic carved detail with a pointed apex above curved intersections.

CYLINDER-FRONT. The quarter-round front of a desk or secretary so mounted that it pivots.

CYMA-CURVE. A continuous curve, one half of which is concave, the other convex.

DOVETAIL. A type of joining with interlocking flaring tenons which resemble the tailfeathers of a dove.

DOWEL. A circular wooden pin used to fasten two pieces of wood.

DOWEL JOINT. Where the two pieces are strengthened by the insertion of a short length of dowel. If completely concealed, this is called a "blind dowel joint."

DROP-FRONT. A full-size hinged writing flap, which drops to the middle of a piece.

EBONIZED. Wood stained black to simulate ebony.

ESCUTCHEON. A brass keyhole plate.

ÉTAGÈRE. Large piece similar to a whatnot. Has a large mirror flanked by small graduated shelves above a projecting base.

EXTENSION TABLE. A table with split top which opens to ccommodate extra leaves.

FALL-FRONT. Writing flap of a desk or secretary which hinges from the upright to the horizontal.

FLUSH. Even or level with the surrounding surface.

FLUTING. A series of rounded furrows or channels, cut vertically on a column shaft, pilaster, leg or frieze. (Reverse of Reeding.)

FIELDING PANEL. A panel with plain surface framed by molding, beveling or grooving; or a panel composed of smaller panels.

FRETWORK OR FRETTED. An interlaced ornamental pattern, either in silhouette and pierced, or carved in low relief. Frequently done in foliated scroll or geometric motifs.

FRIEZE. The flat surface beneath a cornice.

FINIAL. A decorative finish that terminates the back uprights of a chair or the corners and center of a pediment. Generally turned or carved in urn, vase, ball or steeple form.

FINGER GRIP. A groove cut in lower edge of a drawer front, replacing a handle or knob.

FINGER-HOLE. A pierced opening in the cresting or top rail of a chair back, for ease in handling.

FINGER-MOLDED. An incised, concave continuous molding, cut into the face of a chair or sofa frame. Used especially in the Louis XV substyle.

FLARE. Outward spread, as with a chair seat that is wider at the front than at the back.

GALLERY. A railing of wood or brass rods at the rear, or rear and sides, of a top or a shelf.

GATE-LEG. A swinging leg that supports a table leaf. (Resembles a fence gate in outline, hence the name.)

GEOMETRIC. An abstract pattern evolved of interlacing squares, triangles, circles or arcs.

GESSO. A mixture of plaster of Paris, glue and water applied to wood surfaces to fill pores and obtain a glass-like smoothness. Used where surface is to be gold-leafed, or painted to simulate veneer.

GOTHIC ARCH. *See* Arches.

HIGH RELIEF. *See* Relief Carving.

INCISED CARVING. Cut into the surface ornamented.

INSET PILASTER. A pilaster inset in a flat surface. (Most frequently at the front corners of a case piece.)

JOINT. The joining of two members in the structure of a piece.

KEYHOLE ESCUTCHEON. A decorative brass plate with centered keyhole.

KEYHOLE ROSETTE. An applied wooden disk with beaded rim.

KEYHOLE SURROUND. Cast-metal inset of keyhole shape, used instead of an escutcheon.

KEYSTONE BACK. A chair or sofa back shaped like a keystone. (Used in Louis XVI substyle.)

KNEE. The outcurved upper portion of a cabriole leg. (*See* Cabriole.)

KNOB-AND-RING FINIAL. A turned finial with knob shaping above one or two elements of ring turning.

KNOB TURNING. Turning done in a series of knobs.

KNUCKLE-CARVED. Carving that resembles the knuckle of the human hand.

LACQUERED. A special finish (*see* Lacquer Furniture, Section XVI) done in gilt and colors on a black background.

LAMINATED WOOD. Made of thin layers of wood glued together with a grain of each layer at right angles to that above and below. (Used especially on Belter furniture.)

LANCET ARCH. *See* Arches.

LAP JOINT. A joint where the two pieces are cut to half-thickness and lapped one over the other.

LATTICEWORK. A crisscross pattern formed by narrow bars, either carved from one piece of wood or assembled and joined.

LAZY SUSAN TABLE. A table with circular top surmounted by a smaller revolving top, also circular. Designed to reduce passing of dishes or condiment bottles, hence the name.

LOOSE SEAT. *See* Slip Seat.

LOUNGE. *See* Couch.

LOW RELIEF. *See* Relief Carving.

LOZENGE. Diamond-shaped.

LUNETTE. A semicircular or half-moon element in a decorative design, either carved or done with lines of inlay.

LYRE. A decorative design based on the classic Greek form.

MEDIUM RELIEF. *See* Relief Carving.

MITERED POINT. A joint cut at an angle, generally 45 degrees.

MOLDED BASE. The base of a case piece formed with molded elements.

MOLDED PANEL. A panel formed by applied carving.

MOLDING. A narrow continuous surface, projecting and applied or incised, used for decoration.

MORTISE. A slot cut into a wooden member, generally half of a mortise and tenon joint.

MOUNTS. The brass handles, escutcheons and other decorative details applied to pieces of furniture. Also turned wooden knobs or carved wooden handles.

MUNTINS. The wooden separations that retain the panes of glass in a glazed door.

MUSHROOM-TURNED KNOBS. Circular wooden knobs with fronts flatly carved, resembling mushroom cap.

NESTED TABLES. Tables three or four in number of graduated sizes fitting one inside the other.

OGEE. A molding with a single or double cyma-curve. (*See* Molding, Cyma-curve.)

OTTOMAN. A backless, armless seat, usually about chair-seat high.

OUTROUNDED CORNERS. The corners of square or rectangular tops, if semicircular curves replace the usual right angles.

PAINTED AND GRAINED. A finish done by first painting with a ground coat and then applying a dark shade resembling the natural grain of wood.

PANEL. A square or rectangular board held in place by stiles and rails.

PAPIER-MÂCHÉ. A wood substitute made of paper by special processes. French meaning "chewed paper."

PEDESTAL TABLE. Having a central pedestal instead of legs.

PEDIMENT. The ornamental top surmounting a tall piece of furniture. Frequently has a scrolled or straight triangular profile, broken at the center. An adaptation of the triangular space forming the gable end of a roof in classic Greek and Roman architecture.

PEG FOOT. A small, short turned foot. (*See* Turned.)

PEMBROKE TABLE. A drop-leaf table where central fixed leaf is widest, generally about twice as wide as the drop leaves.

PENDENT FINIAL. A downward-projecting finial.

PIER GLASS. A narrow tall mirror designed to be hung on a wall between windows.

PIER TABLE. A table originally designed to stand in front of a wall space between windows.

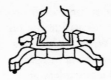

PLINTH. The base of a column, pedestal or finial.

PLINTH BASE. A base without feet which rests directly on the floor.

PULL BRACKETS. Located on either side of the top drawer of a desk or secretary and pulled out to support the writing flap.

QUADRANT BRACKETS. Quarter circle cast brass brackets which support the fall-front of a desk or secretary.

QUATREFOIL. A Gothic ornamental detail having four balancing lobes. Done either incised or pierced. Is the conventionalized four-leaf clover without stem in shape.

RAIL. A horizontal connecting member in furniture construction.

RAISED PANEL. A panel which projects slightly from the surrounding surface.

REBATE. A rectangular slot or groove.

REBATE JOINT. A joint where the two parts have matching slots.

REEDING. A series of rounded, continuous, closely set beading done in parallel lines. The opposite of Fluting.

RELIEF CARVING. Where the design is raised by having background cut away. Varies in degree. Low relief where design is raised less than a quarter of the full round. Medium relief, from a quarter to less than one half of the full round. High relief, raised half or more.

RETURNS. An architectural term used to designate the horizontal moldings on the sides of large bookcases and wardrobes.

RING-AND-BALL. Turning composed of elements in ring shapes and ball shapes.

RING TURNING. A turning in which one or more narrow rings provide the decorative treatment.

ROCOCO. Elaborate ornamentation with many curves combined with shells, rocks and other conventionalized rustic details. Is derived from a combination of two French words, *rocaille* (rockwork) and *coquille* (shell).

ROLLED ARM. A sofa or chair arm with an outward curve or roll from the perpendicular.

ROSETTE. A circular ornamental detail with flower or foliage carving or concentric beading.

ROSETTE KNOB. A circular knob centering a bead-rimmed rosette.

ROSETTE KEYHOLE. *See* Keyhole Rosette.

RUDIMENTARY FOOT. A plain uncarved foot terminating a cabriole leg.

RULE JOINT. Resembles the central joint of a carpenter's or cabinetmaker's folding rule. Also known as a "Knuckle Joint."

RUNNERS. The wooden strips attached to the inner sides of a case piece, on which the drawer slides.

SABER LEG. A front chair leg with a perpendicular curve like that of a saber.

SAUSAGE TURNING. A turning that resembles a length of short plump sausages.

SCROLL. Shape of an unrolled roll of paper—a spiral role ornamentation.

SCROLLED. Ornamented with scrolls.

SCROLL-SAW CUT. An outline of curves and scrolls or pierced openings done with a scroll saw.

SERPENTINE FRONT. The front of a case piece, chair or sofa having a balanced wavy curve that is convex at center and ends, and concave between.

SETTEE. A light open seat, for two to six persons, with a low back and arms.

SHAPED PEDIMENT. A pediment in which the plinths of the central and corner finials are connected by two members, the upper edges of which are concave, convex, cyma-curved or triangular. Made either fixed or removable.

SHELL-CARVED. Ornamented with shell motif carved in relief or incised. The shell ornamentation most used generally resembles the scallop shell in form and outline.

SKIRT. A cross member, frequently valanced, found on case pieces at bottom of carcase, on tables under top connecting legs; under seats of chairs. Also called "Apron."

SLIP SEAT. A removable, upholstered seat.

SOCKET CASTER. A roller with an offset tapering shank, which fits into an inset metal socket.

SPANDREL. An applied triangular decorative detail, used in pairs above an arched panel.

SPLIT-BALL MOLDING. An applied molding formed of repeating ball segments.

SPOOL-TURNED. Turning like that done to make a length of spools prior to cutting apart into individual units, always identical. Chief shapes are ball, ball-and-ring, bobbin, knob, spool, sausage, urn and vase.

SWAG. A pendent, carved detail. With Victorian furniture, done in flower, fruit or leafage motifs, applied.

TAMBOUR. A flexible, sliding shutter made of thin strips of wood glued to a coarse textile backing.

TENON. A thin, projecting tongue fitting into a corresponding groove or mortise.

TESTER. *See* Canopy.

THREE-QUARTER GALLERY. A gallery on back and sides of a top or shelf.

TILT-TOP TABLE. A tripod table with circular, square or octagon top, hinged to tilt to the perpendicular.

TONGUE-AND-GROOVE JOINT. Used for joining two boards. On the side of one is a continuous beadlike molding and on the other a continuous channel into which the former fits.

TOP RAIL. The top horizontal rail of a chair or sofa back.

TORUS MOLDING. A bold convex molding, usually semi-circular but sometimes slightly flattened.

TREFOIL. A Gothic ornamental detail having three balancing lobes. Either incised or pierced. Shape is that of a conventionalized three-leaf clover, without stem.

TRESTLE TABLE. One with fixed leaf, supported by trestles instead of legs.

TRESTLES. Postlike or pierced uprights supporting a table top. Are usually mounted on block or shoe feet.

TRIPLE BEAD MOLDING. A projecting molding formed of three bead units, with the center one overlapping the other two.

TRIPOD TABLE. A table with pedestal supported by three out-curved legs.

TROPHY SWAG. An applied swag carved in medium or high relief to represent game, such as a brace of birds or a string of fish.

TURN BUTTON. A small oblong wooden button mounted loosely with a screw or nail, as substitute for a door latch.

TURNED. Shaped by turning.

TURNING. Shaping of wood on a lathe, done with turning chisels.

URN. A turned decorative detail, largely used as a finial.

VALANCE. Decorative shaping, done in balancing scrolls on lower edge of a cross member. Is a conventionalized representation of drapery.

VASE-AND-RING TURNED. Turning that combines elements of vase shape and ring shape.

VASE-SHAPED SPLAT. A chair-back splat with vase outline.

VASE TURNED. Turning where the principal elements have a vase shape.

VENEER. Any thin layer of wood glued on a base wood for decorative effect of grain or contrasting color.

VIGNETTE. A small painted decorative detail, either scenic or floral, framed by scrolls.

VOLUTED. Having a spirally scrolled end.

WAVY MOLDING. A machine-cut applied molding with face done in repeating ripples. Made in flat or triangular form. Especially used on pieces of Transitional and Gothic substyles. Sometimes it is known as "Ripple Molding."

WEBBING. Jute, woven in bands about three inches wide. Tacked in a latticelike pattern to the foundation of an upholstered seat of chair or sofa, generally supporting the coil springs.

WHATNOT. An open tier of shelves, with slender turned or scrolled supports. Used for display of curios in Victorian period.

WHORL FOOT. An up-curved, carved foot done in scroll motif, terminating a cabriole leg. Used on Louis XV substyle pieces.

WRITING ARM. A wide wooden tablet, attached to right arm of a chair.

Field Guide
TO
AMERICAN
Victorian Furniture

SECTION I

How to Use This Book

THIS is a specialized book, devoted to the designs and types of Victorian furniture made in the United States of wood and cast iron and to the papier-mâché and lacquered novelty pieces so extensively imported during their vogue. It adheres to the same plan as my *Field Guide to Early American Furniture* and, like it, is intended to do for the collector of this mid-nineteenth-century furniture what "field guides" on birds or animals do for their devotees.

Although several excellent books have been published within the past few years on the Victorian they have not been complete: one is left with a hazy impression of horsehair upholstery, curved outlines, carvings in grape or rose motifs, marble-topped center tables and what-nots; whereas such details actually represent only one of eight substyles which overlapped, followed, or even ran along with each other. Naturally some of the designs are better than others, and I believe that an accurate and comprehensive inventory of the furniture made in these eight substyles will show the collector which they are.

Here, the furniture has been grouped, section by section, according to the ten major forms in which it was made. With each, the examples shown and described are arranged as near chronologically as the overlapping or contemporary timing of the eight substyles permit. Although the reign of the queen whose name this period bears was from 1837 to 1901, herein the years from 1840 to 1880 have been fixed as time limits, since in this country during that forty-year span the bulk of Victorian furniture was made.

True, it was gaining admirers earlier and some scattering examples were made. Similarly, for about ten years after 1880, catalogues of some furniture factories showed "survival" pieces in the Victorian style; but by then in the main it was outmoded by the designs of the Art Nouveau, the Mission and the Modern Colonial.

The pieces selected are those which the collector may expect to find in private collections, museum displays of Victorian period rooms or in dealers' shops. Elaborate show pieces made for display in nineteenth-century exhibitions here and in Europe, and later illustrated in contemporary books on decoration, have been omitted intentionally. They are too large and overpowering to be used in present-day homes; and besides, most of them seem to have disappeared.

Consequently, this field guide is limited to such examples of the Victorian as are still in existence, such as one may remember seeing in old established homes years ago and such as might possibly be retrieved from some storeroom or acquired from an old house's contents by way of the auction block.

Except for Belter furniture and unusually fine custom-made beds and bureaus in the Gothic and Louis XV substyles, or for certain Renaissance sideboards, Victorian pieces are reasonable in price compared with those of earlier furniture periods. Because of this and because the supply is still ample, it has not attracted the furniture copyists who sell their handiwork as original. So far, the reproductions are mostly of spool-turned beds, Louis XV chairs and some tables with the characteristic cabriole legs, and these are frankly offered as copies in regular furniture stores.

Some foundries have revived the making of metal garden furniture, either of cast iron or of lighter aluminum alloys, and advertise it as such in home decorating and garden magazines. Here again there is no intent to deceive, and the copies can be readily recognized.

First Step in General Preparation

Before going on a Victorian furniture hunt or trying to identify a specific piece, it is advisable to read and digest the two sections that follow this one. Section II gives one a quick look at the eight substyles, tells the outstanding characteristics of each, the principal pieces made and the wood or woods most frequently used. In ten to twenty minutes' reading, will be found the essential characteristics from the Transitional Early Victorian through the Turkish, a span of forty years during which the United States pushed its western boundary to the Pacific Ocean, was rent asunder, became reunited and was able to celebrate the one hundredth anniversary of its founding with the Centennial Exposition of 1876 at Philadelphia, city of its birth.

The chief characteristics of the substyles are reduced to a few essentials. Get to know these as well as you know the variety and meaning of highway markers. This will be of material help in placing the pieces you see as to kind, and approximate years within the period.

Second Step in General Preparation

In Section III will be found the explanation for the shift that was already under way at the start of the period — that from the individual craftsman's handwork to furniture factories with the first power-driven tools and mass production. How mechanization of furniture making progressed and design and workmanship became more stereotyped are told.

For instance, inspection of a chest of drawers of the Transitional Early Victorian span will show indications of at least some handwork, such as dovetail joints and rough planing of back boards, in contrast to the Eastlake substyle where there is a uniform mechanical exactness. It is this degree of machine work which marks the difference between the furniture made in the early, middle or late years of the period. Along with this, careful fitting and finishing are characteristic of the fine pieces, made to order in the cabinetmaking shops of the larger cities, where there still existed custom work. Compared to them, the workmanship of the interior parts of quantity-produced cottage furniture is decidedly slapdash in character.

With a little practice and patience you will soon find it not too difficult to spot an early piece, one made in a custom cabinet shop or the out-and-out mass-factory product.

After you have become familiar with the various style influences, which at first seem hopelessly confusing, and have learned to tell the good from the bad in workmanship, you are ready for a try at field work. For instance, in a shop, at a country auction or at an antiques show you may see a piece of Victorian furniture of a type or design that is new to you. It is interesting — but you aren't sure whether it is early or late, desirable or something to let alone. Since you have your copy of *Field Guide to American Victorian Furniture* in your pocket or purse, you look for a picture in it similar to the piece in question among the numbered line drawings. Nearby in the text, with an identical number, will be a description. Compare it with the piece you have just seen.

That short description gives a *typical* example of that particular kind of chair, table or the like, and its essential characteristics are set forth. If it is a case piece, the proper kind of handles and whether the top is wood or marble will be stated. These specifications also include the kind of wood or special material, tell whether it was the work of a cabinetmaker, custom made, or the product of an early or late factory; they state its design and approximate dates, and give, finally, a coded indication of its comparative value.

For a specific demonstration we might take an unusual but not rare piece, a small stool having a hinged top covered with needlework or other upholstery and containing a slipper box. You turn to the section "Chairs, Ottomans and Footstools" and toward the end find a line drawing of just such a piece.

Its number is 50, and the description with corresponding number reads:

50. Eastlake Slipper Box Stool

Design with slipper compartment beneath hinged top like the preceding. About 20 inches long, eight to 10 inches deep, and 16 inches tall. Carcase formed of trestle ends joined by sidepieces with conforming molding-framed panels. Upper ends of trestles match these sides. Below trestles are scroll-cut in concave curves, with conforming shaped openings done in balancing segmented curves.

Black walnut or ebonized maple, by furniture factories as an occasional piece only. *Ca. 1870–1880.* AA to AAA

The capital letters at the end are part of a four-symbol code giving comparative dollar value of any piece (explained later in this section). Thus, AA to AAA runs from a low of $10 to $25 for such a stool in the rough, needing refinishing, possible minor repairs and reupholstering of the top, to a high of $25 to $50 for one in good condition with original needlework top.

After a very little practice, anyone can duplicate this identification for the rest of the 274 pieces illustrated.

Especially with chairs, two or three variants of the same design are sometimes shown side by side. There are also some pieces that are described but not pictured, since they closely resemble others that are illustrated.

Some pieces are designated as "survivals." As the name indicates, a survival example is a piece of furniture of an earlier style which continued to be made after other furniture forms in it had become obsolete. One of the best examples is the spool-turned day bed (*see No. 72*), illustrated in furniture-factory catalogues as late as 1880 although the use of spool-turned furniture was at its height twenty to thirty years earlier. There are also late forms of the Windsor, the least recognized as such being the common U-back kitchen chair, which continued to be made well after the close of the Victorian period.

In Sections IV to XVII, the ten main furniture forms

are treated, as well as such special types as the melodeon, spinet and early piano, papier-mâché and lacquered wood pieces, and cast-iron furniture. Placing these three groups in separate sections was done to high-light their distinctiveness. Examples of each furniture form are presented chronologically by the substyles of the period. In a few instances overlapping or contemporaneousness would make such an arrangement confusing, as in the case of the spindle-back turned chairs and the desks designed for library or office use. These have been presented as special groups according to their construction.

Section XIV, Mirrors, is of necessity presented primarily according to types of frames, since making the latter was a specialized trade of its own, not particularly influenced by the design trends of the substyles.

In selecting the typical pieces to be illustrated and described, I have intentionally given preference to forthright examples I believe most representative of the period and best adapted for present everyday living in the average home. They are the kind I would acquire and dealers tell me they are the ones which most of their customers prefer.

However, there are those impressive pieces, such as the chairs and sofas, made by Belter, which are high-priced and becoming so rare they are now found chiefly in museums or private collections; these have been included not only because they are essential to a well-rounded whole, but because it is well to recognize such rarities, which have been known to crop up sometimes in unusual places where their worth is not appreciated.

Every description is complete in itself, as to identification, but to show how the pieces within the group are interrelated, each section begins with some brief observations about that particular furniture form and what changes it underwent during the period. Immediately following, when germane, are a few notes under the heading "Special Comments," explaining construction and special details.

I believe readers who study these sections may be saved from acquiring pieces of doubtful merit, those damaged by unwise attempts to restore them, or mutilated by removal of structural parts or decorative trim. That each piece has certain distinct characteristics is just as true of Victorian furniture as of that which was made earlier.

In Section XIX the limited variety of woods used for making Victorian furniture is briefly discussed and special combinations of them are commented on, together with the years when they were most widely used. Likewise, in Section XVIII, details concerning handles and hardware used in the various substyles are given. (Since many Victorian case pieces have lost their original handles, this section should be of help in deciding on replacements.)

In gathering source material over 5000 photographs of furniture from the files of dealers who specialize in the Victorian have been inspected, and many of them loaned to me for further study. Some represent examples handled by these dealers over a period of twenty years or more. These have been amplified by study of furniture trade journals and illustrated factory catalogues of the period. From these sources, plus examination of Victorian pieces in museums, private collections, historic houses and shops, I have been able to select typical examples and have tried to keep the accent on those which are available in fair quantity today.

As to value: Victorian furniture prices are not subject to the stabilizing influence that exists for earlier antique furniture: the auctions held by large galleries which publish handsomely illustrated catalogues, completely priced. As yet, except for Belter furniture and a very few specialized collections, relatively few examples of the Victorian have been part of such sales. However, as with earlier furniture, values for the Victorian are determined individually, factors involved including rarity, design, condition and, most important of all, *collector demand*.

Experienced dealers and collectors specializing in the Victorian are guided by a schedule of comparative values which they recognize and understand as basic. Generally this holds year in and year out, with the ratios between the price levels for differing grades remaining fairly constant. Relative values for fine quality pieces stay more or less the same. Average pieces are more readily affected by other factors such as temporary fads, inspired by some decorator's novel effects. But long-range comparative values are little changed by such crazes.

To show how comparative values apply, we take a simple pine chest of drawers as a common denominator. It has four drawers, the lower ends of the corners are scroll-cut to simulate bracket feet, the front skirt is simply valanced and its sides have large, slightly sunk panels. It is about 38 inches wide by 34 inches tall and 18 inches deep, made between 1850 and 1870, probably as part of the cottage bedroom set. It is just a plain usable piece, frequently found in dealers' shops since there is a steady demand for it.

We give it an arbitrary value of fifty dollars, which is very close to what it sells for in average shops in good condition, properly refinished and fitted with mushroom-turned wooden knobs.

Now, compare this price with that of other Victorian chests of drawers and bureaus. A similar one with solid ends and, probably, an added shallow top drawer, but still made of pine, would be worth a fourth more. If of mahogany, with marble top and attached mirror, it is worth a half more; if of rosewood without a mirror, the same. But if it is of mahogany, has a mirror supported by scrolled and pierced brackets resting on a recessed cabinet, and its front is serpentined, the value is doubled.

For other comparisons, a love seat of the Louis XV substyle with cabriole legs and finger-molded frame of black walnut would be worth two to three times as much as our common denominator chest of drawers. A drop-front desk with table base would be between two and three times as much. As we go up the scale, a Renaissance substyle sideboard with marble top and shaped pediment is worth four to five times as much, and a pierced and carved Belter armchair six to eight times.

The same relation exists through the entire gamut of Victorian furniture. The value of any piece, except one of unusual rarity, is directly related to that of an average simple piece. This forms what is known as a standard of comparative value, and is not to be confused with actual prices for specific pieces. It is only a gauge against which individual prices may be checked for an average of several years under normal *uninflated* price levels. As such, it serves as an indication as to whether the price asked for a particular piece is high, low or average. It is a composite of average fair prices for pieces of the same sort bought in good repair, refinished if necessary. Added refinements would increase value and crudities or worn condition would decrease it. Also, since much of the Victorian furniture was made in room sets, the value of each individual piece if in such a set — all matching and obviously made together — increases 10 to 20 per cent, simply because the whole is still intact *as a set*.

For the convenience of the collector, a simple four-symbol code of comparative values has been devised. It aims to reflect average prices the country over, and does not take into consideration special conditions in certain sections. The code symbols appear after the descriptions of all pieces discussed elsewhere in this book.

The low is for a simple example of a particular piece in the rough, requiring refinishing and possibly minor repairs. The high is for a piece with fine detail, needing no repairs or refinishing. For upholstered pieces, it is assumed that only recovering with new material is required. If the condition is such that springs must be retied or webbing replaced, the prospective owner must take this added expense into consideration in determining his opinion of worth.

Code Symbols and Table of Comparative Values

A	Under $15
AA	$15 to $40
AAA	$40 to $75
B	$75 to $125
BB	$125 to $175
BBB	$175 to $250
C	$250 to $400
CC	$400 to $600
CCC	$600 to $900
#	Over $900

Note:

Fine, authentic Belter armchairs, side chairs, sofas, etc., in original unrepaired condition have a comparative value approaching double that indicated for Belter furniture in general.

SECTION **II**

The Substyles of Victorian Furniture

AMERICAN furniture design of the Victorian Period is a composite, adapted from eight earlier furniture styles which became eight subsidiary style expressions at the hands of Victorian furniture makers between 1840 and 1880. To make it still more complicated, there is repeated overlapping of these subsidiary style spans. Some did more than overlap: they were entirely contemporaneous. Nor were all the major forms of furniture made in each style.

Through constant striving for novelty plus elegance on the part of furniture producers and their designers, Victorian furniture styles were always in a state of flux with new adaptations either consorting with or crowding out those already in vogue. Viewed from present-day distance, the result is at least surface confusion. But at the risk of possible oversimplification, these eight subsidiary styles, with their approximate years, are listed as a kind of blazed trail for the Victorian furniture hunter.

TRANSITIONAL EARLY VICTORIAN	1840–1850
GOTHIC	1840–1865
SPOOL–TURNED	1850–1880
FRENCH, LOUIS XV	1845–1870

RENAISSANCE   1855–1875
FRENCH, LOUIS XVI   1865–1875
EASTLAKE   1870–1880
TURKISH   1870–1880

TRANSITIONAL EARLY VICTORIAN
1840–1850

Wood — mahogany, rosewood and black walnut.
Also maple, butternut and other native hardwoods for country-made pieces, often stained
red or brown

Construction — turned posts, for beds; turned
legs or shaped pedestals, for tables; carved
bracket feet and crestings, for sofas; saber
legs, for chairs; rectangular carcase supported by bracket feet, for chests of drawers, desks and sideboards; drawer fronts
always flush

Decoration — wavy molding, applied carving in
flower and leafage motifs, marble tops for
some tables and chests of drawers, crotch-
grain mahogany veneer for pedestals, cornices and sofa skirts, often with medallion
of applied carvings; applied split finials

Handles — mushroom-turned wooden knobs
with inset keyhole surrounds or applied
wooden keyhole rosettes

Size — proportions ponderous and lines often
heavy

General design clearly reflects the American Empire
period but with Victorian details, such as the wavy
molding, medallions and smaller details of applied carving. Much of the furniture in this decade was made by

cabinetmakers who continued to use American Empire forms and worked with hand tools. There are also the simple country pieces, some of them made by cabinet-makers who had migrated West and settled in various communities in Wisconsin, Illinois, Indiana, Ohio, Kentucky and western Tennessee. Characteristics of their work are simplicity of line, sturdy construction and utilitarian design without carved detail.

Lastly there are the examples produced by small early furniture factories in which a combination of machine sawing and planing with handfitting and finishing can be observed. Chairs, tables, sofas and some chests of drawers and desks are among these. If a marble top is present, it can be either white or colored and richly mottled. All the major furniture forms appear in the Transitional style. New pieces include the ottoman, the Lazy Susan table, the wardrobe and bookcase.

GOTHIC
1840–1865

Wood — mahogany with crotch-grain veneer, rosewood or black walnut

Construction — pointed arched panels for glazed doors, chairbacks and pilasters; deeply cut spiral turnings, legs and uprights; pierced and carved arabesque chairbacks; beveled or cove-molded cornice with pronounced over-hang; low triangular or arched pediment; short bracket feet or plinth base for case pieces; Gothic paneled or ogee-molded drawer fronts; white marble or wooden tops

> *Decoration* — carved cusp, steeple-turned finials;
> incised or pierced trefoils and quatrefoils;
> incised or pierced spandrels; carving sharply
> cut and in medium relief; bold raised mold-
> ings, always applied
>
> *Handles* — mushroom-turned wooden knobs or
> finger grips on lower edge of drawer fronts
>
> *Size* — ample proportions for elaborate or archi-
> tectural pieces; chairs of standard size ex-
> cept for tall backs

This style coincided with the height of the Gothic
Revival architecture, widely used for city mansions,
country homes, churches and other public buildings
which superseded the Greek Revival of the early nineteenth century. Many of the best examples of Gothic
furniture were designed by architects to conform to
that of their structures and consequently were custom-
made. This occurred with large pieces, such as sideboards and bookcases, and with some of the finer side
chairs.

Simpler pieces are the product of early furniture factories, notably the secretary with fold-over writing flap.
Matching sets in this style for the bedroom are well
known, as are sets of chairs. Side chairs predominate;
it is not uncommon to find a combination of the Gothic
and spool-turned. Armchairs are much less numerous;
most of these which have survived are probably of the
type designed for churches or for the use of presiding
officers in the meeting rooms of masonic lodges and
similar organizations.

Not all of the major furniture forms are found in the
Gothic style. Tables are noticeably absent, and sofas occur

more frequently in the form of the armless love seat. In general it was a style fitted for larger buildings or cities and apparently not attempted by cabinetmakers in the smaller towns of either the Eastern Seaboard or the Middle West.

SPOOL-TURNED
1850–1880

Wood — black walnut, maple, birch or other common native hardwoods; mahogany for small occasional tables

Construction — spool turnings for legs, trestle supports, bedposts, uprights and spindles, always in identical repeating units; motifs bobbin, knob, button, sausage, vase-and-ring and two balls separated by thin rings; pieces structurally simple with rectangular outline

Decoration — chiefly that of spool turnings; contrasting turnings for spindles; steeple-turned finials; spool-turned quadrants connecting posts and top rails of some beds and day beds; moldings of split spool turnings; spool-turned crestings

Handles — mushroom-turned wooden knobs

Size — average

This style was the first consistently factory-manufactured and mass-produced. It is simple of design, and of usable size. There are three typical variations for the low beds. Tables are of two kinds — the four-legged and trestle; the latter in a small size often part of a matching bedroom set. Not all furniture forms found in this group; beds and tables most numerous pieces.

FRENCH, LOUIS XV
1845–1870

Wood — black walnut, rosewood, occasionally mahogany, also native hardwoods for simple pieces

Construction — curved outline, balanced serpentine and cyma-curves; slender, restrained cabriole legs, terminating in rudimentary or whorl feet; balloon-shaped chair backs; table tops cartouche shape and of marble — tall cabriole table legs, braced by X-shape stretcher with central finial; semiconcealed drawer often in base of chests of drawers or bureaus; oval panels; bedstead-type beds; drop-front or slant-front for desks and secretaries; laminated, pierced and carved work for Belter pieces

Decoration — carving in rose or grape motifs with leaves and tendrils done in medium to high relief on top rails of chairs and sofas; on other furniture in low to medium relief as applied work; finger molding on frames of chairs, sofas and kindred pieces; boldly done scroll carving on knees of ornate table legs; applied moldings and carved spandrels; pierced gallery parts; large mirror panels; arched carved and sometimes pierced pediments; crestings carved and solid or pierced; all pierced and carved details in ornate intertwining designs with flower or fruit motifs combined with leaves, tendrils and S- or C-shaped scrolls

Handles — wooden, fruit-and-leaf carved —
turned rosette or mushroom knobs with
keyhole rosettes or scroll-carved medallions

Size — tall and ample of proportion except for
side chairs

This substyle is the best known of all types of Victorian furniture. A survival of Louis XV decorative designs with outlines and proportions altered to include the British ideal of comfort, it began in 1830 with the reign of Louis Philippe, who gave his whole-hearted approval to a change in furniture style from the Napoleonic designs. This new French fashion reached America only a little before another political upheaval in 1848 sent Louis Philippe into exile in England, but it expressed the general Romantic movement so well that it continued to dominate furniture design for over twenty years.

Its curvilineal outlines are in marked contrast to the perpendicular ones of the preceding substyles, as are its characteristic finger molding and decorative carving. Among the new pieces are the parlor center table with cabriole legs and marble top, the whatnot and étagère, the low-armed upholstered "lady chair," and small boudoir pieces. Along with these is the matching parlor set. A standard one includes a sofa or love seat, gentleman's armchair, lady chair, four side chairs, an ottoman and center table. A drawing room set would add two or more side chairs; sofas, couches or love seats would probably be in pairs, and there might be one or more matching étagères or whatnots. At the other extreme, a very simple matching set could have as little as a sofa or love seat, a gentleman's armchair, a lady chair, and perhaps four side chairs. (Sideboards and extension tables not found in this furniture form.)

RENAISSANCE
1860–1875

Wood — black walnut, often with burl-veneered panels; ash, with black walnut trim, or pine, painted and grained, for simpler pieces; satinwood with rosewood trim with some custom-made pieces

Construction — outline stiff and heavy; designs adapted from Renaissance architecture, mainly late German serpentine arched pediments and semicircular arched panels; bold moldings flanking overlapping raised cartouches; raised and shaped small incidental panels, larger ones framed with applied moldings, boldly rounded corners for footboards of beds, high headboards; all case-piece carcases rectangular and resting on low bracket or block feet or having plinth bases; extension table has split pedestal; parlor center table is supported by four tall scrolled brackets surrounding a baluster-turned shaft; other table supports, pierced and scrolled or shaped trestles; marble tops for most case pieces; tall bureau mirrors fixed, shorter ones tilting; finials turned or quadrilaterally shaped; all moldings and carved details applied

Decoration — medallions and swags in flower or fruit motifs, carved in medium to high re-

lief; animal heads in full relief on sideboard
pediments; door panels hung with sporting
trophy swags in high relief; boldly carved
and shaped cartouches surmounting pediments; turned and conventionalized flower
rosettes; applied moldings sometimes ebonized

Handles — wooden, carved in fruit and leafage,
scroll or straplike motifs; pendent pear-
shape knobs — wooden keyhole rosettes

Size — elaborate pieces oversize and tall; simpler
ones standard size

The structural and decorative features of this substyle
are based on those of Renaissance architecture instead of
any previous furniture form. They include tall arched
pediments, semicircular arched panels, large carved cartouches, boldly done cornice moldings and cyma-curved
or scrolled brackets.

This style developed in Europe shortly before the
middle of the century and was dramatized by ultra-
elaborate attention-drawing pieces at such exhibitions as
the Crystal Palace of 1851 in London. American pieces
were soon being influenced but were reduced in scale and
of plainer ornamentation, largely for dining room, library and bedroom use. Among them are the sideboard
with tall arched pediment, the pedestal-base extension
table, large secretaries and desks for library or office —
one, the Wooten Patent Desk, a triumph of Yankee in-
genuity. In addition, there are the circular, marble-topped
parlor table, the rectangular library table with baize-
paneled top and full-width drawer, and the trestle sewing table.

FRENCH, LOUIS XVI
1865–1875

Wood — black walnut and, less frequently, ebonized maple or similar native hardwoods

Construction — slender tapering turned legs; plain or fluted and terminating in small peg feet, generally with large bun turning at upper end; upholstered keystone-shaped chair and sofa backs; upholstered, nearly circular chair seats; open or rudimentary arms; molded, slightly arched top rails; bead-molded frames; table legs braced by turned H-shaped stretchers with urn or vase-shaped central finial; tops rectangular with bowed sides and ends; surface plain or with conforming inset marble panel

Decoration — burl-veneered incidental panels; small realistic carved masks; turned rosettes; fine incised and gilded straight lines or scrolls

Size — average; chair and sofa backs of standard height; more love seats than full-length sofas; tables medium-sized

Soon after her marriage to Napoleon III in 1853, the Empress Eugénie fostered a Marie Antoinette cult; with it came a revival of the Louis XVI fashion for furniture design. This appeared in America about 1865 and lasted about ten years. Chiefly parlor furniture, it has two grades of workmanship — fine custom-made, and average factory-made examples. Pieces are not as numerous as those of the Louis XV style, nor are they in as great demand with collectors.

EASTLAKE
1870–1880

Wood — black walnut; ash, cherry, maple, chestnut and oak for late examples

Construction — straight lines and rectangular structure for chairs and tables with tapering legs square or turned; rectangular paneled head and footboards with flat molded cornices for beds; case pieces mainly stile and rail constructed, with large rectangular sunk panels, molded bases, marble or wooden tops, scroll-cut supporting brackets, flat or simply arched molded cornices; panels of walnut furniture faced with burl veneer

Decoration — reeded edges; fine incised lines frame paneling and drawer fronts; low relief, machine-done carving of geometric motifs or simple foliated scrolls and rosettes

Handles — pendent ring or bail with chased and shaped plates and matching keyhole escutcheons of oxidized or plated brass

Size — average

Named for Charles Lock Eastlake, English architect who wrote *Hints on Household Taste in Furniture, Upholstery and Other Details* in 1868. Eastlake was a reformer rather than an originator of furniture designs. He championed a revival of the Jacobean with its sturdy rectangular outlines and urged abandonment of shoddy factory work. That it could be done was proved by a restricted number of excellent and expensive pieces produced in London cabinet shops doing only custom work.

American furniture factories and their designers capitalized on the Eastlake popularity by producing furniture in all major forms of rectangular outlines which approximated the Jacobean but ignored his warnings about quality of workmanship. It was during this final span of the Victorian period that American furniture making became a mass-production industry and both design and quality of workmanship suffered accordingly. At the Centennial Exposition of 1876 in Philadelphia fine examples of better than average factory pieces were shown. People from all parts of the country looked at these and later became ready purchasers of the mass-produced American Eastlake.

TURKISH
1870–1880

Wood — native hard and soft woods for up-holstery-covered frame, black walnut or maple for turned legs

Construction — rectangular or shaped frame completely concealed by overstuffed upholstery for chairs, sofas and similar pieces; seats supported by coil springs; back and arms deeply padded and made with or without coil springs; short baluster or vase-turned legs, castered and concealed by deep fringe-enclosed arms, flaring or bolster-shaped

Decoration — plain or figured upholstery material with corresponding fringe from seat to floor and arm tassels; upholstery material including plush, velour, brocatelle, tapestry, brocade and, less frequently, leather

Size — always oversize with large low seat

Interest in Mohammedan art and architecture, the increased importance of Turkey in diplomatic affairs and the building of the Suez Canal all contributed to a vogue for furniture which resembled that of a Turkish divan. The American interpretation is limited to side and armchairs, sofas, couches and ottomans, the double or "conversation" chair and the circular sofa. Made originally in sets for parlor or library, this Turkish style is the predecessor of the overstuffed furniture of present-day manufacture. (Incidentally, at the time Turkish furniture was being produced in English and American factories, the palaces and fine residences of Constantinople and Cairo were being refurnished with carved and gilded furniture, chiefly imported from France.)

Special Groups within the Victorian Substyles

COTTAGE FURNITURE
1850–1880

Factory production of simple utilitarian Cottage style pieces was indirectly brought about by Mrs. Sarah Josepha Hale, editor of *Godey's Lady's Book*. Beginning in 1849, she instituted a "Cottage Furniture Department" which was illustrated each month with line drawings. Within a year, a few furniture manufacturers took the hint and began making simple painted "cottage bedroom sets" in quantity — either spool-turned or a simplification of the Louis XV style. These were enough in demand so that with slight modifications they still appeared in manufacturers' catalogues thirty years later, especially the spool beds, and became the Cottage style.

Cottage furniture production was further expanded with simple spool-turned tables, chairs and sofas. Included in this group, too, were tables of basic design with plainly turned legs, such as the drop-leaf or the five-leg extension dining tables. Chairs for use with such tables were either the turned type with spindle-back and cane seat or wooden-seated survival versions of the Windsor loop-back or rod-back chairs.

The simplicity of this furniture gives it a charm that some of the more ornate Victorian examples lack, and makes it the most usable today.

BELTER FURNITURE
1844–1863

At the other end of the scale is the formal pierced and carved furniture made by John Henry Belter of New

BELTER DRAWING ROOM SET

York. Born and trained as a cabinetmaker and wood carver in Germany, he migrated to New York where, by 1844, he had his own business. He continued it until his death in 1863. His furniture is always of laminated rosewood with distinctive pierced and carved decoration. The design falls entirely within the French, Louis XV substyle. Best known for his chairs (*See Nos. 6 to 10*) Belter also made some matching tables, sofas, couches, beds, cabinets and secretaries. The drawing room set shown on page 28 includes sidewall and corner sofas and three sizes of chairs.

SECTION **III**

The How and Who of Victorian Furniture

QUEEN VICTORIA had little interest, direct or indirect, in creating a new furniture style. The period was later associated with her name more through the times. She was England's debutante queen when it began, and its dowager monarch with two more decades to reign when it petered out.

The span we call the American Victorian Period is from 1840 to 1880, dates that are approximations rather than rigid limits; a leeway of five years or more should be allowed for special instances and localities. During the first of the four decades, the transformation of American furniture making from an individual craft to an industrial art came about, although there were certain craftsmen shops in the larger cities where specially designed pieces continued to be custom-made.

This shift to quantity-produced furniture had started in the American Empire Period, notably in chair shops like that of Lambert Hitchcock. Now came invention and perfection of early power-driven woodworking machines. Outstanding among them were the automatic lathe of Thomas Blanchard of Philadelphia, Hall's circular saw, the planing machine of William Woodworth of Poughkeepsie, the closely related machines for cutting mortises and tenons invented and pioneered by George Page and J. A. Fay of Keene, New Hampshire.

Later came the power-driven band saw, which replaced the hand fret saw for making brackets and shaping the blanks for applied carving, as well as machines for cutting moldings and for producing the plain chair stretchers known to furniture makers as "rounds." With these and kindred machines available, furniture factories multiplied rapidly and spread inland from the Atlantic seaboard.

Another change was the appearance of the furniture dealer. With him, the time-honored relationship between the cabinetmaker who made specific pieces and his customers ceased.

But these shifts did not come all at once. Duncan Phyfe did not close his New York shops, where he had employed as many as a hundred workmen at the height of his business, until 1846. He is credited with having made, or supervised the making of some furniture of the Early Victorian Transitional design. According to the inventory of his household effects, made soon after his death in 1854, 16 out of 110 pieces of furniture were Victorian. Included among them were eight mahogany French chairs, four of carved rosewood, two rosewood center tables, a rosewood work table and a gilt chair.

Thomas Goddard of Newport, Rhode Island, last of the Goddard-Townsend family group of block-front furniture fame, was active as a cabinetmaker and furniture repairer until close to his death in 1858.

The outstanding Victorian furniture maker, Belter was established in New York by 1844, just as Duncan Phyfe was considering retiring, and Belter continued active until his death in 1863.

Philadelphia had two well-known makers of Victorian furniture — George J. Henkels and Daniel Pabst. Henkels maintained a large furniture warehouse at 173 Chestnut Street, opposite Independence Hall, from about 1850 to 1870. His catalogues and advertising, as well as specific pieces attributed to him, show that his furniture was made in the Gothic and French substyles, especially the Louis XV, and that the woods used were "rosewood, walnut, mahogany, satinwood and maple all of superior construction." One outstanding piece is a low bed with ornate side canopy and drapery hangings which he presented to Jenny Lind on her first visit to Philadelphia. Daniel Pabst, who was a little younger, is best known for his sideboards and pedestal extension tables in the Renaissance substyle. Some of these have been exhibited from time to time at the Philadelphia Museum in Victorian Period rooms.

In Boston, A. Eliaers maintained shops at 12 to 24 Cornhill from about 1840 to well into the 1860's and was one of the leading exponents of the Louis XV style. He came originally from Paris; his advertising stressed "French Cabinetmaker" and claimed "This is the only establishment in the United States where persons can be furnished in every article belonging to furnishing insides of Churches, Hotels and Private Dwellings at a moment's notice." (Eliaers also built graceful, double-curved staircases of the flying type which he installed in handsome mansions in many parts of the country.) Contemporary with him was J. S. L. Babbs (about 1850 until after 1860) who was a wholesale manufacturer of chair and sofa frames of the Louis XV style in his steam-powered factory on Albany Street.

Cabinetmakers working in smaller cities who produced furniture, principally in the Louis XV substyle, included Elijah Galusha of Troy, New York. He worked as late as 1869 and was a native of Shaftsbury, Vermont, where he was born in 1804. A fairly sizable amount of his work is still owned in and around Troy, especially by descendants of his partner, J. Crawford Green. Also, for the wealthy Ohio–Mississippi River trade, S. J. John of Cincinnati made a specialty of parlor sets in this style.

In New Orleans there were naturally cabinetmakers whose furniture was distinctly in the French manner. This they made not only for the fine homes of the city but shipped in considerable amount up the Mississippi as far as Prairie du Chien, Wisconsin.

François Seignouret came from Bordeaux before 1820 and was active in New Orleans until the 1860's, making many of the tall-post beds with partial testers, handsome bureaus and large wardrobes with mirror-paneled doors. There was A. Seibrecht (about 1840–1860), whose parlor sets are similar to those by Belter save that the carving is solid and the cresting not pierced. Another leading craftsman was Prudent Mallard (about 1835–1860), who came from Sèvres and is considered by some to have been the most expensive of all New Orleans furniture makers of the period. (One of his bedroom sets might be priced as high as $3000.)

Two New Orleans craftsmen of French birth working later were A. Debruille and Pierre Abadie. They both advertised to "sell, buy or repair." These are but a few of the names that can be gleaned by studying old advertisements, catalogues and trade cards of the period. Also there were those makers of very fine pieces such as Herts & Company and Potter & Stymus of New York, Allen and Brothers of Philadelphia and others whose work is known from illustrations of pieces which they exhibited at the New York Crystal Palace in 1853 and at the Centennial Exhibition of 1876 at Philadelphia. The actual pieces, fine as they were, seem to have disappeared.

Cabinetmakers in the communities west of the Ohio River Valley stayed active longer than those further east. When the first legislature of the new state of Wisconsin met in 1848, its members sat at small taper-legged desks, one of which still survives in the museum of the Wisconsin State Historical Society (See No. 150). These were made by a local cabinetmaker. Factory-made furniture was too bulky for easy transportation at that time, so many of the essential household pieces were produced locally.

Jamestown, New York, was one of the first communities in the Great Lakes Basin to have a furniture industry. Between 1850 and 1860 furniture factories had also arrived in many of the larger Western cities — such as Cincinnati, Cleveland, Chicago, Indianapolis, Grand Rapids, Muscatine, Iowa and San Francisco.

Some idea of the development of furniture making in the United States from the beginning to the end of the Victorian Period is indicated by these census figures: in 1840, 18,003 workers were employed in cabinetmaking shops and early factories (elsewhere estimated at 1500) and the annual value of furniture made is given as $7,555,405; forty years later, the census of 1880 reports 4843 furniture factories and 384 chair shops. Together they employed 53,018 "males, 16 years old or over"; 2216 "females 15 years or over"; 3068 boys and girls below these ages. The annual value totaled $77,845,817, of which $68,037,992 is credited to the furniture factories and $9,807,825 to the chair shops.

Section IV

Chairs, Ottomans and Footstools

COMFORT AND USEFULNESS are the dominating characteristics of Victorian chairs. There are more than forty different types, ranging from light side chairs to fringed
Turkish upholstered armchairs. There are innovations
like the Morris chair, and ornate oddities.

The group most easily identified as Victorian had its
heyday from about 1850 to 1870. French in feeling, with
design elements of the Louis XV Period, the chief characteristics are a curvilinear outline, finger-molded and
carved frame, simplified cabriole legs, carved crestings
done in flower, fruit and vine motifs.

From the dainty side chair with crested open back to
the gentleman's armchair, the French-style chairs, singly
or in sets, have proved most adaptable for present-day
use. Hence they are the most sought-after. This group
also includes the Belter chairs, which, then as now, top
all others because of superior workmanship.

Antedating those in the French style are the carry-
overs — with design and construction like the American
Empire pieces but with distinctive Victorian details. Of
these, there are more side than armchairs. Made in the
decade between 1840 and 1850, they form a readily recognized group.

Ranking also as Early Victorian are the spool-turned
and Gothic chairs. These two styles, sometimes combined, overlap both the Transitional (American Empire

to Victorian) and the French styles of Louis XV and XVI. Both types were produced in rather limited numbers, chiefly as occasional chairs instead of in sets. Consequently they are more unusual today.

Along with the stylized chairs are the turned chairs, mostly spindle-backed. Those with cane seat are of the Cottage type, often made as part of a cottage bedroom set or in sets of six or eight as dining room chairs. Others with solid wooden seats are Windsor survivals, intended for use in kitchen or fire-house. Chairs made after 1875 are mostly of Eastlake design save for the completely upholstered examples inspired by the Turkish divan.

Since the Victorian Period was one of distinct masculine domination, the widely-made parlor sets consistently included an ample upholstered armchair, known as a gentleman's chair, but with it was usually a companion lady chair. The distinguishing marks of this are low flaring arms and reduced height of seat, both in deference to the voluminous hoop skirts in vogue at the time.

The ottoman, as an auxiliary seat in American parlor furnishings, dates from a little before the start of the Victorian Period and remained in favor for practically its entire span. The high point came with the French,

Louis XV substyle when the ottoman with slender cabriole legs was a standard unit of many matching parlor sets. Used with its companion armchair, the two
pieces could do duty as a chaise longue — an arrangement for comfort lacking with ottomans made earlier
or later.

As the name indicates, the ottoman is a furniture form
inspired by the Turkish — the original a pile of small
rugs used as a low seat — and first came into use in
Europe during the late eighteenth century. The Victorian
version of this backless, armless chair form is 14 to 16
inches high and, like the chairs of the period, has a
crowning upholstered seat and coil springs.

The Victorians liked variety in stools. Some are low
footrests; others are chair-seat high with a slipper box
beneath the hinged top. With few exceptions both ottomans and stools are all factory-made.

Special Comments on Chairs and Their Construction

With enough exceptions to prove the rule — such as
the Lincoln presentation armchair and those made to
order after designs by architects with a flair for furniture, like A. J. Davis of New York — Victorian chairs
consist of part fashioned by simple or more complicated
power-driven machines and then assembled and finished
by hand. They fall into two groups — the turned and
the shaped.

The turned are mostly side chairs, spindle-backed.
The diameter of the uprights is about twice that of the
spindle and stretcher members. Joining is by socket joints
made fast with glue, seldom pegged.

The seat is either caned or solid. If caned, there are

four shaped rails, joined by glue dowel joints and made fast to the rear uprights by two or more dowel joints. The solid in early examples are one-piece and about an inch and a half thick; later ones are about an inch thick and made of two or three pieces glued together. With a solid seat, the four legs are usually socket-jointed to it as are the back uprights and spindles, if full-length.

With shaped chairs, the parts of the frame are consistently joined by concealed dowel joints. This includes not only the framing of back and arms but legs and seat rails. Sometimes the seat rails are strengthened by corner blocks held fast by screws or nails. Many of the upholstered armchairs have a concealed vertical brace at the center of the back. This and the enclosed frame is generally of some other wood than that of the exposed framework.

The carved cresting of the back and other parts of a shaped chair is usually cut from the member so decorated, rather than applied. It varies from low to high relief, with much of it done in medium relief. If a cresting is carved in silhouette, it may also be pierced to accentuate the design.

The upholstered seat has a crowning top, five to six inches high, and contains five to seven coil springs, tied to a bottom of interwoven webbing straps, then slightly compressed and anchored in place by a network of string (front to back, side to side and diagonal), with ends fastened to the seat rails by large tacks. The springs are then covered with burlap, curled horsehair, cotton padding, and finally the muslin that is immediately under the upholstery material. Upholstered back and enclosed arms have no springs but the same webbing base, horse-hair, burlap, padding and muslin. The edges of the material are tacked to the frame and shaping is accomplished by tying with stout upholsterer's twine. If upholstery is tufted, the individual depressions are held in place by tying and ornamenting with buttons. Untufted upholstery may also be ornamented with buttons, generally set in rows about three inches apart.

Side chairs, whether shaped or turned, vary in height from 32 to 36 inches and in width from 16 to 18 inches, with seat about 17 inches from the floor. When such a chair is found with a lower seat, it has probably been cut down to serve as a slipper chair. Most upholstered armchairs have the same seat height and the legs are fitted with socket or cup casters. Rocking chairs have a seat about 15 inches from the floor and the rockers are usually from 30 to 34 inches long.

1. Transitional Side Chair (A and B)

So called because the lines of some of its parts, particularly the legs, are a hold-over from those of the vase-splat side chair of the American Empire period.

Open back with elongated U-shape; may have a slight upward flare from the seat. Top rail usually arched, in a flat curve, but can have slightly serpentined outline. Pierced with a central finger-hole flanked by low-relief carving in leaf, flower and fruit motifs.

With the more usual arched top rail, edges are deeply rounded, it may be plain or crested. An uncrested top rail sometimes has a centered conventionalized flower or fruit detail carved in low to medium relief. If the top rail has a cresting it can be either a simple molded element or a larger central carved detail perhaps including leaf-age or bunch of grapes. Rounded front surface of the top rail is either plain or, more generally, finger-molded.

Back uprights generally shaped so that upper ends

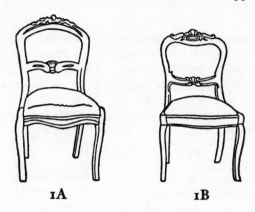

1A   1B

curve outward very slightly to join the top rail. Uprights joined about halfway from the seat by a narrow concave, horizontal splat slightly serpentined.

This splat can be plain with molded edges (A), serpentined (B) with a centered carved detail. With some examples, instead of the horizontal splat there is a narrow vertical one that flares upward and is pierced. It is supported by a plain cross rail placed just above the seat.

Seat front either bowed or slightly serpentined. With former, rail is either plain or finger-molded. With both, lower edge straight and unmolded. The serpentined front has either a plain rail with lower edge finished with a small projecting molding or a simply valanced one outlined by shallow finger-molding. A slip seat, slightly flaring with conforming front, is usual; some examples have a fixed upholstered seat.

The front legs, flat with rounded fronts, are shaped in reverse ogee curves without feet; rear ones canted in saber curve.

Most frequently mahogany or rosewood, sometimes black walnut, in sets of four, six or more. Originally used as parlor or dining room chairs, quite often part of a matching set. Plentiful — in pairs, or in sets of six. *Ca. 1850–1870.* AAA to B

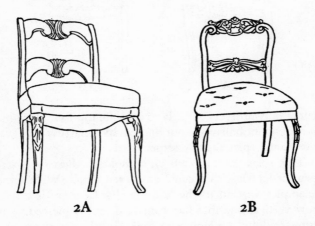

2A   2B

2. Side Chair with Simple Cabriole Legs (A and B)

Open slightly concave back 31 to 33 inches high and formed in two ways: top rail, placed between uprights, about three inches high and composed of two opposing scrolls, crotch-grain veneered, and a central detail of balancing curved beading carved in low relief; below, a corresponding horizontal cross splat (A); slightly arched top rail surmounting uprights which curve outward just below the joining and give the back a U shape; rail carved with a central rose flanked by leafage and scrolls; beneath may be a pierced finger-hole; horizontal cross splat below is also carved with matching motifs (B).

With both types of the back uprights are flat, with front and rear surfaces rounded; there is a slight cyma-curve from seat to upper ends. The shield-shaped upholstered seat is about 18 inches wide with serpentined front. The lower half of seat rails is exposed. Seat is crowned and fitted with coil springs. Cabriole front legs taper slightly, have flat sides, leafage-carved knees and are set diagonally. With later examples, they are fully shaped. The rear legs are square, tapering and canted.

Originally intended for parlor use, and sold in sets of four or six. Most frequently found today singly or in pairs.

Generally mahogany, sometimes rosewood or black walnut. *Ca. 1840–1860.* AAA to B

3. Louis XV Open U-back Side Chair (A and B)

Has arched crest rail shaped in a continuous curve, rounded face decorated with carved flower or fruit and leafage motifs; horizontal cross splat with scrolled outline, either leafage-carved or with central carved detail repeating that of the crest rail (*see A*). Back uprights, surmounted by crest rail, curve outward at the joining. They are sometimes joined to the side seat rails by short, down-curved arms which are about half the depth of the seat (*see B*).

Upholstered seat, rectangular and bowed or shield-shape and slightly serpentined. Top crowned. Cabriole front legs either footless or with rudimentary feet.

3A   3B

Black walnut, sometimes rosewood or mahogany. *Ca. 1860–1870.* AAA to B

4. Louis XV Balloon-back Side Chair (A and B)

So named because the outline of its open, slightly concave back somewhat resembles that of a spherical ballon. Its basic design is a continuously curved top rail over uprights shaped to form an unbroken balloon-shaped loop which flares upward in balanced cyma-curves. These uprights are connected where the back is narrowest by a slender cross splat.

There are three typical variations of this design — simple; more elaborate (A); ornate (B). With simple type, the loop is rounded and finger-molded. There is no carved cresting. The back splat has a slightly serpentine arching and is molded to match the top rail. At the level of the splat, the uprights are joined by conforming, bracket-like arms, also finger-molded, which extended from a third to half the depth of the seat.

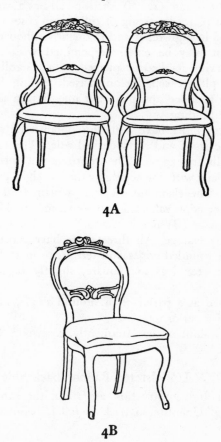

4A

4B

With the elaborate type (*see A*), the arched top rail has a carved cresting done in grape, plum or pear motif with leafage. The serpentined cross-splat has a central carved flower or fruit motif, flanked by leaves. The loop is rounded but not finger-molded.

With the ornate (*see B*), the top rail has a carved and sometimes pierced cresting of full-blown roses with leafage carved in high relief and frequently silhouetted. The cross splat may be either serpentined with a central flower carving flanked by pierced leafage scrolls or concave and plain except for an incised beading. The loop is usually rounded and plain but may have a single line of incised beading.

All three types have a flaring upholstered seat with serpentine front and cyma-curved sides. The lower half of seat rails are exposed. The front seat rail of the simple type is plain with lower edge either straight or slightly valanced. The elaborate (A) has a plain front rail but with lower edge valanced and sometimes molded. That of the ornate (B) has a carved flower detail at center, flanked by leafage. All three types have cabriole front legs with rounded edges and terminate in rudimentary feet. The rear legs are square, slightly tapering and canted.

Designed as a parlor chair. Found single, in pairs or as part of a parlor set.

Black walnut or, less frequently, rosewood. *Ca. 1850–1870*. AAA to B

5. Louis XV Upholstered Balloon-back Side Chair

Design and construction are about the same as the preceding. Upholstered back is taller, balloon shaping more pronounced. The frame is finger-molded. The arched top rail may be otherwise plain or surmounted by a carved and pierced cresting with a central cartouche done in flower or fruit motifs flanked by scrolls and leafage. When such cresting is present, the front seat rail has a matching but smaller centered cartouche and the

5

undulating curve of the rail is more pronounced. The slightly concave back may be canted. The seat is shield-shaped and crowned. Was usually part of a parlor set. Now found single, in pairs or sets of four.

Black walnut or, when carved cresting is present, frequently of rosewood. *Ca. 1860–1875.* AAA to B

BELTER CHAIRS

Belter discarded the time-honored back construction of top rail, uprights and cross rail and replaced it with a one-piece concave back of laminated wood. This was fabricated of six or eight layers, each about a quarter of an inch thick and *all of the same wood*. His favorite material was rosewood although he made some open-back chairs of black walnut and fewer of oak, sometimes using burnished gold leaf.

With all Belter chair backs, the wood grain of the outside layers runs vertically, but is alternately horizontal in the interior layers. Laminating a back was accomplished in four successive steps, beginning with the thinly-cut wood received from a veneer sawyer. The layers were first planed and sandpapered satin-smooth. They were soaked and steamed until cloth-pliant. Next, layer by layer, the back was built up on a convex form, using violinmaker's glue for the bonding agent. Finally, the back was covered with a matching concave form and the two pressed together with powerful screw clamps which were periodically tightened during drying. After it was removed from the forms, the back underwent still further drying before it was ready to be pierced and carved.

Belter kept his method of laminating a trade secret for about fourteen years. Not until 1858 did he patent it. Then, shortly before his death in 1863, he made doubly sure that chair making according to his designs and methods would cease with him: at a time when work-men were not around he destroyed his patterns and wrecked his pressing molds. As was his intent, he took the know-how with him and left only damaged equipment behind.

In many ways he was as talented a designer and cab-inetmaker as Duncan Phyfe who retired about the time Belter opened his shop. He took pride in the combined delicacy and strength of his chairs, now the best known and most distinctive of any American Victorian. He maintained that despite being elaborately pierced and carved, they were unbreakable. There is a tradition, long current with old-time antique furniture repairers, that he kept two demonstration side chairs in the second-story office of the cabinet factory of J. H. Belter & Company at 76th Street and Third Avenue. Occasionally he would toss one of them out of a window — as proof.

Belter chairs were always expensive, made in limited quantity. Today they are scarcer and still expensive. Their designs reflect the French, Louis XV substyle: Their main distinguishing characteristics are:

1. A one-piece concave back of laminated wood.
2. Entire rear of back faced with finished wood. Down this there is a barely visible central hairline where the two widths of facing join. This is more readily observed on the back of an armchair or lady chair.
3. Total absence of straight lines. This curvilineal form is further accented with the back by a pattern of intertwined pierced scrolls.
4. Elaborately pierced back. Except for the scroll-back dining chair, piercing is done in graduated curved or scrolled units resembling tracery.
5. Elaborate carving, finely executed and deeply cut. Motifs are (1) flowers, full-blown roses and sometimes lilies; (2) a single pendent bunch of grapes; (3) sharply defined foliage and (4) small or large scrolls, C-shaped, S-shaped and cyma-curved. If back has a flora cresting, it is carved in high relief and well silhouetted. Flowers on knees of cabriole legs and front seat rails are carved in higher relief than usual. All finger-molding is deeply cut and cabriole legs frequently terminate in carved whorl feet.

6

6. Belter Scroll-back Side Chair

Only type of Belter chair *not* ornamented with floral or leafage carving. Has arched open back framed by two overlapping U-shaped continuous bands from which branch large balanced scrolls ending in volutes. Back has arched cresting with ample finger-hole above two C-shaped scrolls flanked by cyma-curved scrolls of conforming size. The only carved detail is the curl of the volutes.

Has shield-shaped upholstered seat, front slightly serpentined. Conforming seat rails plain, except for the lower edge of the front one which is slightly curved. Slender cabriole front legs. Rudimentary feet, frequently fitted with brass cup casters. At the knees are conventionalized bosses with pendent raised beading downward about half the length of the legs. Rear legs square, slightly tapering, cyma-curved, giving ample spread and backward cant.

Sometimes one has open arms. These have a down-swept curve and are rounded, with boldly shaped hand grips. They are supported by extensions of the front legs that are slightly cyma-curved and rounded. (Also made in miniature as a child's chair.)

Rosewood. In sets of eight, two armchairs and six side chairs would be of rosewood or oak with natural finish or, infrequently, burnished gold leaf. These side chairs of rosewood or oak seem also to have been used as side chairs for Belter bedroom sets since they are sometimes found equipped with rockers, 30 inches long. *Ca. 1844–1863.* B to BB

7

7. Belter Carved-back Side Chair

Designed to be used separately or as part of an extensive drawing room set. Has balloon-shaped back framed by a continuous rounded scroll that is arched at the top and has cyma-curved ends. This is surmounted by a cresting of carved full-blown roses. Inside the outer scroll is a conforming carved and pierced band about three inches wide of conventionalized foliage motif with small volute scrolls. This frames a central carved and pierced medallion defined by a rounded frame with overlapping and balancing C-scroll extensions. The medallion is scrolled down-curved leafage and tendrils, from which hang a pair of sharply carved grape leaves and a single pendent bunch of grapes.

The upholstered seat has a modified shield shaping with bowed front. The conforming seat rails are plain with upper half covered by upholstery. At the center of the front rail is a flower carved in relief, flanked by leafage. The front legs are a modified form of cabriole and terminate in rudimentary feet. The square rear legs are plain, tapering and canted.

Rosewood. *Ca. 1844–1863.* BB to BBB

8. Belter Side Chair with Carved and Upholstered Back

Larger than preceding, from 38 to 40 inches tall and 20 to 22 inches wide. Upholstered panel of tall arched back may be either oval or of cartouche shape. Framing it, a carved and pierced border with sides that flare upward in continuous rounded curves surmounting smaller balancing C-shaped curves. Upper ends join downswept curves of arched top, which is surmounted by a small carved flower or shell cresting. Immediately below this, a solid medallion bearing full-blown roses carved in high relief.

Upholstered seat, shield-shape, front slightly serpentined or bowed. Conforming front rail valanced, with central carved foliated rose; is finger-molded. Molding continues down slender cabriole legs. Carved whorl feet fitted with brass cup casters. The knees of legs have small carved foliated bosses with pendent beading. Rear legs

8

are plain, square, tapering and cyma-curved, giving them ample spread and cant. Frequently part of a drawing room set.

Rosewood only. *Ca. 1844–1863.* BB to BBB

9. Belter Gentleman's Armchair

This is 44 to 48 inches tall, 22 to 24 inches wide, in design and construction like the preceding, with addition of padded open arms. Back taller, more pronounced arching. Surmounted by carved cresting, either single scallop shell flanked by rococo cyma-curved framing, or bouquet of roses in full bloom with foliage carved in high relief and silhouetted. Below cresting is (1) yoke-shaped uncarved scroll or (2) solid medallion of roses carved in high relief flanked unit of curved tendrils with leafage from which hang grape bunch.

The oval or cartouche-shaped upholstered panel framed by conforming pierced and carved band done in foliated

9

cyma and C-shaped scrolls, graduated in size. Open arms flat, with nearly full-length upholstery pads. Arms end in hand grips, finger-molded to conform to that of the arm supports which are cyma-curved extensions of the front legs. The wide, deep seat is shield-shaped with serpentined or bowed front.

The finger-molded front seat rail has a balanced concave curve with central decoration carved either in a rose or small cartouche motif. Finger-molding continues unbroken down the front cabriole legs. Rudimentary feet, fitted with brass cup casters. Between the knees and base of the arm supports are either rose-carved or foliated bosses with pendent beading. Rear legs plain, square, tapering and cyma-curved. Formed part of matching drawing room set as with the preceding chair.

(Miniature child's chair also, generally mounted on rockers).

Rosewood only. *Ca. 1844–1863.* BBB to CC

10

10. Belter Lady Chair

Companion to the preceding. Chief differences: (1) smaller size, most dimensions reduced from an eighth to a quarter; (2) absence of arms or their lowness, little more than short extensions of scrolls framing the back; (3) distance of seat only 14 to 15 inches from floor, (20 inches wide at front); (4) upholstered back panel, either balloon-shaped or an elongated oval.

The back is either perpendicular or has a very slight backward cant. The pierced carving surrounding the upholstery panel can be graduated cyma and C-shaped scrolls with lilies and leafage instead of roses and grapes with foliage. The cabriole front legs generally have rose-carved knees, are finger-molded and terminate in rudimentary or whorl feet, castered. Infrequently found in pairs today.

Rosewood only. *Ca. 1850–1863.* BB to C

11. Balloon-back Armchair

An ample upholstered chair, 44 to 46 inches tall by 22 to 24 inches wide. Exposed frame of the back may be (1) two to three inches wide and finger-molded, with or without a wide carved cresting of a fruit and leafage motif, or (2) so narrow that little more than its outer edge is visible. With this second type, the top rail is surmounted by a cyma-curved cresting of a flower motif flanked by scrolls, done in silhouette.

The upholstered and padded arms are integral parts of the back and are about 10 inches high, supported at front by scrolled and finger-molded extensions of the front legs, usually terminating in short molded hand grips. Seat deep, U-shaped; slightly serpentined front. Lower edge of conforming seat rail may have undulating curve. Finger-molded, as is the rest of the lower frame, and sometimes further decorated with a central flower or fruit detail, flanked by scrolls. Cabriole front legs; either rudimentary or carved whorl feet, frequently castered. The rear legs are square, tapering and canted. Often part of a parlor set.

Black walnut; rosewood. *Ca. 1855–1870.* B to BB

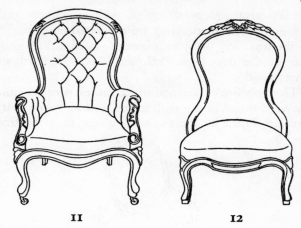

11   12

12. Balloon-back Lady Chair

Like the preceding in design and construction but on smaller scale being from 34 to 36 inches tall with cyma-curved sides that may extend forward from a third to half the depth of the seat to form low flaring arms. The seat is from 20 to 22 inches wide and has either a serpentine or bowed front. It is noticeably lower than most chairs, only 14 or 15 inches from the floor. Once part of set, now single or in pairs.

Black walnut, rosewood. *Ca. 1860–1875.* B to BBB

13. Oval-back Armchair

Of the French, Louis XV substyle. About 38 inches tall. Oval upholstered back with exposed frame about three inches wide; boldly finger-molded. Plain or surmounted by a carved cresting. Is supported at bottom by extensions of rear legs, also finger-molded. The flaring scrolled arms are usually open, with or without pads, but may be enclosed. Arms are supported by extensions of the front legs or by arm stumps placed a little to the rear of the front legs. Both are slightly scrolled and finger-molded.

The upholstered seat, 20 to 22 inches wide, is either rectangular and flaring with serpentined front or a nearly circular ellipse. Of the conforming seat rails, the front

13

one is finger-molded with serpentined lower edge; the side and back ones are plain with straight lower edges. Front legs cabriole, finger-molded with carved knees, rudimentary feet. The rear legs are square and canted. Chair is fitted with cup casters.

Sometimes made as lady chair with characteristic low arms. These are cyma-curved and finger-molded, to match the rest of the frame.

Mostly black walnut; some, with flower-carved cresting, rosewood. *Ca. 1850–1875.* B to BB

14

14. Sleepy Hollow Armchair

Popular but expensive; the favorite chair of Washington Irving, author of *The Legend of Sleepy Hollow*. Known in Europe as "gondola chair." Upholstered. About 36 inches tall by 22 to 26 inches wide. Semicircular arched and boldly concave back has a conforming U-shaped, finger-molded frame about three inches wide. The ends may be (1) cyma-curved and extend forward to surmount the exposed arm supports or (2) may slope downward to the side seat rails and define the rear of enclosed rolled arms.

The arm supports (extensions of the front legs) cyma-curved and finger-molded. If arms are rolled, the supports have a backward flare and terminate in small carved volutes. Deep seat is U-shaped with serpentined

front. Conforming front seat rail finger-molded. Side
and rear rails plain. Cabriole front legs finger-molded;
rudimentary feet. Cartouche-shape carved details at knees.
The rear legs are plain, square and canted. Chair is
fitted with socket casters. Also made as a rocking chair
with shorter legs mounted on well-curved rockers from
32 to 34 inches long. Original upholstery was predomi-
nantly black horsehair.

Frequently black walnut, sometimes rosewood. *Ca.
1850–1870.* B to BBB

15. General Lee Armchair

A chair of this design was owned by General Robert
E. Lee. Chair is 46 to 48 inches tall by 22 inches wide,
has a rectangular upholstered back, slightly canted,
framed by an arched top rail and uprights cut in an
unequal reverse serpentine curve. Top rail may be either
finger-molded or plain with centered carved detail of
grapes or roses balanced by leafage; uprights finished
with triple bead molding. Open arms; full-length, overhanging arm pads. Cyma-curved extensions of front legs
form arm supports. These are bead-molded and terminate in either rounded ends or small bead-molded
hand grips.

Upholstered seat, rectangular and flaring with a slightly
bowed front. Conforming front rail either cove or bead-
molded. Lower edge straight or with leaf-carved central
pendent finial. From legs may follow the pattern of back
uprights in reverse serpentine curve with fronts triple
bead-molded, or be ring-turned. The rear legs are square,
plain and canted.

Black walnut, occasionally rosewood or mahogany; fitted with socket casters, upholstered in black horsehair. *Ca. 1860–1875.* B to BB

Lee Lady Chair

Like the preceding in design but smaller, 38 to 40 inches tall by 20 inches wide with seat 14 to 15 inches from the floor. The open arms are noticeably lower, recessed in a downswept curve and not fitted with arm pads.

Black walnut, rarely rosewood. Frequently found separate from matching armchair. *Ca. 1860–1875.* B to BB

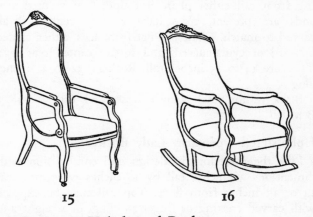

15   16

16. Open-arm Upholstered Rocker

Has approximately the same lines as the General Lee armchair but arms are downcurved. Is 38 to 40 inches tall by about 22 inches wide. The frame of the upholstered back has either a curved or arched top rail which may be surmounted by a carved cresting done in flower or fruit motifs with leafage or may be uncrested and finger-molded. With a curved top rail the back has an elongated U-shape and when arched is rectangular with slightly serpentined ends. The back uprights are either straight or slightly cyma-curved with fronts rounded or finger-molded.

Open arms either flat or slightly curved, equipped with overhanging arm pads; possibly supported by curved extensions of the front legs or may join the seat rails in boldly shaped and carved volutes. Upholstered seat rectangular with straight or slightly bowed front. Conforming front rail either plain or rounded; if voluted arm ends are present, may have applied central detail carved to match. Chair has flat front legs, either canted forward or cyma-curved, and square canted rear legs. They are 14 to 15 inches tall. Rockers, 32 to 34 inches long.

Black walnut, mahogany or rosewood. *Ca. 1860–1875.* B to BB

Upholstered Open-arm Lady Rocker

Like the preceding in design and construction with dimensions 36 inches tall by 18 inches wide and seat 14 or 15 inches from floor. Top rail may be exposed with carved cresting or finger-molding, or straight and covered by upholstery material. Open arms low, sometimes only an inch higher than seat top, in either a flat concave or cyma-curve. Rockers generally from 30 to 32 inches long.

Black walnut, occasionally rosewood or mahogany. *Ca. 1860–1875.* B to BB

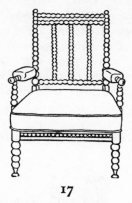

17

17. Spool-turned Armchair

All parts, except seat rails and possibly rear legs, spool-turned. A Victorian revival of the turned spindle arm-chair of the seventeenth century. Spool turnings of legs, back uprights and cross rails about two inches in diameter; spindles from a third to a half less.

This chair is from 36 to 38 inches tall by 22 inches wide. Uprights of the open back terminate in spool-turned finials. Ends of single or double top-rail socketed into uprights just below finials. Between this and a cross rail, placed a little above seat level, are three to five slender spindles. The arms are of two types: (1) extend full depth of seat, have four or five short spindles beneath and are socketed onto the front uprights; (2) shorter, have upholstered arm-pads; arm stumps attached to side rails behind the front legs.

The rectangular seat flares slightly, has a straight front and is covered with either leather or fabric. May be either slip seat or coil-spring type. With the latter the upholstery is attached to seat rails and finished with rows of brass-headed tacks. Front legs are of the same diameter as back uprights or slightly larger and somewhat tapering. Small button or knob feet. Rear legs are generally square and canted. (In America this type of chair is said to have been first made in Baltimore, copied from a Scandinavian example brought in by a returning diplomat.)

Black walnut. Not numerous. *Ca. 1850–1860.* B to BB

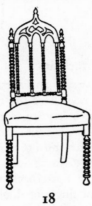

18

18. Spool-turned Gothic Side Chair

Turnings of front legs, back uprights and spindles are like the preceding, but top rail of the back forms a Gothic arch with pierced openings below. Tapering steeple-turned finial above is generally matched by the finials of the back uprights. Chair is about 40 inches tall from central finial to floor. Open back, usually formed by four slender spindles supported by a cross rail a little above the seat. These connect with lower edge of top rail, forming three units like the lancet windows of Gothic architecture.

Rectangular upholstered seat, flaring slightly; a bowed or straight front. Upholstery material is attached to the upper part of the flat, plain seat rails. Front legs match back uprights and terminate in knob or spool-turned feet. Rear legs are square and canted. Used chiefly for hall, parlor or library in private houses; for pulpit or chancel in churches, and for the presiding officer in lodge rooms.

Black walnut. Not numerous. *Ca. 1850–1860.* B to BB

19

19. Gothic Hall Chair

From 36 to 40 inches tall and about 18 inches wide, with consistently low seat about 14 or 15 inches from floor. Back either stiffly perpendicular or slightly sloping, consisting of one-piece shaped and pierced panel supported by turned uprights. Considerable variation in design and ornamentation of back panel; main details much like those of the chair illustrated.

Panel may be either plain, with shaped outline pierced in an elaborate arabesque design and surmounted by an ogee-arched and molded top rail having carved crotchets and central carved trefoil finial, or rectangular with pierced and carved all-over pattern of balancing cyma-curves combined with conventionalized leafage scrolls.

In place of a top rail, the panel itself is cut in a tri-angularly arched outline and is surmounted by three short steeple-turned finials. The uprights are either baluster-turned with vase-ring-and-urn elements termi-nating in urn-shape finials, or spirally-turned with steeple-shaped finials.

The rectangular flaring seat may be wooden or up-holstered. If wood, it is slightly overhanging with molded edge and is hinged at the rear to give access to a shallow storage well beneath. When upholstered, may be either fixed or hinged. Seat rails are plain or molded at top and lower edge valanced in a series of small arches. Front legs match turnings of uprights; back legs plain, square, tapering and canted. Sometimes in pairs, usually single chair.

Generally black walnut. Not numerous. *Ca. 1850–1870.* B to BB

20. Photographer's Studio Chair

Combines ornamental details of Gothic and Renais-sance substyles. From 34 to 38 inches tall by 16 to 20 inches wide. Back surmounted by elaborately shaped cresting, a central cartouche carved in relief of either flowers or fruit with flanking foliage or a grotesque mask flanked by convex or cyma-curved elements, sometimes with scrolled tendrils that extend downward to frame the central panel. Cresting is supported by two slender, free-standing uprights having cylinder, ring and knob-turned elements.

Back panel may be boldly pierced in pattern of S-scrolls with conventionalized leafage in elongated, oval molded

20

frame, or upholstered with a similar frame. Back uprights and seat rails joined by low, scrolled rudimentary arms, either finger-molded or carved. Upholstered seat either flaring with bowed front, or forms nearly circular ellipse. The lower edge of the front seat rail is slightly valanced and either finger-molded or edged with bead molding. The front legs either have a restrained cabriole shaping terminating in rudimentary feet, castered, or may be slender, turned ones with cylinder and ring elements, terminating in small ball feet. Rear legs are square, slightly tapering and canted.

A parlor chair, but used extensively in posing daguerreotypes. (A photograph of Mrs. Abraham Lincoln, taken shortly after her husband's first inauguration, shows her standing beside a chair of this type.)

Black walnut, sometimes rosewood. *Ca. 1850–1870.* AAA to B

21. Gothic Armchair

Is from 38 to 42 inches tall and 20 to 24 inches wide. Back is surmounted by an arched, molded and carved cresting consisting of either a centered pierced quatrefoil flanked by smaller trefoils, or three tracery-like pointed Gothic piercings, the center one higher than the flanking ones. Cresting joins molded uprights just beneath steeple finials which surmount them. Back panel is rectangular, upholstered.

Rectangular, slightly flaring arms have nearly full-length arm pads and terminate in rolled ends. Plain cyma-curved arm stumps attached to the side rails a little behind the front legs. Upholstered seat rectangular and flaring, with straight front. Seat rails about three inches wide covered by upholstery material. Their straight lower edges may be decorated by brass-headed tacks. Front legs either tapering and spirally turned, or turned in inverted vase-shape with plain peg feet. Rear legs square, tapering, slightly backward-curved. Plain brass casters. Upholstery generally black haircloth tufted and decorated with haircloth-covered buttons.

Used as library, pulpit or lodge-room chair. Found single usually, but sometimes in pairs.

Black walnut; some early examples mahogany or rosewood. Not numerous. *Ca. 1850–1880.* B to BB

21   22

22. Louis XVI Chair

Is 34 to 36 inches tall by about 20 inches wide. Concave sloping back, slightly arched top rail, a central applied rosette turned or carved, which forms semicircular cresting. Flanking it usually oblong applied panels of burl veneer; at shaped ends of top rail, smaller matching rosettes. Supporting back uprights plain, connected by a plain cross-rail just above the seat level. Keystone-shape upholstered back.

Back and seat joined by small, short, down-curved open arms. Upholstered seat nearly circular, with seat rails entirely covered. Front legs turned and tapering, with bun elements at upper ends and ring turnings above plain peg feet, frequently castered. Rear legs plain, canted, slightly flaring. Sometimes in a set of six one is an armchair, with open flaring arms, small pads and simple shaped or turned arm stumps, not quite to front legs.

Black walnut, sometimes with burl veneer. *Ca. 1865–1885*. AAA to B

23

23. Curule Armchair

Indirectly inspired by Roman *sella curulis* or curved chair. Legs replaced by two segments, either semi-circular or flatly arched, which support the curved side-pieces. Plain or molded top rail with a slight back-roll, or one that is simply arched and carved with foliated fruit or flowers, connects upper ends of sidepieces. These have a marked backward slope and extend downward in a deep concave curve to join the boldly rounded front seat rail.

About halfway from the top the sidepieces are joined by cyma-curved open arms, which terminate in rolled hand grips and are supported by concave recessed arm stumps. Arms sometimes have arm pads nearly full-length. Upholstered back and seat usually one piece, without a transverse line or crease in the upholstery to mark the normal joining of the two.

When Vassar College was opened, in the 1860's, the curule armchair was among the furnishings of many of the dormitory studies.

Black walnut, some early examples of mahogany or rosewood. Usually upholstered in black haircloth. *Ca. 1850–1875.* AAA to B

24

24. Curule Lady Rocker

A variant of the preceding. Segments have less pronounced curve, and are on rockers about 30 inches long. Open arms, low, without arm pads. Rectangular back arched, and frame has carved cresting done in flower or fruit motif, with foliage. Back and nearly square seat upholstered as separate units. Low seat, 12 to 15 inches from floor.

Black walnut or other native hardwoods, stained brown. *Ca. 1865–1875.* AA to AAA

25

25. Wing Chair

The Victorian version of an armchair made in considerable quantity from about 1730 to 1810. Main points which distinguish this from those of earlier periods are: (1) one-piece sides so shaped as to combine wing and arm in a single unit; (2) very low arms, often little higher than seat cushion; (3) turned front legs taper noticeably; (4) deep fringe often hung from front and side seat rails.

An ample chair with upholstered body. Seat is rectangular and slightly flaring with front either straight or bowed. The turned front legs are of inverted vase shape, with ring turnings. Small knob or peg feet, generally castered. Rear legs square, canted.

Black walnut, mahogany or rosewood legs; concealed frame of assorted hard and soft woods. Unusual. *Ca. 1840–1865.* B to BB

26

26. Cane-seat Transitional Side Chair

Design is similar to Chair No. 1 but simpler, with cane instead of upholstered seat. Open back; flat, slightly concave top rail, about three inches wide, with scrolled outline. Ends mortised into the supporting cyma-curved uprights, as are those of the scrolled-back splat placed halfway between top rail and seat. Top rail may have central scroll-cut finger opening three to four inches wide with carved detail of balancing volutes above, or may be plain.

Seat rectangular and flaring, slightly serpentined front. Front legs — either flat and shaped in reverse ogee curves or turned, like those of a Hitchcock chair, in shallow ring or spool elements; tapering; small button feet. Rear legs — rectangular, continuations of the cyma-curved back uprights, canted in saber curve. Legs braced by a box stretcher with front member a flat, slightly concave bar about two inches wide or simply turned. Other stretcher members are plain turnings, two on each side and one in rear. Used as simple parlor, dining room or bedroom chair. Plentiful in pairs or sets of four.

Maple, sometimes partly yellow birch. Painted to simulate mahogany or black walnut, or finished in black lacquer. *Ca. 1860–1875.* A to AA

TURNED CHAIRS

27

27. Spindle-back Cottage Side Chair

Slightly concave top rail about three inches wide with upper edge either a continuous flat curve or a central cresting flanked by serpentine curves. The lower edge scroll-arched to conform to number of spindles forming the open back. Ends of rail extend beyond those of vase-and-ring turned back uprights; scroll-outlined. Between this rail and a conforming cross slat are from two to four spindles, vase-, knob- and ring-turned.

Cane seat, either rectangular and slightly flaring with bowed front, or simplified shield-shape. Tapering front legs cylinder, knob- and ring-turned; small button feet. Rear legs plain, canted. Plain turned stretchers brace the legs at sides and back; at front there is a vase-and-ring turned stretcher. Original finish of chair is a light brown graining with freehand scrolls, sometimes including a small landscape vignette in darker tone on top rail. Striping in the same tone is found on cross slat, seat rails and front legs.

Maple. Sometimes partly white birch. Less expensive ones of pine can be identified by light weight — five to five and a quarter pounds as against six to six and a half pounds for one of all maple. Generally used as part of a cottage bedroom set. One of the cheapest of the Victorian chairs but always in demand by collectors. Plentiful. *Ca. 1860–1875.* A to AA

Cartouche-crested Side Chair

Similar to No. 26 but top rail has a centered applied cresting, cartouche-shaped, either carved intaglio or faced with burl veneer. Also back uprights are flat, and project about half an inch above the top rail. Cane seat an eccentric ellipse with rear acutely curved. The tapering front legs knob-and-ring turned. Small peg feet.

Black walnut, or ash with cartouche and spindles of black walnut. Used as either dining room or bedroom side chair. May be found in pairs or sets of four or six. *Ca. 1870–1880.* A to AA

28

28. Bar-back Side Chair

Construction of open back similar to that of earlier Sheraton painted fancy chairs. Top rail about three inches wide, arched in a flat curve, and two narrow crossbars of conforming shape placed about three inches apart. Back is supported by slightly flaring uprights, set a little on the diagonal with backward cyma-curve where they join the elliptical cane seat. Leg and stretcher turnings are like those of No. 26.

Black walnut or ash, crossbars of black walnut. Used mostly as a dining chair and originally sold in sets of six to twelve. Not as numerous as chair No. 26. *Ca. 1870–1885.* A to AA

29. Eastlake Side Chair

Slightly concave back formed by two tiers of spindles separated by crossbars. Straight top rail which may be plain, faced with burl veneer or ornamented with a shaped panel of it. Upper spindles short, ball-and-ring turned, varying from four to six. Tall lower ones, usually two, vase-and-ring turned. Back supported by square, slightly flaring uprights with rounded ends which surmount the top rail about an inch. They are joined to the seat by short, square open brackets set at a 45-degree

29

angle. These are bead-molded as are the top rail, crossbars and uprights.

Cane seat — rectangular, flaring. Beneath the slightly bowed front is a recessed triangular skirt. Tapering front legs turned in cylinder, ball-and-ring elements. Small peg feet. The rear ones are plain, square, tapering and canted. Two box stretchers brace the legs. The front ones have a central ring turning; the others are plain.

Sold in sets of four to twelve, used either as dining or living room chairs. For the latter purpose a set sometimes included a rocking chair of larger proportions with a rectangular cane panel replacing the lower back spindles.

Black walnut, with or without burl-veneered ornamentation; occasionally ash or cherry. *Ca. 1875–1890.*
A to AA

30A   30B

30. Parlor Side Chair

Made chiefly of turned parts, usually with spindle
back and rush or upholstered seat. Top rail: (A) slender,
turned, often surmounted by row of seven to nine small
ball finials; (B) flat, slightly concave, upper edge shaped
in a continuous arc ending in scroll-cut ears, lower edge
arched to correspond to the number of back spindles, or
triple-arched to conform to a back splat of conventional
lyre design.

Turned parts may have ring-and-vase or ring elements.
Spindles vary from four to nine in number. With the
latter, the back is usually composed of a row of short
spindles and two equispaced cross-members, turned to
match the top rail. The rectangular seat is flaring with

slightly bowed front, rush or upholstered. The turned front legs are tapering. Small peg feet, braced by vase-and-ring or ring-turned stretcher. Other stretchers at sides and back usually plain; where a chair has only ring turnings, these may occur on all parts except the rear legs. Intended to simulate bamboo, it reflects the vogue for Japanese art and handicrafts which began in the 1880's.

Maple or beech, finished in black lacquer. Occasionally mahogany with rush seat, either gilded or painted cream yellow. Late examples are sometimes oak; natural finish. The popular "occasional chair" for parlor use. An Astor, Vanderbilt or similar mansion would be provided with a quantity to be held in reserve for formal dinners or "musical soirées." *Ca. 1870–1890.* AA to AAA

31

31. Desk Chair

Open back, surmounted by arched top rail ending in scroll-cut ears. May have a carved cresting. It is supported by (1) plain flat uprights and three equally placed narrow vertical splats extending to the rear seat rail; (2) shaped flat uprights framing a cane panel with a cross rail just above the seat. Open rounded arms flare outward and are down-curved, ending in scrolled rolls. They are supported either by extensions of the front legs or by short turned arm stumps.

The seat may be U-shaped or elliptical with either cane or leather panel. Tapering front legs cylinder-and-ring turned, with small ball feet; rear legs plain. Braced by double box stretcher, plain members except for front which are vase-and-ring turned. Sometimes the turned legs are replaced by four flaring scrolled legs with upper ends joined tripod-like. A supporting iron screw, attached to the underside of the seat, fits into the joining. By means of this mechanical device, the chair revolves and the height of seat is adjustable.

Black walnut or, less frequently, mahogany, cherry or oak. *Ca. 1870–1890.* AA to B

Cane-back Rocker

Oval or rectangular back, carved detail of flower or fruit motif framing cane panel. Slightly flaring arms, low, may have downward cyma curve and join the side seat rails a little to the rear of the front legs or be flat with rounded hand grips supported by extensions of front legs.

Seat either elliptical or rectangular with bowed or serpentined front. Front legs baluster-turned with vase or cylinder-and-ring elements. Rear ones plain as are the turned stretchers, except for front one which is vase-and-ring turned. Plain rockers, from 30 to 34 inches long.

Black walnut, maple, birch or, occasionally, cherry. If of maple or birch, sometimes painted and grained as part of a cottage bedroom set. Examples found today may have upholstery in place of the original cane. An armless chair of this type was also made and listed in contemporary manufacturers' catalogues as a "nursing rocker." *Ca. 1865–1880.* A to AAA

32

32. Victorian Boston Rocker

With slight simplification of line and decoration, continues the design of the American Empire period. Tall back, shaped top rail about five inches wide with rounded corners, sometimes surmounted by low rolled cresting. It is supported by plain turned uprights which flank five or six slender tapering spindles, either straight or slightly conforming.

The seat may be oval, solid and saddled or rectangular, upcurved at rear with boldly rolled front and cyma-curved sides. (With this shaping the seat often has a large panel of woven cane.) Open recessed arms about two inches wide, cyma-curved with rolled ends that are supported by spindle-turned arm stumps. A single spindle is placed midway between stumps and back uprights. The short turned legs, front ones ornamented with ring elements, are mounted on narrow rockers about 26 inches long. Legs are braced by a box stretcher with front element sometimes ring-and-ball turned.

Was also made about a fifth smaller, without arms, as a lady chair.

Ralph Waldo Emerson favored a Boston rocker. A simply turned one stood in the study of his Concord home beside his writing table, the hardness of the oval seat alleviated by a cushion.

Maple with seat of pine. Made in same early chair factories that produced Hitchcock-type chairs. Painted and grained to simulate rosewood, with striping. Top rail sometimes has gilt stencil design. *Ca. 1840–1860.* AA to AAA

33. Painted Rocking Chair and Matching Side Chair

A Pennsylvania Dutch version of the Boston rocker, with U-shaped open back, and arched top rail with curved central finger-hole, down-curved to meet the slightly flaring and rounded uprights. Simple vase-shaped back splat that extends from top rail to seat. Cyma-curved arms ending in convex scrolls, supported by turned arm stumps. Solid wooden seat an inch and a half to two inches thick, rolled at front and upcurved at rear, supported by short turned legs, braced front and rear by turned stretchers. Rockers about 28 inches long.

Maple and assorted hardwoods, seat of pine or white wood. Painted with a body coat of brown or black. Top

33

rail, back splat and front of seat are decorated with
flower and foliage motifs and striping, in polychrome
colors. Striping with yellow also decorates other parts.
A variant lady chair generally armless. *Ca. 1840–1880.*
AAA to B

34. Eastlake Platform Rocker

Also called a "patent rocker," this is a mechanical
version of the usual upholstered rocking armchair invented about 1870. Chair has open arms fitted with pads;
lower edges of side rails are cut in bold convex curves
so that it rocks on a low-shaped platform or base, usually
fitted with socket casters. Body of chair is attached to the
platform by a pair of yoke springs.

Frame has Eastlake decorative details including
arcaded or molded cresting of back top rail. Upholstery
material is plush or tapestry.

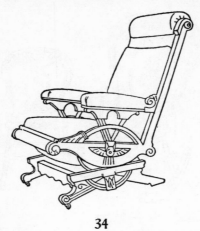

34

Black walnut, ebonized maple or cherry. By furniture factories, sometimes as part of parlor set. *Ca. 1870–1880 or after*. A to AAA

Turned Platform Rocker

A less expensive type of above, the frame of turned members. Padded upholstery of back and seat is replaced by carpet panels tacked to the frame members. Has turned arms and the usual platform base with yoke or compression coil springs.

Maple, birch or cherry, finish natural or sometimes ebonized. By furniture factories in quantity. Was very popular in rural sections. Numerous. *Ca. 1870–1880 or after*. A

SURVIVAL WINDSOR CHAIRS

As it originated in England, the Windsor chair was a simple sturdy piece of furniture for country tavern or farmhouse use. Transplanted to America about 1725, our craftsmen added refinements of turnings and niceties of line to such an extent that it became suitable for use in any setting except that of a sophisticated mansion where the furniture was in keeping with stylized architecture.

With the Victorian Period the Windsor reverted to its original status and was again made as a simple chair sturdy enough to withstand the rigors of common use. Large quantities of these Victorian versions of the Windsor were produced by chair factories throughout the period.

Except for the low-back firehouse chair, the Windsor relationship has been generally disregarded by enthusiasts of Victorian furniture, but many pieces have Windsor characteristics: solid wood saddle-seat, splayed legs, open spindle-back.

Kitchen U-back Windsor

A simplified form of the loop-back; the plain U-shaped bent loop is about an inch and a quarter in diameter and frames four or five turned tapering spindles. U-shaped wooden seat with either straight or slightly bowed front. Saddling either very slight or missing entirely. Upper edge of seat sometimes finished in simple bead molding. Thickness of seat not over an inch and a quarter — only about half that of early Windsor. Plain turned and slightly tapering legs have little or no splay;

rear ones canted backward slightly, braced by a double box stretcher of plain turned members.

Cheapest of all Victorian chairs, this was made in quantity of machine-formed parts by chair factories in all sections and sometimes retailed for as little as fifty cents. An earlier or better-made example has a one-piece, thicker seat, sometimes of pine; a later and less well-made chair has a thin seat of two or three pieces glued together.

Assorted hardwoods; finish natural or painted. Plentiful, but often found in bad order. Not worth structural repairs. *Ca. 1870–1880 or later.* A

35. Spindle-back Dining Room Windsor

Has open back, framed by U-shaped rail about three inches wide with centered finger-hole. Lower ends of rail flare forward in simple cyma curves to join the middle of the seat rails. Back has four or five vase-and-ring turned spindles, the two outer ones slightly heavier, being continuations of rear legs.

Cane seat, U-shaped with bowed front. Front legs turned in vase, ring and cylinder details. Small knob feet. The rear legs plain, tapering and canted. Legs are braced by two box stretchers about five inches apart. Front members are vase-and-ring turned; others plain.

Generally oak, sometimes all or partially ash. Original finish natural with varnish, but may be found painted or stained to simulate black walnut. Cane seat sometimes replaced with a thin upholstered one. Popular in its day because of sturdy construction and ease in handling, was used in restaurants and country hotels as well as in the home. *Ca. 1870–1885.* A to AA

35   36

36. Spindle-back Side Chair

Survival of the rod-back Windsor, but may also have details characteristic of the Hitchcock chair. Back has a slightly arched top rail, three inches wide, with rounded ends and straight or shaped lower edge. Supported by flaring uprights, either baluster-turned or plain with flattened fronts, framing either four or five plain spindles; or there may be a flat horizontal splat about halfway between top rail and seat with three or four simply turned short spindles beneath it. Wooden seat, saddled, rectangular and flaring with straight rolled front, or shield-shaped. The legs turned and splayed, front ones either plain and tapering or baluster-turned. Small ball feet. Legs braced by a box stretcher with front member vase-and-ball turned.

Maple or birch, seat of pine or other soft wood. By early chair factories. Painted; back, seat, front legs and stretcher striped in yellow, top rail of back sometimes stencil-decorated. More desirable in sets of six. *Ca. 1840–1870.* A to AA single; sets, BB

37

37. Splat-back Windsor

A survival design; back spindles are replaced by a vase-shaped central splat that is solid and much wider than the pierced splat typical of many English Windsors. Has same top rail as kitchen chair, as well as a flaring rectangular seat and splayed tapering legs braced by a box stretcher of turned members. Made in early chair factories, widely used in farmhouses and village homes.

Maple, birch or assorted hardwoods, with solid one-piece seat of pine or other softwood. Generally painted or stained and striped with yellow. Chair of this type was in the Lincoln residence at Springfield, Illinois. Mr. Lincoln sold it to a neighbor in 1860, shortly before he left for his inauguration as President. *Ca. 1840–1865.* Except for those with historical associations, singly, A to AA; sets, BB

38

38. Firehouse Windsor

Also called a "captain's chair," this is the Victorian revival of the low-back Philadelphia Windsor of 1725–1760 and takes its name from its extensive use in quarters of the Volunteer Fire Companies of the period. Many other uses.

An early example has a heavy horseshoe-shaped continuous arm with low cresting and terminates in rounded ends. It is supported by from seven to nine simply turned spindles. Deep, U-shaped seat, either flat or slightly saddled. Legs have only a moderate splay with front ones ring-turned and tapering and rear ones plain and canted. They are braced by a box stretcher of turned members with front one either ring-turned or replaced by a flat cross stretcher about two inches wide.

With a later chair, the horseshoe arm may be of bent wood with finger-hole in center of low cresting. Ends are bent at right angles and replace the front supporting spindles. U-shaped seat of cane, with conforming seat rails; either bowed or serpentined front. The turned and tapering legs have practically no splay and are braced by a single or double box stretcher of turned members.

Both early and late examples also made for children, two styles: High chair, splayed legs, usually a narrow foot rest attached to the front legs about eight inches below the seat; child's miniature chair, sometimes equipped with rockers.

Early examples were made with seat and arm of pine, legs, spindles and stretchers of maple or birch, painted, grained and striped. Late ones are of oak, finish natural, and date from about 1880. *Ca. 1840–1880.* AA to B

39

39. Writing Armchair

Design, construction, size and wood are same as No. 38. But a broad, boldly curved fixed writing tablet is attached at the right side of the horseshoe-shaped arm, and a small shallow drawer is under the tablet and another larger and deeper one beneath the solid U-shaped seat. A late example, with bentwood arm and cane seat, has a rectangular tablet with rounded front but lacks drawers and was used as a classroom chair.

The chair illustrated once belonged to Franklin Pierce, who gave it to a close friend about 1850. *Ca. 1840–1880. Late type after 1875.* A to BB

40

40. Upholstered Camp Chair

Folding chair with upholstered back and seat, either with or without arms, sometimes fitted with rockers. The armchair has a pair of X-shaped supports that cross at the seat level where they are pivot-joined. The side chair has a pair of long supports that slope forward and a shorter pair that slope backward, joined by pivots at the seat level. With both, the supports, whether ring-turned or square and molded, are braced at front and rear by ring-turned or vase-and-ring turned stretchers.

The armchair has a concave enclosed upholstered back with plain top rail covered by the material. Arms are upholstery-covered straps; upholstery of the U-shaped seat covers the rails. The side chair has a flat back with shaped top rail; supports frame an upholstered panel. Its upholstered seat is rectangular with conforming rails exposed. Rockers, if present, are pivot-joined to the supports.

Made by furniture factories. Slightly varying designs.

Black walnut, cherry, oak; sometimes maple or birch, ebonized. Upholstered with tapestry or similar materials. *Ca. 1870–1885.* A to AA

41

41. Corner Chair

Is so named because, with the diagonally placed seat, the back forms a right-angled corner. First made in the Queen Anne Period, it has appeared with variations of style through subsequent furniture periods.

In general the Victorian type is like the occasional parlor chair (*see No. 30*). Back is supported by three slender turned extensions of the three rear legs. Into these are socketed the two turned top rails and matching lower cross-rails. Two groups of five to nine vase-and-ball spindles complete the open back. The square seat may be upholstered, rushed or caned. The seat-high leg at the front corner is turned to match the three uprights. Turned stretchers brace the legs. Frequently, the turned parts have incised ring elements to simulate bamboo.

Maple, finish natural, mahoganized or gilded; oak, finish natural. Factory-made. *Ca. 1875–1890.* AA to AAA

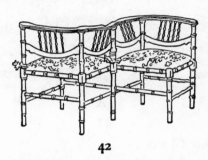

42

42. Conversation Chair

Also known as a "tête-à-tête chair." Design originated in France. A double corner chair with opposite seats, construction similar to the preceding. Has flat, boldly S-curved arm, with outcurved or rounded ends. This may be surmounted at the center of each opposing curve by a low shaped or carved cresting. Arm supported by five slender turned uprights.

The two backs are deeply concave to conform to the double curve of the arm and are completed by groups of five to nine vase-and-ball turned spindles or narrow splats. The upholstered twin seats are either square or elliptical with conforming seat rails either enclosed or exposed. Legs are braced by twin box stretchers. Also made as an upholstered chair, with enclosed double back and cabriole legs, in the Turkish substyle.

Black walnut or maple, the latter mahoganized, painted white with gilt striping or gilded. *Ca. 1865–1885.* AA to BB

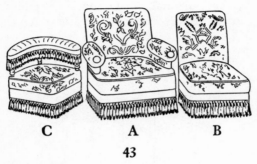

C   A   B

43

43. Turkish Chairs

All overstuffed, with upholstery-covered frames and, frequently, pendent fringe concealing legs. Boxlike with rectangular or slightly curved outline and of large size, varying from 36 to 40 inches tall by 20 to 26 inches wide with seat about 14 inches from floor. Both seat and back have coiled springs covered with curled hair and padding. The front legs are either turned in inverted vase shape or are spool-turned. Rear ones square and canted backward. Legs are fitted with socket casters. The concealed frames are of assorted native hard- and softwoods and legs are of black walnut or of maple or birch, stained brown or ebonized. Original upholstery materials include plain deep-pile velvet in brown, Nile green or Victorian red, brocade, velour, brocatel or Wilton carpeting. *Ca. 1865–1880 or after.* (Values below.)

A. Armchair

Back is either rectangular and flat or arched and concave with flaring recessed arms that are (1) low and bolster-shaped, (2) enclosed and outcurved or (3) open with arm pad and supported by turned arm stumps. Seat is either rectangular or U-shaped. If not trimmed with pendent fringe, front seat rail is molded or reeded. AAA to B

B. Side Chair

Smaller than the preceding. Has plain rectangular back with matching seat or is flaring and concave and seat has a conforming curve at rear. Made also slightly larger as a lady chair. AA to AAA

C. Corner Chair

Seat is square and placed diagonally. It is surmounted by a low concave padded arm with fringe that is supported by the turned upward extensions of the three rear legs. AA to B

There is also a Turkish conversation chair that has same design and structure of frame as other conversation chairs (*see No. 42*). Its S-curved back can be plain or flaring and seats are U-shaped with bowed fronts or circular. Rear of backs always covered with same material as rest of chair.

Variants of the Turkish chairs were known as "Spanish" or "Persian."

44

44. Morris Chair

Bears name of William Morris, English artist, architect and poet who was also interested in furniture and decorative arts. It is claimed that this chair was first made about 1875 for Morris's own home. It subsequently became very popular in the United States.

It is a large armchair about 38 inches tall by 26 inches wide, back and seat rectangular and either upholstered or fitted with thick conforming cushions. The tall, adjustable back is joined to the seat rail by a pair of hinges, and its slope is controlled by a metal cross rod that fits into grooves on the rear extensions of the arms.

Arms are either flat or convex-curved, with or without arm pads, supported by extensions of the square or shaped front legs; space between arms and side seat-rails is usually fitted with turned spindles. Front seat-rail is plain or molded, with plain or valanced lower edge. The side seat-rails either straight or extend to the floor in a deep convex curve, replacing square rear legs. Chair is fitted with socket casters.

Black walnut or cherry; late examples oak or mahogany. Arms may terminate in carved knuckle or animal-head hand grips. Factory-made in large quantities. Plentiful, found in most secondhand stores. *Ca. 1875–1900.* AA to AAA

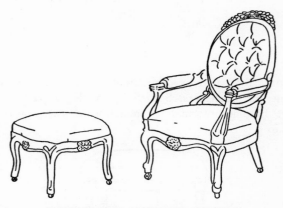

ARMCHAIR AND MATCHING OTTOMAN

OTTOMANS AND FOOTSTOOLS

45. Bracket-foot Ottoman

Has upholstered rectangular top, usually about chair-seat size (20 inches wide by 16 inches deep); sometimes large as a love seat (48 inches wide by 18 inches deep). About 16 inches tall; cushion-like seat supported by a rectangular base with either ogee-molded or serpentined skirt, the latter plain and edged top and bottom with a wavy or concave molding. The four low bracket feet are plain or ogee-molded, fitted with casters.

Mahogany, with crotch-grain veneer, or, less fre-

45

quently, rosewood by cabinetmakers or chair and sofa-frame manufacturers. Sometimes made in pairs or as large fireplace ottoman to match sofa. *Ca. 1840–1855.* AA to B

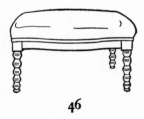

46

46. Spool-turned Ottoman

Rectangular upholstered seat, 20 to 24 inches wide by 18 to 20 inches deep, with plain straight rails partially covered by upholstery. Is from 14 to 16 inches tall and supported by four spool-turned legs, sometimes with small button feet.

Made by early furniture factories or chair and sofa-frame manufacturers. Black walnut or, with less expensive examples, native hardwoods stained brown. *Ca. 1850–1865.* AA to AAA

47

47. Cabriole-leg Ottoman

Has upholstered seat, 18 to 22 inches wide by 14 to 16 inches deep and is 14 to 16 inches tall. The four seat rails are serpentined, finger-molded and have central medallions of flowers or fruits, flanked by leafage in low or medium relief. It is supported by finger-molded cabriole legs with either conventionalized bosses or carved flowers at knees, terminating in rudimentary or carved whorl feet.

Black walnut or occasionally rosewood. Generally part of parlor set, gentleman's armchair and ottoman of corresponding size. Found today more often as a separate piece. Was also made with longer legs (18 to 22 inches high) for use as a dressing table seat or a piano stool. Quantity-produced by furniture factories and manufacturers of sofa and chair frames. (Belter included an ottoman of this type in some of his parlor sets.) *Ca. 1850–1865.* AAA to BB

48

48. Lyre Trestle Ottoman

Rectangular upholstered seat, 22 to 24 inches wide by 16 to 18 inches deep, and is 14 to 16 inches tall. Seat rails are straight, plain and partially covered with upholstery. Is supported by a pair of open lyre-shaped trestles with down-swept cyma-curved feet.

Rosewood, black walnut or, infrequently, mahogany, by cabinetmakers or manufacturers of chair and sofa frames. *Ca. 1850–1875.* AA to AAA

49

49. Early Slipper Box Stool

Beneath the upholstered lid there is a slipper compartment which is contained within the frame. Is from 14 to 16 inches tall, has an overhanging top 16 to 20 inches long by eight to 10 inches deep is hinged at rear. Six-inches deep slipper box. The sides are plain and their straight lower edges may be banded with wavy molding. Is supported by four tall plain cyma-curved scroll-cut bracket legs terminating in incurved volutes.

Made by cabinetmakers or early furniture factories of mahogany, with sides and legs crotch-grain veneered, or of rosewood. Decorative needlework in flower and foliage designs generally the original material of upholstered top. *Ca. 1840–1855.* AA to AAA

50

50. Eastlake Slipper Box Stool

Design with slipper compartment beneath hinged top like the preceding. About 20 inches long, eight to 10 inches deep, and 16 inches tall. Carcase formed of trestle ends joined by sidepieces with conforming molding-framed panels. Upper ends of trestles match the sides. Below they are scroll-cut in concave curves, with conforming shaped openings, done in balancing segmented curves.

Black walnut or ebonized maple, by furniture factories as an occasional piece only. *Ca. 1870–1880.* AA to AAA

51. Upholstered Footstool

Oval or rectangular top 12 to 14 inches long by eight to 10 inches deep, six to 10 inches tall. Upholstered top, frequently finished by row of brass-headed tacks, is of pine or whitewood about an inch and a half thick into which are socketed the four legs. These are baluster-turned, terminate in small peg feet and flare at about a 60 degree angle. Legs are of maple or other native hardwood and often painted a dark color, sometimes striped with gilt or yellow paint. Numerous. *Ca. 1840–1865.* A to AA

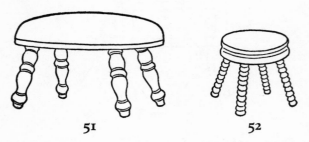

51   52

52. Spool-turned Footstool

Like the preceding but top not upholstered. Has circular top about 12 inches in diameter, about two inches thick with simply molded or rounded edge. Legs are spool-turned. Finish natural or sometimes stained brown to simulate black walnut. Produced by early factories making other spool-turned furniture. Not as numerous as the preceding. *Ca. 1850–1870.* A to AA

Sofas, Love Seats and Couches

SOFAS, love seats and couches are among the best-known and most readily recognized pieces of Victorian furniture. The earliest examples are carry-overs in design and construction from the American Empire Period, with the addition of decorative touches. Sometimes the outline is partially Gothic, especially in the arching of the back.

Close upon this Transitional phase is the French, Louis XV substyle, characterized by short cabriole legs, finger-molded frame and carving done in flower or fruit motifs with foliage, often grape leaves. Acknowledged as the height of the Victorian, some eight typical variations of design are to be found which date between 1850 and 1870. Within this span are the ornate sofas and couches of laminated construction by Belter.

This style is followed by one inspired by the Louis XVI substyle, sometimes combined with Eastlake details. In addition to sofas and kindred pieces of this type, a few of the upholstered Turkish sort, as well as the couch known as a "lounge," appear during these late Victorian years.

Throughout the entire period, most sofas and love seats were originally part of a parlor or drawing room set. Belter made many fine ones for the handsome city mansions of his New York clients. His sets included a pair of sofas, a couch, a gentleman's armchair, a lady chair, six side chairs, one or two ottomans, a marble-top center table and a child's chair, frequently a rocker. Occasionally, too, a shipowning family brought home a set, made of carved teakwood from India, which was distinctly Victorian although Oriental in execution.

For the householder of very limited means, there might be a simple, factory-made parlor set consisting of a sofa or love seat, an armchair, and four side chairs; more often the furnishings were mainly a lounge or spool-turned sofa and an assortment of simple Cottage-style chairs.

Special Comments on Sofas, Love Seats and Couches

The distinction between a sofa and a love seat is one of length and height of seat. A sofa varies from over five to nearly seven feet in length; a love seat is three feet four inches to five feet long. The sofa seat is 16 to 18 inches from the floor; that of the love seat can be as low as 14 or 15 inches. Except for these differences in dimensions, both are alike except for some early love seats, which are armless. All sofas, like their close relative the armchair, have either enclosed or open arms.

A couch is a luxurious form of the earlier "day bed" and has either a forward extension of the back or a head-rest at one end from which the back sweeps down in a conforming shaping to the seat level of the opposite end or foot.

With all three pieces, the legs and exposed parts of the frame are of mahogany, rosewood or, more often, black walnut. Parts of framework concealed by upholstery are usually of pine or other softwoods. For extra strength, internal back braces and seat cross braces may be of such hardwoods as maple, birch or chestnut. Frame parts are joined by glued dowel joints for back top rail and open arms and by butt or dowel joints for interior parts which are generally strengthened with glued blocks.

Construction of a sofa or similar piece is the same as that of an upholstered armchair (*see Nos. 13, 14, and 15*). The upholstered seat is finished with a slight crowning curve and is supported beneath the padding by coiled springs. These vary in number from 16 to 24 and are placed in two or three lengthwise rows. They are usually mounted on interlaced bands of webbing and tied to a uniform height. Seat, back and arms are often deeply tufted and fitted with buttons for decorative effect and to retain the shaping of the upholstery. Back and enclosed arms have padding but not springs. If the back has one or more removable panels, these are upholstered separately and then held in place with concealed screws.

Carved medallions and molding bands on the veneered skirt of a Transitional sofa (*see No. 53*) are applied. Likewise, the carved cresting of the back is separate and attached by dowels. With the French Louis XV substyle, the carved decoration, usually of flower and fruit motifs with leafage, is cut from the part so decorated and the finger-molding of frame and legs is incised. Fine examples have carefully done hand carving and finger-molding. With simpler ones, the work is not as well executed and is partially machine-done.

The pierced carving on Belter sofas, love seats or couches are always handwork done on laminated rosewood; the backs of his pieces are solid, faced with rosewood veneer instead of the usual textile panel.

On the late Victorian sofas, love seats and lounges all

carved decorations, rosettes, incidental raised panels and moldings are applied and glued in place, as are the parts of an arcaded cresting or any projecting ornamental brackets.

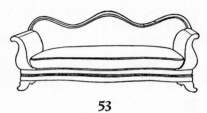

53

53. Transitional Serpentine-back Sofa

Serpentined-arched top rail, serpentine front with skirt trimmed with wavy molding, show Victorian influence. Half-lyre curve of ends and bracket-like feet belong to the earlier American Empire Period and mark this design as Transitional.

Five feet, eight inches to six feet, six inches long by 32 to 36 inches high by 22 inches deep; seat sometimes as low as 15 inches from floor. The serpentined top rail of the back may be either plain or have a cresting of foliated flowers and fruits. It is full-length if sofa has straight ends, or about a third shorter if they join back in concave curves. Upholstery is full-length, or formed of three panels of conforming outline partially framed by the top rail.

The half-lyre ends are faced with conforming uprights that are either plain or carved with foliated scrolls and flowers matching the carving of top rail. Ends join back either at right angles, frequently with top rails exposed, or curve to back with top rails covered. The seat is rectangular; serpentine front. Feet castered, may be plain or carved with foliated scrolls.

Mahogany, with crotch-grain veneer. Some later examples black walnut. *Ca. 1840–1855*. AAA to B

LOUIS XV SUBSTYLE SOFAS

54

54. Serpentine-back Enclosed-arm Sofa

Has an exposed partially carved frame, five feet, six inches to six feet, four inches long by 34 to 38 inches tall by about 22 inches deep. Continuous top rail, serpentine arched, curves in unbroken line to enclosed arms. Frequently has a cresting of carved flowers and fruit. Flanked by leafage, done in medium relief.

Back and arms are upholstered as a unit. Rounded, rudimentary hand grips; sometimes arm pads. They are supported by cyma-curved extensions of the front legs, often with simple bosses between. The front of the upholstered seat is either straight or slightly serpentined with conforming seat rail, sometimes carved in addition to finger-molding. Cabriole front legs, rudimentary feet; rear ones plain, square and canted. Also made as a love seat, with same dimensions except length, which varies from three feet four inches to four feet six inches. Both were frequently part of parlor or drawing rooms sets.

Made of rosewood, black walnut; infrequently, mahogany. By cabinetmakers and early factories. Plentiful. *Ca. 1850–1870.* B to BB

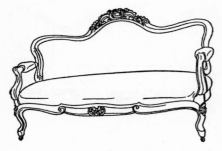

55

55. Serpentine-back Open-arm Sofa

Like preceding but has open arms. The rounded ends have a less pronounced curve and do not project as far forward. The serpentine arched top rail curves downward to the seat and serves as rear supports of the open arms. Its cresting of foliated flowers and fruits is carved in silhouette and may also be pierced.

The open arms have nearly full-size arm pads and are supported by boldly cyma-curved extensions of the front legs with either a leaf or shell-carved detail between. The finger-molding at center of the serpentined front seat rail may be interrupted by a small flower-carved medallion or a shell-shaped cartouche. Is also of love-seat size. Probably made a few years later than enclosed-arm type. Rosewood or black walnut. Numerous. *Ca. 1855–1870.* B to BB

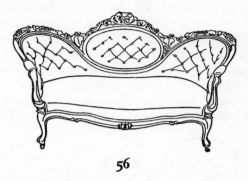

56

56. Medallion-back Sofa

Size and lines are same as other serpentine-back sofas (*see No. 54*), but design is elaborated by a large upholstered medallion of either oval or cartouche shape, in the center of the back.

The serpentine, arched top rail surmounts both medallion and rounded ends, curving downward in an unbroken line to the enclosed arms. It also forms the frame of the medallion by a secondary element that sweeps from the rounded ends beneath it in an unbroken and deeply curved line. Top rail may be undecorated, except for finger-molding, or be surmounted by a simple or elaborate pierced cresting of foliated flowers and fruits that sometimes extends over the rounded ends in bunches of grapes and tendrils in medium relief.

Finger-molding of front seat rail is sometimes interrupted at center by a carved floral or conventionalized detail. Cabriole front legs. Rudimentary or, infrequently, small pad feet. Also love-seat size. With late example, foliate carved crest is replaced by an oval medallion flanked by small, rectangular panels, faced with burl veneer.

Most frequently black walnut, sometimes rosewood. Quantity-produced with plain finger-molded frame in black walnut, by furniture factories as part of a medium-priced parlor set. Dealers sometimes call this design "mirror-back," from resemblance of medallion to an oval mirror frame. Numerous. *Ca. 1855–1870.* B to BB

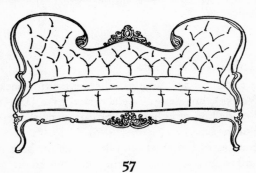

57

57. Triple-arch Sofa

Small — four feet two inches to four feet 10 inches long, by 40 to 44 inches tall, by about 20 inches deep. Triple-arched back with outline of two tall chair-backs joined by a lower central section with less pronounced arching. The chair-backs form rounded ends, and the serpentine top rail curves down to the enclosed arms in an unbroken line. Plain, with only top exposed and surmounted by carved leafage-scrolled crestings; sometimes wider with finger-molding, and carvings in medium relief at top of the three archings.

Shaped back and arms upholstered as unit, plain or finger-molded, with arm pads and rounded rudimentary hand grips. They are supported by cyma-curved and finger-molded extensions of the front legs, frequently with a simple boss or other carved detail at joining. The serpentined front seat rail is valanced or curved and has either a scrolled molding with central medallions of foliated scrolls or finger-molding only. Cabriole front legs, finger-molded; either rudimentary or whorl feet. Square rear legs, plain and canted.

The famous midgets, General and Mrs. Tom Thumb, had a miniature, specially made triple-arch sofa as part of the stage properties for their P. T. Barnum tours.

Black walnut, rosewood or, less often, mahogany. By cabinetmakers and manufacturers of sofa and chair frames. *Ca. 1855–1870.* B to BB

58. Scroll-curved Sofa

Five feet to six feet eight inches long, by 40 to 44 inches high, by about 22 inches deep. Back outlined in undulating scrolls, carved cresting, exposed frame all or partially finger-molded. Top rail and cresting make scroll-arched unit — motif, foliated flowers and fruits in medium or high relief. Ends of top rails are boldly rounded and extend downward to enclosed arms.

The upholstered back flat. Conforming scrolled top. Enclosed arms flare slightly, have covered top rails supported by cyma-curved, finger-molded extensions of front legs. Rounded and finger-molded hand grips. Between arm supports and legs, usually a small boss or leaf-carved detail. Seat rectangular. Scroll-valanced skirt beneath has central carving like cresting of back, either edged with scrolled molding or finger-molded. Cabriole front legs finger-molded. Rudimentary or whorl feet, rear ones square and canted. Sometimes love-seat size.

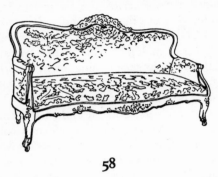

58

Rosewood, black walnut or, with early examples, mahogany. By cabinetmakers, furniture factories or manufacturers of sofa and chair frames. *Ca. 1840–1865.* B to BBB

59. Triple-back Sofa

General lines and construction of open-arm sofa (*see No. 55*), but back has three curvilinear upholstered panels set in chair-back frames. Small-sofa or love-seat size.

Details vary from plain finger-molded framing, conforming to shaping of panels, raised about two inches from the seat, to elaborate carved and crested decoration. Shaping of panels may be three ovals, the center one horizontal and those flanking it vertical, or cartouche-shaped with central panel widest. Open padded arms, supported by cyma-curved and finger-molded extensions of front legs. Rounded hand grips and boss or other carved detail at joining.

Upholstered seat. Front seat rail has restrained serpentine curve; either finger-molded with straight lower

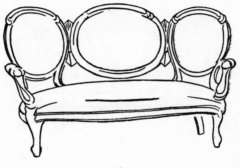

59

edge or valanced, cyma-curved and elaborately molded with leafage-carved branching scrolls at center. Front legs cabriole, finger-molded. Either rudimentary or carved whorl feet. Rear ones plain, square and canted.

Black walnut, rosewood or, less often, of mahogany. Simple finger-molded sofas were made in quantity. Elaborate examples were custom-made by cabinetmakers. Part of matching parlor set. *Ca. 1855–1875.* B to BB

60. Belter Triple-arch Sofa

Made to match his gentleman's armchair (*see No. 9*), its dimensions are six feet, four inches to seven feet, two inches by 46 to 50 inches tall by about 22 inches deep.

The triple-arched back and recessed rounded ends are of one-piece laminated construction with a continuous band of pierced carving in place of a shaped top rail. This is in two designs: (1) three large C-shaped scrolls, surmounted by arched crestings pierced and carved with foliated full-blown roses in high relief and separated by

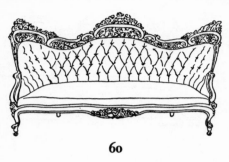

60

matching cyma-curves, forming upper edge of pierced band carved in leafage and grape motifs; (2) molding shaped in curved units, with central arch surmounted by a small scroll-carved finial, forming top of the pierced and carved band of intertwined foliated scrolls.

The shaped back and enclosed arms are upholstered as a unit. The arms have cyma-curved and finger-molded supports — extensions of the front legs — and terminate in rounded hand grips. Between supports and legs, either carved roses or scrolled bosses. Front seat rail serpentined and finger-molded. Central carved detail is either shell-shape or branching leafage scrolls surmounted by a small rose in medium relief. Front legs are cabriole, finger-molded. Carved whorl front feet; rear ones plain rounded, canted. Back may be finished with a large upholstery panel. In a drawing room set with two sofas, one was sometimes made triangular to fit in a corner.

Rosewood. Rare. *Ca. 1844–1863.* CC to #

61

61. Belter Graduated Triple-arch Sofa

Like the preceding except for graduated triple-arched and scrolled asymmetrical back; smaller. Arch-shaped crestings, carved elaborate flower-garlanded cartouches and leafage scrolls, partially pierced, are scrolled downward to join enclosed arms and concave C-shaped scrolls which separate back and ends.

Back and arms are upholstered as a unit. The arms have exposed finger-molded top rails, rolled ends, supported by cyma-curved, finger-molded or leafage-carved extensions of the front legs. Front seat rail serpentined, molded and carved with trailing roses and leafage. Short, cabriole front legs, ornamented with a carved pendent bunch of grapes at each knee and carved whorl feet.

Rosewood. Unusual. *Ca. 1844–1863.* CC to #

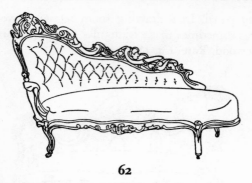

62

62. Belter Couch

Design is a modification of the Louis XV substyle. Has an armchair back, rounded end with single enclosed arm, and a triangular back that slopes downward to a rounded, armless foot. All of one-piece laminated construction.

Six feet long by 44 inches tall at highest point, and 28 inches deep. Top rail is surmounted by elaborate pierced and carved design. Above the chair-back end, a high arch with cartouche finial; beneath, full-blown roses with leafage carved in high relief. Pierced carving curves downward to join the enclosed arm supported by cyma-curved and finger-molded extension of the cabriole leg, which has a scroll-shaped boss at the joining.

Upholstered seat, straight front, semicircular ends. Front seat rail has a central carved cartouche flanked by conventionalized leafage scrolls. Conforming end rails are finger-molded. Four finger-molded cabriole legs, rudimentary feet.

Rosewood. Depicted in contemporary book and periodical illustrations, but few examples still extant. *Ca. 1844–1863.* CC to #

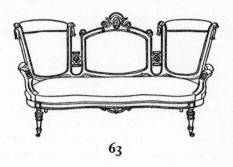

63

63. Louis XVI Eastlake Sofa

Usually made with open arms, reflecting late French style with Eastlake details. Four feet four inches to five feet eight inches long, by 36 to 40 inches tall, by about 22 inches deep. The upholstered back may be formed of (1) single panel, (2) three shaped panels separated by exposed framing, or (3) half-length panel flanked by low, armlike curved ends. The full-length panel is surmounted by an arched and carved top rail with central cartouche of conventionalized leafage scrolls surrounding a shield-shaped or oval medallion in medium relief, terminating in short leafage-carved finials. Top rail supported by conformingly carved uprights, with or without projecting side brackets at upper ends.

With the three-panel back, the central one is lower and rectangular, with curved upper and lower edges and molded frame with arched top rail and central carved cartouche. The taller flanking panels are keystone shaped with either corresponding exposed top rails or nearly flat, covered ones. The half-length panel type is rectangular with arched upper edge, molded frame, conforming top rail and either central carved cartouche and small finials at ends or central rosette and smaller ones at ends. It is flanked by low rounded ends serving as enclosed recessed arms.

If sofa has open arms, they are either straight or curve forward and are padded. Either rudimentary molded hand grips or carved lionheads in high relief, supported by cyma-curved, molded arm stumps or extensions of the front legs. Enclosed arms have concave curve; are recessed, covered, and have molded supports ending in rosettes. Upholstered seat rectangular; either straight or slightly curved front and straight or conformingly rounded ends. Molded front seat rail has either a straight lower edge with central demicartouche pendent finial or is valanced and ornamented with carved leafage scrolls and a central medallion.

Usually, turned front legs that taper from a large bun-shaped element to ring turnings and peg feet. An ornate example has four front legs, shaped like flaring beakers, leafage-carved, and small button feet. Rear legs always square, tapering and canted.

Black walnut, burl-veneer trim; maple, birch or beech ebonized; less frequently mahogany; carvings sometimes touched with gilt. Simple black walnut ones quantity-produced by furniture factories and plentiful; elaborate black walnut, ebonized hardwood or mahogany examples work of cabinetmaking shops. *Ca. 1870–1880.* AAA to BB

64

64. Circular Sofa

Also called *causeuse* — a place for small talk — like many of French origin. Always circular in its American form, four to seven feet in diameter and 40 to 48 inches tall. The flat circular top has a molded edge for a palm or other potted plant or may be in two parts and fit around a structural column. Sometimes there is a low frieze beneath, either molded or carved with leafage scrolls.

The upholstered back is either plain and circular or quadrangular with each side forming a tall flaring panel, sometimes with a molded frame. Four open, recessed and upholstered arms project from the corners, frequently trimmed with deep pendent fringe, and terminate in down-curved molded hand grips, supported by cyma-curved and molded or carved arm stumps. The uphol-

stered seat, about 18 inches deep, is circular and has a
molded or leafage-scrolled seat rail with straight lower
edge. This may be plain, have a series of small pendent
finials or be trimmed with a deep fringe. Four, six or
eight legs, baluster-turned with peg feet; or cabriole,
finger-molded, with rudimentary or carved whorl feet.

Also made in the Turkish style like a Turkish chair
(*see No. 43*). Used extensively in ornate drawing rooms
or hotel lobbies and similar public places, but few examples have survived. *Ca. 1850–1880.* AAA to BB

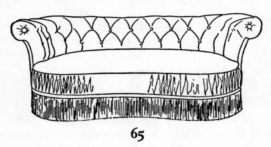

65

65. Turkish Sofa

Construction and upholstery are the same as with
Turkish chairs (*see No. 43*). Two types: (1) low upholstered back, boldly rolled top and recessed curved ends,
a conforming seat with nearly semicircular curved ends.
Dimensions from five feet six inches to six feet long by
about 30 inches tall; (2) taller, plain back divided into
two or three square panels with full-depth bolster arms
and rectangular seat with square corners (frequently
small-sofa or love-seat size). Both have deep pendent
fringe below the seat concealing short, baluster-turned
legs. *Ca. 1870–1880.* AAA to B

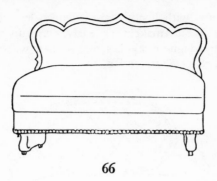

66

66. Armless Love Seat

Frame is similar to that of the Transitional Sofa (*see No. 53*), but without arms, seat is only 14 to 15 inches from floor. It is 40 to 44 inches long by 28 to 32 inches tall by about 17 inches deep. Back has triple, serpentine or flatly arched top rail, generally about two inches wide and faced with crotch-grain veneer. Ends boldly rounded and continue down to seat level. May also have arched leafage-scrolled central cresting, finger-hole opening.

Upholstered back, rectangular with conforming top, slightly incurved ends. Rectangular seat; straight front; square corners. Seat rails either plain or ogee-molded and crotch-grain veneered. Plain, scrolled bracket front feet, veneer-faced, at rear square, tapering legs or brackets.

A late example may have a slightly serpentined front-seat rail trimmed with a central carved medallion in flower or shell motif flanked by leafage scrolls and short cabriole legs, with plain or flower-carved knees and rudimentary or carved whorl feet.

Mahogany, with liberal use of veneer, less often rosewood; by cabinetmakers or early furniture factories. Favored by daguerreotypists for women wearing hoop skirts. *Ca. 1845–1865.* B to BB

67

67. Oval-back Love Seat

Construction and design similar to open-arm sofa (*see No. 55*), but back consists of large single panel, usually oval. Dimensions are from 42 to 52 inches long by 30 to 32 inches tall by about 20 inches deep. Upholstered back panel has conforming finger-molded frame, with or without a carved cresting in low relief.

Open arms, slightly recessed, curved outward from back; padded and supported by cyma-curved finger-molded extensions of front legs. Carved boss or other detail at the joining. Rectangular, upholstered seat, about 14 or 15 inches from floor. Straight or restrained serpentine front. Front seat rail serpentined and finger-molded, sometimes interrupted by a central band of carved leafage scrolls in low relief. Cabriole front legs finger-molded with either rudimentary or carved whorl feet; rear ones square, tapering, canted.

Rosewood, black walnut or, infrequently, mahogany. Ornate examples work of cabinetmaking shops, generally rosewood; simpler factory-made ones are black walnut. Plentiful. *Ca. 1855–1870.* B to BB

68

68. Double-chair Love Seat

General design that of two gentleman's armchairs joined in Siamese-twin manner. Dimensions are 40 to 48 inches long by 36 to 42 inches tall, depending on arch of twin chair backs, by about 20 inches deep.

Chair backs either balloon-shaped with triple arched and molded top rail surmounted by a carved cresting of foliated flowers or fruits (*see No. 11*) or of the Sleepy Hollow type with semicircular arched top (*see No. 14*). The outer sides of both types join enclosed arms supported by cyma-curved and finger-molded extensions of the front legs. Rounded hand grips. Often, between arm supports and legs, a carved boss or other ornamental detail. On inner sides the twin backs curve downward to join (1) a common central arm, (2) a low upholstered back surmounted by a pierced and carved cresting of foliated flowers combined with cyma-curved scrolls or (3) a low balustrade, consisting of spool or baluster-turned horizontals and short spindles, which may be surmounted by a shallow shelf.

If the common central arm is present, it forms a pair of U-shaped seats with bowed fronts. Otherwise the seat is rectangular with straight or slightly bowed front. The seat rail is serpentined, finger-molded and trimmed with a central carving of leafage scrolls or, infrequently, is enclosed by the seat upholstery. Cabriole front legs, finger-molded and terminating in rudimentary feet or, with enclosed seat rail, short baluster-turned tapering ones with ring elements. Rear legs square, tapering and canted.

Rosewood, mahogany or black walnut. Elaborate examples by cabinetmakers, simpler ones by manufacturers. Belter is credited with making a double-chair love seat that matched his armchair. Longfellow's study in the Craigie House, Cambridge, Massachusetts, included one of the central-arm type. *Ca. 1855–1865.* BB to BBB

69. Medallion-back Couch

Like the Belter couch (*see No. 62*), its design is derived from the Louis XV substyle. Has rounded headrest with single enclosed arm, and a back similar to the medallion-back sofa (*see No. 56*), which curves down to a rounded foot. Medallion and headrest surmounted by pierced and carved crestings. Continuous top rail forming asymmetrical serpentine curve terminating in in-

curved volutes; may be finger-molded or plain. Upholstered seat, straight front with rounded ends. Seat rails
serpentined and finger-molded. Finger-molded cabriole
legs. Rudimentary feet, castered. Dimensions five feet

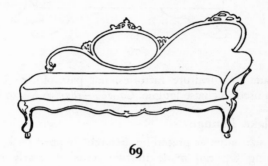

69

10 inches to six feet eight inches long, by 34 to 44 inches
tall at head, and about 24 inches deep.

Sometimes part of a matching parlor set. Black walnut
produced by manufacturers; early examples, rosewood
or mahogany, work of cabinetmakers. *Ca. 1855–1870.*
B to BB

70. Mid-Victorian Lounge

General design like the foregoing, but simpler lines.
Six feet to six feet six inches long, by 32 to 36 inches tall,
and 24 inches deep. Body enclosed by upholstery. Large
outcurved scroll-bracket feet faced with mahogany, black
walnut, rosewood or cherry veneer. Convex overhanging
headrest; no footrest. Shaped back has sweeping cyma-
curved outline, high where it joins the headrest and low
at the foot, terminating in a convex curve.

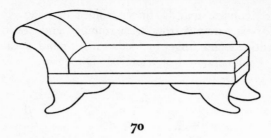

70

Made by furniture factories, not part of set. Today often used as chaise longue. *Ca. 1840–1875.* AAA to B

Eastlake Lounge

In size same as preceding. Straight stepped back, conforming top rail made in two units of nearly equal length, generally surmounted by arched and partially carved crestings. Front of convex headrest generally faced with a triangular wooden panel decorated to match top rail. Foot of lounge is either straight or bowed. Seat rail straight and molded, or covered by upholstery and banded on lower edge by simple molding. Scroll-bracket feet or flaring carved paws. Sometimes made to open and serve as a three-quarter bed.

Black walnut, cherry or other native hardwoods, ebonized or stained to simulate walnut or mahogany. Upholstery was tapestry or figured damask, Brussels carpeting, haircloth or leather. Produced by furniture factories specializing in upholstered pieces. Late examples often have oversize bolster headrest. *Ca. 1875–1890.* AA to AAA

Special Comments on Settees and Spool-turned Day Beds and Sofas

A settee has the same construction as the wooden-seat spindle-back side chair. If with solid one-piece seat, the legs, back uprights, arms and spindles are socketed into it and glued. If seat is cane, these parts are socket-joined to seat frame.

Glued socket joints are used with the uniformly turned uprights, arms and spindles of a spool-turned day bed or sofa. Seat is supported by plain side and end rails which are joined to the spool-turned uprights by mortise-and-tenon joints. The ends are assembled as units with all joints glued tight. Side rails and ends are held by bed screws or inset iron bed latches.

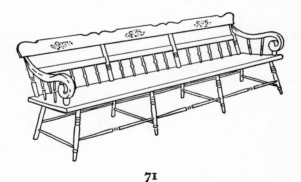

71

71. Painted Settee

Is similar to painted chair and rocker in construction (*Nos. 32 and 33*). Full size has eight legs and is five feet six inches to seven feet long by 30 to 32 inches tall, and about 18 inches deep. Also love-seat size, with six legs and length of four to five feet.

Back has top rail four to seven inches high with straight or slightly shaped upper edge; it is supported by three or four turned and slightly canted uprights. About half the distance to the seat is a narrow horizontal splat in two or three sections. Beneath it are frequently 12 to 15 turned spindles with ends socketed into splat and seat. Has down-curved arms about two inches wide, ending in convex scrolls, and supported by short turned arm stumps and spindles matching those of back.

Has a solid, slightly body-conforming wooden seat with rounded front edge. Front legs ring-turned; rear ones plain, braced by a double or triple box stretcher of turned members. May have four legs mounted on rockers about two inches wide by 28 inches long.

Original finish brown, black or dark green, often decorated with polychrome medallions on top rail and striping in gilt or yellow on turned parts. Made of maple or assorted hardwoods with one-piece pine seat; sometimes unpainted; late example may have seat of woven cane.

Quantity-produced by chair shops and from about 1870 by furniture factories. Many available today made in small Pennsylvania Dutch chair shops and furniture factories. Underside of seat sometimes stenciled with maker's name. *Ca. 1840–1890.* AAA to BBB

72. Spool-turned Day Bed

Also known as "Hired Man's Bed." Not fitted with springs, the mattress rests on eight wooden slats. Is about six feet long by 24 inches wide and 28 inches high. The ends have spool-turned posts surmounted by quarter-circle, bead-molded segments that join the spool-turned top rail. Posts are joined at seat level by plain cross-rails about six inches high; space between rails is filled by four to six spool-turned spindles. Ends are connected by

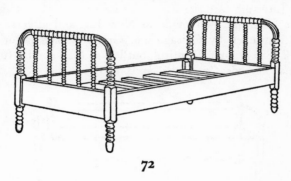

72

plain side-rails; posts, below, either spool or baluster-turned, taper slightly and terminate in double button feet.

A more sophisticated early variant has full-height, spool-turned tapering posts surmounted by slightly projecting spool-turned top-rails with simple rosetted ends. Another variant, dating from about 1870, is a combination day bed and settee. With it, only the front posts are surmounted by the quarter-circle segments. The rear ones are full height and may terminate in short spool-turned finials. The ends have the usual spool-turned top-rails with spindles beneath. The back posts are joined by a flat top-rail with arched upper edge, and the space beneath is filled with from 10 to 15 spindles matching those of the ends. This type is sometimes made with a secondary front-rail, equipped with folding turned legs, which pulls out to form a double bed.

All are made of maple, birch or assorted native hardwoods; finish is natural or stained to simulate black walnut. Quantity-produced by Eastern and Middlewestern furniture factories as part of assortment of Cottage-style furniture. Not made in New England after 1870, but continued by Chicago and Grand Rapids factories until 1880 or later. Plentiful, but less so than similar full-size spool beds. *Ca. 1840–1880.* B to BB

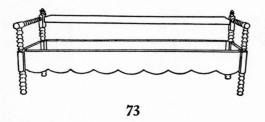

73

73. Spool-turned Sofa

This is the only type made with spool turnings. A simple sofa, lacking elaborate pierced and carved details characteristic of some spool-turned Gothic chairs. About six feet long, 28 inches high, 20 inches deep. Posts uniformly spool-turned, except for square sections at seat level and shorter ones at upper ends where back rail and arms join them. Back posts terminate in low spool-turned finials and are connected by a straight top rail with deeply rounded upper edge.

Back either upholstered or open. The open ends have spool-turned arms of the same height as back. These surmount the front posts, and have plain turned ends.

Upholstered seat, rectangular with frame fitting inside seat rails. Rails plain, about six inches high, forming skirt with lower edge valanced in a repeating simple curve.

Cherry, maple, birch or, occasionally, black walnut; by a few early furniture factories, chiefly in New England. Unusual. *Ca. 1840–1855.* B to BB

Chests of Drawers, Bureaus and Parlor Cabinets

THE CHEST OF DRAWERS with or without its attached mirror was always a part of the Victorian bedroom set. It shared all the style influences of the period. The term "bureau" early in the Victorian Period became attached to a chest of drawers surmounted by a large tilting or stationary mirror. The word "bureau," although everyone knows its Gallic origin and that to the French it means "desk," is by now an accepted misnomer. It was a taken-for-granted part of any bedroom set, even the painted Cottage-type, but the plain chest of drawers must also have had plenty of public favor, since there are twice as many of them to be found today.

The painted Cottage-style bureaus and chests of drawers were produced in great quantity, and are still plentiful. Many still retain their original finish, even to the decorative vignettes and scrollings. Least plentiful are those in the Gothic manner, and those with spool-turned ornamental details. Among truly handsome pieces are serpentine-front chests of drawers with white marble tops produced during the Louis XV substyle years.

Special Comments on Chests of Drawers and Bureaus

A chest of drawers consists of an enclosed carcase containing three or more tiers of drawers, the upper one sometimes of two half-width drawers and the balance full width. A bureau has a similar carcase but is surmounted by a swivel or fixed mirror supported by shaped or turned brackets or contained in a shaped pediment, usually with flanking bracket shelves.

Early Victorian chests of drawers and a few bureaus, dating before 1850, the work of cabinetmakers working with hand tools, are recognized by hand-cut dovetails on drawer sides, roughly smoothed backboards and similar finish for the underside of drawer bottoms.

Some elaborate examples were custom made cabinetwork done in the larger cities, hand-tooled except for planing and sawing.

Otherwise, Victorian chests of drawers and bureaus are of factory origin. Some, made in early or small local factories, may show evidences of handwork since these establishments had little machinery besides power-driven saws and planes. With more extensive mechanization, drawer dovetails became rounded rather than flaring; backboards about a half-inch thick, machine-finished and narrow so that the back is formed of from five to seven pieces, placed vertically and overlapping.

Carcase parts (sides, bearer strips and top) are generally joined by glue butt or dowel joints instead of dovetails or mortise and tenons. These joints are frequently strengthened by glued blocks.

Wood or marble top consistently overhangs the carcase from one half to an inch on front and sides. Marble top is held in place by its weight; the wooden one is fixed and usually retained by small glued blocks, six to 10 in number, attached to underside and sides of carcase.

Drawer openings are separated by bearer strips, about

three-quarters of an inch thick. If piece has a serpentine front, the strips are shaped to conform. Drawer runners are placed to the rear of the bearer strips and are glued and sometimes nailed to the sides of the carcase.

Drawer fronts fit flush into the openings and are never finished with an overlapping molded lip. With some examples, drawer fronts are edged with a slightly raised applied molding. So that drawer fronts will be flush with the openings, a pair of small stop blocks are glued to the upper sides of the bearer strips. When a drawer slides in beyond the opening, it indicates that the stop blocks are missing and should be replaced.

The top drawer may be shallower; otherwise drawers are of uniform depth, usually from six to seven inches. Drawer fronts are fitted with (1) mushroom-turned or rosette-turned knobs, (2) carved wooden handles, usually of a fruit motif with leafage or a strap loop, or (3) metal bail or ring handles with shaped plates. With all except the metal drawer-pulls, either inset metal keyhole surrounds or wooden keyhole rosettes are used.

Carcase sides may be plain but more often are stile-and-rail constructed with rectangular panels. With Cottage-type chests of drawers or bureaus, the lower ends of sides and front corners are scroll-cut to simulate bracket feet. More elaborate examples are supported by low bracket feet or by molded block feet. Some have plinth base. All are fitted with casters.

A skirt, when present, may be either valanced in balancing curves or straight. It may also serve as the front of an additional drawer in the base. This semiconcealed drawer is sometimes part of a plinth base and is without handles or knobs.

Turned uprights or scroll-cut mirror brackets frequently rest on a recessed cabinet containing small drawers or on corner handkerchief boxes with hinged lids. Shaped pediment tops sometimes have these corner boxes.

Turned mirror-supports are socketed into the carcase top; scrolled brackets or shaped pediments rest on it and are held in place by a pair of braces, about two inches wide by 18 to 24 inches long, which are screwed to the back of the piece.

All moldings, carved or turned details — pilasters and finials, bracket shelves, incidental raised panels, arcades and galleries — are applied work. Crotch-grain veneer may be found on mahogany drawer fronts and burl veneer on the raised panels and drawer fronts of black walnut examples. With ash pieces, the applied carving and moldings are of black walnut.

Except for cabinet- and custom-made early pieces, which are 20 inches front to rear, practically all are 16 to 18 inches deep.

A bedroom set usually included a double bed, two to four side chairs, a rocking chair with low arms or armless, a washstand and a small table. A more elaborate one added a wardrobe, a pair of bedside stands, a dressing table, shaving stand and both a bureau and a high chest of drawers.

74. Transitional Chest of Drawers

Has a slightly overhanging top, 36 to 40 inches wide by about 18 inches deep, with square edges and square or slightly rounded front corners. There is either a plain backboard or gallery about three inches high or a pair of recessed cases connected by a plain backboard of conforming height. Each case contains a shallow drawer about eight inches wide, fitted with an inset brass keyhole surround.

The carcase has plain solid sides and contains four tiers of drawers. These are usually of equal depth (about seven and a half inches) but sometimes the top tier is

74

shallower, and may have two half-width drawers instead of one of full-width. All drawer fronts are plain and fitted with mushroom-turned wooden knobs and centered inset brass keyhole surrounds. Sometimes the stiles and rails framing the drawer fronts are finished with a narrow band of wavy molding, either incised or applied. Base has plain bracket feet, five to six inches tall and either simply scrolled bracket at front or a skirt valanced in balancing cyma-curved scrolls. Total height with plain top varies from 38 to 40 inches or with end cases, 42 to 44 inches.

Made of (1) mahogany with drawer fronts crotch-grain veneered; (2) maple or assorted native hardwoods stained to simulate mahogany, with drawer fronts faced with crotch-grain mahogany veneer or (3) black walnut with drawer fronts crotch-grain mahogany or burl walnut veneer. Numerous. *Ca. 1840–1865.* AAA to B

75

75. Chest of Drawers with Recessed Top

Rectangular, slightly overhanging white marble top, 36 to 40 inches wide; square edge, rounded corners. At rear, full-width recessed case four to five inches high; the conforming top, wood or matching marble, contains three or four drawers of equal width, or a wide central drawer flanked by two narrower ones.

Carcase contains three full-width drawers of equal depth with plain fronts, fitted with mushroom-turned wooden knobs and inset keyhole surrounds. The drawers of the recessed case are fitted with similar knobs but are without keyhole surrounds. Front has bulbous, octagon-shaped legs about six inches tall, rear the same or plain brackets.

Made of pine or other softwoods, completely veneered

with crotch-grain mahogany or well-marked rosewood. Drawer knobs of rosewood pieces usually of rosewood. Probably a product of the cabinetmaker's shop rather than the early factory. Not numerous. *Ca. 1840–1860.* B to BB

76

76. Three-drawer Chest of Drawers or Bureau

Rectangular, slightly overhanging marble top, with plain, rounded or concave molded edge and square or slightly rounded corners. Is of two sizes — small, 32 to 34 inches wide, usually without mirror; large, 38 to 42 inches wide with attached oval tilting mirror. Mirror is 32 to 36 inches tall by 16 to 18 inches wide; flat conforming frame about two inches wide, with a band of split ball turnings around outer edge. Mirror tilts on a large scroll-cut, lyre-shaped support with voluted ends and central ornamentation carved in balancing scrolls that terminate in conventionalized leafage. It rests on a scroll-carved rosette base attached to the marble top by concealed screws.

Carcase has chamfered front corners with split turnings, either at top and bottom or at bottom only, and contains three full-width drawers. Drawer fronts are recessed about half an inch and edged with narrow wavy molding, which gives them the appearance of slightly sunk panels. Mushroom-turned wooden knobs and inset keyhole surrounds; ring-turned front feet; back, plain square brackets. Total height, with attached mirror, six feet to six feet six inches, and without mirror 30 to 36 inches. Made of pine or assorted soft woods veneered with rosewood or crotch-grain mahogany. *Ca. 1840–1860.* B to BB

77. Four-drawer Chest of Drawers

Is like foregoing in design and construction. Has overhanging marble top, 38 to 42 inches wide. Carcase contains four tiers of full-width drawers with plain or rounded bearer strips. Drawer fronts fitted with the usual turned wooden knobs and either inset brass keyhole surrounds or wooden keyhole rosettes. Four to five inches high base, with outrounded front corners and skirt valanced in balancing cyma-curved scrolls. Total height is from 37 to 39 inches.

Entirely veneered with mahogany or rosewood or made of maple or other native hardwoods, stained red,

77

with drawer fronts veneered with crotch-grain mahogany. Not as numerous as No. 74. *Ca. 1840–1865.* AAA to B

78. Chest of Drawers with Overhanging Drawer

Rectangular wooden top, 40 to 42 inches wide, plain edge and square front corners. Two cabinets, placed about two inches from each end and connected by a plain backboard of conforming height. Each cabinet contains a drawer eight to ten inches wide and about three inches deep, fitted with a centered mushroom-turned knob.

Carcase has an overhanging, full-width frieze drawer, six to eight inches deep, is ogee-molded with finger grips on lower edge. Beneath, three full-width drawers with flush fronts, mushroom-turned wooden knobs and inset brass keyhole surrounds or wooden keyhole rosettes. Plain base, rounded front corners and skirt valanced in balancing cyma-curved scrolls.

78

Sometimes mahogany, with crotch-grain veneer drawer fronts; more often maple or other hardwoods stained either mahogany or rosewood to match veneer of drawer fronts. *Ca. 1840–1865*. AAA to B

79. Bureau with Octagon Mirror

Rectangular wooden top 38 to 42 inches wide, plain edge and slightly rounded front corners. Two cabinets, about five inches tall and eight to ten inches wide, connected by backboard. Above, octagon tilting mirror, about 24 inches tall by 16 inches wide, set in a conforming molded frame, supported by boldly S-scrolled brackets with voluted upper ends, resting on cabinets. Each cabinet contains a single drawer with one or two mushroom-turned wooden knobs.

Carcase has plain ends and slightly rounded front corners. It has a frieze containing either a full-width or two half-width drawers about five inches deep, edged with wavy molding. Beneath are three full-width drawers, each about seven inches deep, with plain fronts, mushroom-turned wooden knobs and either inset brass keyhole surrounds or wooden keyhole rosettes. Low,

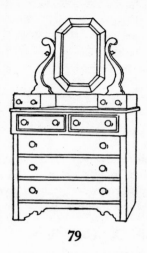

79

simply scrolled bracket feet; narrow plain skirt. Total height from five feet, eight inches to six feet, four inches.

Mahogany, crotch-grain veneer drawer fronts; or native hardwood stained to match veneer. Less frequently, rosewood. Not numerous. *Ca. 1850–1860.* B to BB

80. Bureau with Oval Mirror

Is like foregoing in construction and size. Top has a white marble central section about 20 inches wide, flanked by end cases, each containing a drawer eight to ten inches wide and three inches deep. Their plain fronts are fitted with inset brass keyhole surrounds. The marble section has an oval tilting mirror at rear, about 24 inches tall by 14 to 18 inches wide, set in plain rounded frame sometimes crested with carving. Mirror is held by a conforming lyre-shaped support with voluted upper ends and rests on a low, rectangular base attached to the marble by concealed screws.

Carcase has rounded front corners and sides either plain or stile-and-rail constructed with rectangular,

80

sunken panels. An overhanging frieze contains a full-width drawer about five inches deep with front (1) straight and ogee-molded, with or without a band of wavy molding along lower edge or (2) slightly serpentined and paneled with half-rounded molding that terminates in incurved scrolls and carved acanthus leaves. Drawer has inset brass keyhole surround and invisible finger grips. Three full-width drawers beneath, of equal depth and fitted with mushroom-turned wooden knobs; inset brass keyhole surrounds.

Two sorts of base: (1) plain, with front masking a semisecret full-width drawer about four inches deep, and short bulbous tapering legs; (2) bracket-footed, with conforming rounded edges and skirt either plain and narrow or valanced in balancing cyma-curved scrolls.

Mahogany with drawer fronts and side panels of crotch-grain veneer, or with solid sides of maple or other native hardwoods stained red. Height from five feet six inches to six feet two inches. *Ca. 1850–1865.* B to BB

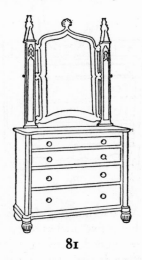

81

81. Gothic Bureau

Rectangular white marble top, 40 to 46 inches wide, molded edge, rounded front corners. Tilting mirror with Gothic arch shaping, about 28 inches wide by 36 to 38 inches tall, set in a narrow molded frame surmounted by a small finial, carved in an anthemion motif. Mirror is supported by square posts that have narrow inset Gothic-arched mirror panels and terminate in tapering spires surmounted by carved cusplike finials.

Carcase has semicircular pilasters at front corners; rectangular paneled sides; four full-width drawers of graduated depth. Plain fronts, mushroom-turned wooden knobs and either brass keyhole surrounds or wooden keyhole rosettes. Slightly projecting molded base. Short, turned and reeded feet. Height from six feet to six feet eight inches.

Mahogany; drawer fronts crotch-grain veneered. Not numerous. *Ca. 1840–1850.* BB to BBB

82

82. Spool-turned Chest of Drawers

Rectangular top, 38 to 46 inches wide; plain edge, square corners; rear gallery, about six inches tall with edge (1) straight with spool-turned molding ending in small projecting finials or (2) scroll-cut in balancing cyma-curves that flank straight sloping sections having spool-turned molding with finial ends.

Carcase has stile-and-rail constructed ends, rectangular panels. Front stiles about three inches wide with full-length split, turned pilasters. These are either spool-turned their entire length or baluster-and-spool turned, ending in standing and pendent ball elements.

The carcase contains four tiers of drawers; top tier frequently has two half-width drawers. All drawer fronts plain, fitted with mushroom-turned wooden knobs; inset brass keyhole surrounds or wooden keyhole rosettes. Corner stiles take place of legs, are usually socket-castered and braced by tall scroll-cut flat brackets. Height from 44 to 48 inches.

Maple, cherry, birch, sometimes black walnut. Not numerous. *Ca. 1840–1850.* B to BB

83. Spool-turned Bureau

Rectangular top, plain edge and square corners, 38 to 46 inches wide; has rectangular tilting mirror, about 22 inches high by 16 inches wide with spool-turned, rosette-cornered frame, supported by spool-turned uprights with steeple-turned finials. Ends of carcase are solid; front contains frieze drawer fitted with inset brass keyhole surround and invisible finger grips. Three other full-width drawers with plain fronts, mushroom-turned wooden knobs and inset brass keyhole surrounds. These flanked by half-round pilasters, either spool-turned or turned in cylinder and ring-and-ball elements. Feet ring-and-ball turned, fitted with casters. Plain skirt, five or six inches high, sometimes masks a semisecret drawer.

83

Carcase is 38 to 40 inches tall. Total height from five feet four inches to six feet.

Mahogany, with drawer fronts crotch-grain veneer; sometimes maple, birch, or combination of both, stained red to simulate mahogany. Not numerous. *Ca. 1840–1850.* B to BBB

84. Cottage Chest of Drawers

Rectangular top, 34 to 40 inches wide; rounded front corners, concave molded or rounded edge; sometimes a gallery board, three to five inches high, with plain, rounded or cyma-curved ends. Straight-front carcase, slightly rounded corners; four full-width drawers, each six to seven inches deep, either mushroom-turned wooden knobs, or fruit-and-foliage carved wooden handles and inset iron keyhole surrounds. Sides solid or with rectangular, slightly sunk panels. Base from three to five inches high, projecting about half an inch at front and sides and fitted with socket casters. It may have either a scroll-valanced skirt or a plain one serving as the front of a full-width concealed drawer.

Pine; interior parts sometimes of other native softwoods. Originally painted to simulate black walnut or

84

grained in light and dark tones of brown with scrolls and stripes in a darker shade. With latter, drawer fronts often had either stripe-outlined panels framing central landscape vignettes or shaped ones of a lighter color with central flower-and-leafage medallions in naturalistic colors. Originally part of a painted bedroom set. Among the least expensive chests of drawers. Plentiful. *Ca. 1860–1870.* AA to AAA

85. Painted Cottage Bureau

Carcase and finish the same as foregoing, but top rear has a tilting mirror with flat frame flanked by scroll-cut supports. Mirror generally rectangular, 20 to 28 inches tall by 14 to 18 inches wide, with curved top and a scrolled and pierced or solid arched cresting. Flat, shaped supports with either tapering or turned finials, flaring downward in pronounced scrolling. A little below the center of each, usually a bracket-like shelf, rounded or shaped, with rounded or molded edge. Base of each support consists of either recessed box, about eight inches wide and three inches high, with molded front and sides,

85

and hinged lid, or of a raised compartment half as deep as top, with single shallow drawer.

With the less usual oval mirror, flanking supports are of conforming shape and terminate in down-scrolled volutes. Their lower ends are joined to pierced triangular brackets attached directly to the top.

Pine with interior parts sometimes of other native softwoods. Besides the usual finish, sometimes enameled in delicate pastel shades or in black decorated with floral medallions and banding done in color. Originally part of cottage bedroom set of six to ten pieces. Now frequently found repainted. Plentiful to numerous. *Ca. 1850–1870.* AAA to B

86

86. Painted Chest of Drawers

Has rectangular top, 36 to 40 inches wide, with rounded front stiles and solid ends which extend to the floor in a flat-arch cutout. The front is without valanced skirt, but the lower ends of the stiles are braced by scroll-cut brackets, to simulate bracket feet. There are five tiers of graduated, full-width drawers with the top one less than three inches deep. All drawer fronts are plain, fitted with mushroom-turned wooden knobs and inset iron keyhole surrounds.

Sometimes top is surmounted at rear by a rectangular tilting mirror, about 20 inches tall by 14 inches wide, which has a plain or molded frame, generally without cresting. Mirror is supported by spool or baluster-turned uprights terminating in button or urn finials. Lower ends of supports are often inserted into molded wooden rosettes about three inches in diameter.

Made of pine, with interior parts sometimes of other native softwoods. Generally painted red to simulate mahogany, brown for black walnut or grained to resemble rosewood. Not as numerous as two preceding pieces. *Ca. 1840–1860*. AAA to B

87

87. Serpentine-front Chest of Drawers

Has rectangular wooden top, 38 to 42 inches wide, with serpentine front, rounded or molded edge and rounded or square front corners. The carcase has solid sides and front stiles are apt to be about twice as wide as usual. Conforming front contains three or four full-width drawers of equal depth, seven to eight inches, with serpentine fronts, fitted with mushroom-turned wooden knobs and inset brass keyhole surrounds.

Is supported by (1) a base about five inches high which masks a semisecret full-width drawer and rests on very low spool-turned feet or (2) plain bracket feet connected by a skirt with lower edge valanced in balancing cyma-curved scrolls. Usually has socket casters. Height varies from 35 to 37 inches.

Mahogany, with crotch-grain veneer drawer fronts;

maple, birch or other native hardwoods, sometimes stained brown to simulate black walnut. *Ca. 1845–1865.* B to BB

88

88. Serpentine-front Chest of Drawers with Marble Top

Rectangular marble top, 40 to 46 inches wide; boldly serpentined front, projecting chamfered front corners and concave molded edge. Carcase has a conforming front and projecting chamfered corners, about two inches wide, ornamented top and bottom with scroll-carved brackets. Four full-width drawers of equal depth, their serpentine fronts fitted with mushroom-turned wooden knobs and either inset brass keyhole surrounds or wooden keyhole rosettes. Sides of carcase are either plain or stile-and-rail constructed. Base is about six inches high with conforming outline. Skirts at front and sides are valanced in balancing scroll-cut cyma-curves. Some-

times socket casters. Height varies from 34 to 36 inches.
Mahogany or rosewood; veneered drawer fronts. *Ca.
1845–1865.* B to BB

89

89. Louis XV Bureau

Rectangular top, 40 to 52 inches wide, of wood or
white marble with rounded corners and edge rounded,
plain or concave-molded. At rear, a tilting vertical mirror, 22 to 28 inches tall by 18 to 22 inches wide. It may
be (1) oblong with undulating frame and rounded
corners, pierced bracket supports consisting of large S-
and smaller C-scrolls, and a serpentine-front case that
contains two half-width shallow drawers or (2) cartouche-shaped with conforming scroll-carved frame, and

supporting scroll-and-leaf carved and pierced framework with arched top surmounted by carved rosette. Carcase has slightly rounded front corners; either plain or paneled ends. Four tiers of graduated drawers, top one either two half-width drawers or one full-width. All drawer fronts plain with mushroom-turned wooden knobs, and either inset brass keyhole surrounds or wooden keyhole rosettes. Drawer openings frequently framed with bands of either half-round or wavy molding. The low base, generally castered, has valanced skirt that is plain or scroll-carved on lower edge. Total height varies from six to seven feet.

Rosewood with veneered drawer fronts; black walnut; or, less frequently, mahogany with crotch-grain veneer drawer fronts. *Ca. 1850–1870.* BB to BBB

90. Louis XV Serpentine-front Bureau

Has rectangular top of marble or wood, 42 to 50 inches wide, with serpentine front, out-rounded corners and molded edge. Is surmounted at rear by a tilting mirror, 24 to 36 inches tall by 18 to 24 inches wide, having molded frame with triple or plain arched top. A shaped, pierced, molded and scroll-carved framework has modified broken-pediment top with either flower-and-foliage or cartouche-shaped central finial. Ends of framework rest on either small rectangular molded plinths or on small boxes about two inches high with serpentine fronts and hinged lids.

Carcase has conforming serpentine front with chamfered front corners, decorated at each end with short scroll-carved brackets either out-rounded or rectangular. Four full-width drawers, of equal depth except for the top one, which is sometimes shallower. They are fitted with either turned or incised wooden rosette knobs. Keyhole escutcheons either wooden rosettes or scroll-carved cartouches. Drawer openings separated by rounded bearer strips. Low base is castered, its conforming front valanced

90

in balancing cyma-curves with central scrolled element. Total height varies from six feet to seven feet, six inches.

Rosewood, black walnut, less frequently mahogany; drawer fronts crotch-grain veneered. *Ca. 1850–1870.* BB to BBB

91. Panel-front Chest of Drawers

Rectangular wooden top, 34 to 40 inches wide, with rounded front corners and rounded or molded edge. Carcase has plain solid ends. Slightly chamfered front corners. Four full-width drawers, top one shallower.

Drawer fronts framed by concave molding and with (1) mushroom-turned wooden knobs (2) incised wooden rosette knobs or (3) carved fruit-and-leafage handles and inset metal keyhole surrounds. Top drawer sometimes has central rosette interrupting concave molding. Plain

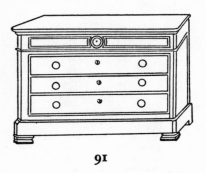

91

base projects about half an inch and is about four inches high, supported by molded block feet, generally castered. Total height varies from 32 to 34 inches.

Black walnut, rosewood or such native hardwoods as butternut or ash; sometimes pine, painted. Usually by cabinet shops and known as a "plain bureau." Not numerous. *Ca. 1850–1865.* B to BB

92. Three-drawer Chest of Drawers

Rectangular top, 34 to 38 inches wide, of wood or marble with rounded front corners and molded or rounded edge. Carcase has rounded or chamfered front stiles, rectangular paneled sides. Three full-width drawers of equal depth or a shallower top one which overhangs the other two. All drawer fronts have single or double horizontal panels with half-rounded ends and wooden carved fruit-and-leafage or leafage-and-scroll handles. Wooden keyhole rosettes. A plain molded base, with or without low block feet; or stiles, braced by scrolled

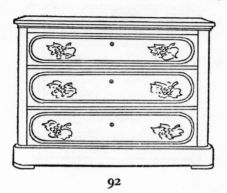

92

brackets, extending to the floor and taking place of feet. Socket casters. Total height from 30 to 32 inches.

Black walnut, sometimes with panels of burl veneer, ash or butternut with black walnut moldings, handles and keyhole rosettes. *Ca. 1860–1875.* B to BB

93. Four-drawer Chest of Drawers

Like foregoing but larger. Rectangular top, either white marble or wood, from 38 to 42 inches wide. If front stiles of carcase chamfered, they may have split urn or teardrop finials top and bottom; sometimes matching ones at centers. Four drawers of equal depth with horizontal paneled fronts fitted with either carved handles or incised rosette knobs and wooden keyhole rosettes. Castered base plain, resting on low block or button feet, with front sometimes masking a shallow full-width drawer; or valanced in balancing cyma-curves, with plain bracket feet.

93

Black walnut; drawer fronts sometimes burl-veneered; ash or butternut with black walnut moldings and handles. *Ca. 1860–1875*. B to BB

94. Three-drawer Renaissance Bureau

Like the foregoing but has an attached vertical mirror with rectangular frame, 30 to 38 inches high by 16 to 20 inches wide, with bold semicircular top, supported either in a framework or, less frequently, by uprights. Framework has molded arched pediment top, solid or pierced, surmounted by cartouche-shaped carved finial, and scroll-outlined sides with small attached bracket shelves. It may rest on a pair of recessed molded boxes, about eight inches wide by two to three inches high, or on a full-width projecting base without boxes. If mirror is flanked

by uprights, these have scrolled finials, are less elaborate
in outline and generally without bracket shelves, but
have recessed molded boxes.

Carcase usually has a rectangular white marble top
with rounded front corners and concave molded edge,
42 to 48 inches wide. The three full-width drawers have

94

molding-paneled fronts, sometimes faced with burl
veneer, and are fitted with turned incised rosette knobs
or leafage-carved wooden handles and usually turned
wooden keyhole rosettes. The upper drawer shallower
than other two and may overhang them slightly. Plain
base from four to six inches high, with concealed full-
width drawer and low block feet. Total height varies
from six feet four inches to seven feet six inches.

Generally made as part of a bedroom set of black

walnut or rosewood. Less elaborate example ash with black walnut moldings and handles. *Ca. 1860–1875.* B to BB

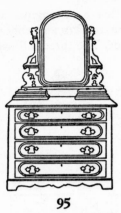

95

95. Four-drawer Renaissance Bureau

Simpler version of the preceding with four full-width drawers of equal depth, and a less ornate mirror supported by scrolled uprights with or without bracket shelves attached to a white marble top. Slightly projecting molded base is without concealed drawer, but has low cyma-curved valanced skirt flanked by simulated plain bracket feet, castered. Total height varies from five feet ten inches to six feet two inches.

Black walnut or ash with moldings and handles of black walnut. *Ca. 1860–1875.* B to BB

96. Eastlake Bureau

Structurally it has a tall shaped framework with fixed or tilting mirror surmounting a carcase which contains either two or three full-width drawers. The mirror is rectangular and is 30 to 48 inches high by 16 to 30 inches wide. The framework surrounding it is partially molded and sometimes has carved details. The top may be (1) flat and arcaded, (2) a scrolled pediment surmounted

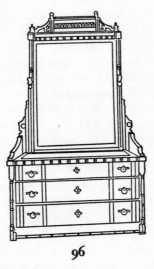

96

by a carved arched or cartouche-shaped central finial or (3) a curved and molded cornice with overlapping central cartouche and pendent S-scrolls at its ends. The sides of this framework are flat with scroll-cut outer edges and fitted with one or more tiers of small bracket shelves. It is sometimes trimmed with wooden rosettes or raised incidental panels, frequently of burl walnut.

The carcase is from 42 to 54 inches wide. Its top of wood or marble is either full-size or consists of a broad central well flanked by raised ends, eight or ten inches high, which contain either single deep drawers, about eight inches wide, or two tiers of shallow ones. Below the top are two full-width drawers of equal depth. All drawer fronts have matching panels that are raised, outlined by molding, or both raised and outlined by molding. Carved handles with turned knobs, or pendent handles; turned keyhole rosettes. The raised end-drawers sometimes have plain keyholes.

Base plain, slightly projecting. Framework and carcase are secured by vertical braces screwed to the back. Total height varies from six feet eight inches to over eight feet.

Black walnut, sometimes with burl walnut paneling; ash or butternut, generally with black walnut trim; or, less frequently, cherry. *Ca. 1865–1880.* B to BBB

97. Eastlake Tall Chest of Drawers

Design like the foregoing but taller and without surmounting mirror. Is from 48 to 56 inches tall, 30 to 34 inches wide and 16 to 18 inches deep. Rectangular overhanging top, surmounted by simple rear gallery or arcaded three-quarter one, two to four inches high. The sides of the carcase have large rectangular slightly sunk panels, and the fronts of the corner stiles are trimmed with either narrow incidental panels of burl veneer or incised stringing combined with conventionalized scrolls. Carcase contains five or six full-width drawers, either slightly graduated or of equal depth. The fronts have small rectangular central panels of burl veneer framed by incised stringing and are fitted with oxidized brass pendent ring handles with square chased plates, placed diagonally.

There is a plinth-like base, with the lower edge of the front member simply scalloped, fitted with socket casters.

Black walnut or cherry; less expensive examples ash,

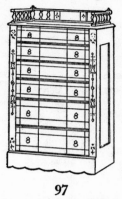

97

chestnut, oak or maple, sometimes trimmed with black walnut. By furniture factories. Plentiful and in demand because of usefulness. *Ca. 1870–1880.* B to BB

98. Louis XV Parlor Commode

An ornamental piece, inspired by similar French ones. Dimensions are 30 to 32 inches tall by 36 to 40 inches wide and 18 to 20 inches deep.

Overhanging, demi-cartouche top, concave molded edge. Carcase has cyma-curved ends with large conforming panels that are rectangular and framed by a raised triple bead molding. Projecting front corners treated like pilasters, carved in combination of molded and foliated scrolls. Full-width drawer of medium depth above a double-door cupboard. Serpentine front with keyhole rosette, below medallion framed and flanked by branching, partially foliated scrolls. Drawer opening and cupboard doors separated by conforming cock-bead molding.

Cupboard doors usually flat, recessed the depth of this molding, with rectangular panels with arched tops framed at sides and bottom by a raised molding and at

98

top by a cresting, which is composed of C-shape and concave scrolls and a foliated finial with pendent flower carved in medium relief. Doors are fitted with carved wooden keyhole cartouches; right-hand one has an overlapping rounded molding. A plain projecting base about two inches high has rounded front corners and is supported by short, bun-turned feet or carved cabriole brackets ending in upcurved whorls.

Rosewood, less frequently mahogany with crotchgrain veneer trim, by city cabinetmakers; late examples black walnut, by a few furniture factories. Not part of a standard parlor set. *Ca. 1850–1865.* C to CC

99

99. Belter Break-front Parlor Cabinet

An architectural piece, designed for either drawing or
dining room. In two parts: open cabinet with two
shelves; an enclosed break-front lower section with one
drawer and three cupboards. Over-all height about seven
feet; width of lower section nine to ten feet; depth
16 inches.

Open cabinet has flat top with serpentined front,
rounded corners and molded edge surmounted by a
serpentine, arched, broken pediment. This is outlined by
balancing molded cyma-curved scrolls; below them intertwining tendrils, leaves and pendent bunches of grapes
are pierced and carved in high relief. Scrolls terminate
at corners in low carved trefoil finials. Cabinet sides
elaborately pierced and carved, in matching grape motif.
The two shelves have conforming fronts, and the shaped
base has molded and valanced skirt with short cabriole

legs terminating in carved whorl feet. Cabinet stands on the raised central section of the lower part.

The enclosed break front is divided into three sections, the central one projecting about two inches and taller by ten inches. All have rectangular tops with rounded front corners and molded edges. Carcase has rounded corners, including those of central section, ornamented by matching grape-and-leaf motif.

Central section contains a full-width drawer, above a double-door cupboard; central medallion of carved foliated flowers surrounds the keyhole and is flanked by matching carved details. Double doors beneath have large, shaped rectangular panels framed by raised balancing cyma-curved scrolls with leafage details at centers and corners. The flanking sections each contain a cupboard with single door paneled and carved to match the central pair.

Base has shallow skirt with molded lower edge, valanced in balancing cyma-curves. Six very short cabriole legs and carved whorl feet.

Rosewood, pediment and open cabinet ends laminated. One of the unusual Belter pieces, probably made on order. *Ca. 1844–1863.* CC to CCC

Tables and Small Stands

To many collectors the marble-top parlor center table represents the Victorian Period. It occurs in two forms: French style with cabriole legs and cartouche-shaped top; Renaissance, with turned shaft flanked by tall scroll-cut brackets, supporting oval or round top.

These are the best-known types of Victorian tables but are only two of over forty different kinds that were made. For this was also the day of the extension dining table, whether made with a split pedestal base or supported by five baluster-turned legs. Its wide favor crowded the drop-leaf table from the dining room. And just as much a part of the period are the small and medium-sized trestle tables, and card and lamp stand drop-leaf tables with spool-turned legs, widely made as part of the popular-priced Cottage-style furniture.

Special Comments on Tables and Their Construction

Height of top from floor is uniformly 27 to 29 inches (unless otherwise mentioned in the description of a particular table).

Handwork construction methods prevail with early Victorian tables, which were made by cabinetmakers or produced on order by custom shops in the larger cities. Mortise-and-tenon joints are used for joining legs to frame and swinging legs to pivoting brackets. These are glued, rarely pegged. The supports of a trestle table are braced by single stretchers. If flat or shaped, mortise and tenon or dowel joints are used. If spool-turned, the ends are socketed into sides of the supporting four brackets.

Table drawers have dovetail joints for joining front, sides and back — hand-done and flaring if the work of a cabinetmaker; machine-cut and rounded if factory-made.

Table tops consistently overhang their beds. With a small table, by not over two inches but with a larger one, from four to six inches. The overhang on a drop-leaf table is two to four inches at the ends. A rule or knuckle joint is used for the drop leaves. This consists of a matching straight-concave and straight-convex finish on the sides of top and leaves. When leaves are down, this provides a molded finish and when raised allows a close fit.

Drop leaves when raised are supported by swinging legs or, more frequently, by pull or pivoting brackets built into the sides of the table frame. They are found on both handmade and factory-produced tables. A swinging leg is attached to the outer end of a bracket that is pivot-joined to the table bed, and swings out at a 90-degree angle to support the leaf. A table's "bed" is the horizontal framework beneath the top, to which legs or pedestals are attached. Drawers, if present, fit within this bed. The wooden top or fixed leaf of a drop-leaf table, if made by a cabinetmaker, is attached to the bed by unseen screws located on the inner sides of it. They fit into tapering curved cuts that extend to within three quarters to an inch of the upper edge of the bed. With a factory-made table, the top is glued to the bed and sometimes strengthened by blocks that are also glued.

A marble top rests on but is not attached to the bed. It may be taken off but should be lifted evenly and never tilted on the bed, since, because of its weight, the strain may crack it. This applies especially to a large top of veined or mottled marble. Further, when shipping other than in a moving van, a marble top should be crated with adequate cushioning to prevent breakage.

The fixed and fold-over leaves of a card table are joined by special toggle hinges, set in shallow recesses cut in the edges of both leaves at the rear. When the top is opened, the fixed leaf rotates 90 degrees on the bed and the hinged one rests on the balance of it.

With a pedestal table, the bed is screwed to an unseen flat crosspiece about six inches wide which is either mortise-and-tenoned or screwed to the upper end of the pedestal shaft.

All extension tables have a concealed telescoping bed. It has two parallel units, spaced about 14 to 18 inches apart, made of three or four sections, each with its grooved slot, so that the whole slides as a unit. The outer ends of the bed are screwed or glued to the underside of the fixed leaves. The removable extra leaves rest on the extended bed. There is usually a fifth supporting leg attached to the underside of the bed to provide additional support when table is extended. If there is a pedestal base, this is made in two vertical sections and is generally hollow to accommodate the central supporting leg.

The tripod legs of an early Victorian pedestal table are joined to the base of the shaft by dovetail joints. With later examples, these legs, whether three or four in number, are attached by dowel joints. This method is also used with the shaped bracket legs of the Renaissance pedestal tables.

Raised carved decoration, moldings, incidental panels,

bosses and rosettes are always applied work but the cabriole legs of Louis XV sub-style tables are shaped and carved from single pieces of wood.

Table-leg casters are generally of the socket type though tapering cup casters are used with some turned legs.

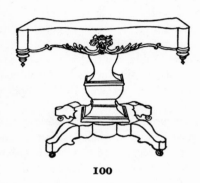

100

100. Transitional Center Table

Retains general lines of a similar table of American Empire period but has a shaped marble top with molded edge and valanced skirt ornamented with characteristic Victorian flower-and-foliage carving.

Table has nearly square top about 36 inches wide, serpentined on all sides with outrounded corners. Marble top rests on conforming bed with crosspiece to which the shaft of the pedestal is attached. Skirt about four inches deep, valanced in balancing scrolls, veneered and with center flower carving flanked by conventionalized foliage or scrolls. Turned pendent finials with teardrops ornament the corners.

The bulbous, veneered pedestal is either square or octagonal and rests on (1) a rectangular shaped and molded base with low projecting bracket feet, castered, or (2) four cyma-curved legs, placed diagonally, that are foliage and scroll-carved and terminate in whorl feet, castered.

Mahogany with liberal crotch-grain veneer or, less frequently, rosewood veneer. *Ca. 1840–1850.* AAA to BB

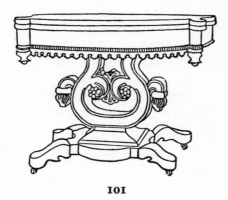

101

101. Transitional Card Table

Has a two-leaf, fold-over rotating top, 36 to 42 inches wide, with bowed front, serpentine sides and outrounded corners. When open, rotates 90 degrees, leaves resting on bed sometimes containing a traylike drawer. Access to drawer is gained by rotating unopened top. Conforming skirt is plain, but has a band of wavy molding at lower edge above an arcaded valance flanked by turned pendent finials at corners.

Large lyre-shaped pedestal, with elaborately carved

volutes and rosettes, rests on a rectangular ogee-molded plinth, wavy-molded top and bottom, that is supported by a bowed base with four diagonally placed projecting ogee-shaped bracket feet, castered.

Mahogany faced with crotch-grain veneer. *Ca. 1840– 1850*. AAA to B

Transitional Pier Table

Like the preceding in design and size but has single fixed top with serpentine front and sides, slightly out-rounded corners and molded edge. Skirt, slightly va-lanced, is ornamented by a central carved detail of flowers flanked by foliage and scrolls and split finial turnings at corners. Similar pedestal and base.

Top is of mahogany or rosewood; other parts of pine with crotch-grain mahogany or rosewood veneering. *Ca. 1840–1850*. AAA to BB

102

102. Transitional Drop-leaf Table

Top 38 to 42 inches wide and, with leaves raised, 42 to 46 inches long. The central overhanging fixed leaf is 16 to 18 inches across and matching drop leaves are 13 to 15 inches across. When raised, these are supported by pull or pivot brackets, built into table bed. Table has four tapering turned legs with some ring turning which terminate in small peg or bun feet, often castered.

Made by cabinetmakers and early furniture factories of black walnut, butternut, cherry, maple or assorted native hardwoods stained brown or red. Known to have been made prior to 1850 as far west as Wisconsin, Indiana, Kentucky and western Tennessee. Examples made by early factories have less tapering, plainer legs, sometimes pine tops. *Ca. 1840–1865.* B to BBB

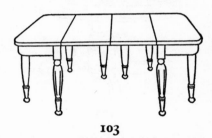

103

103. Two-part Dining Table

A survival from the American Empire and earlier periods. Consists of two matching five-leg tables, each with a single deep drop leaf. With leaves down, the pair provide a top 46 to 52 inches wide and 42 to 48 inches long with leaves raised; the total length varies from six to eight feet.

Each table has a rectangular, slightly overhanging fixed leaf with rounded outer corners; on the inner side a rectangular drop leaf. The skirt beneath is plain, about four inches deep, and may be edged with a bead or wavy molding. The legs are turned, baluster-shaped, tapering, and terminate in small bun or peg feet, castered. The fifth swinging leg supports the raised leaf. The edges of the drop leaves have small matching mortises and tenons so that they fit tightly when pair is joined.

Black walnut; butternut; maple, generally stained brown; cherry; infrequently, mahogany, by cabinet-makers. Made in limited numbers; now scarce. *Ca. 1860–1865.* BB to C

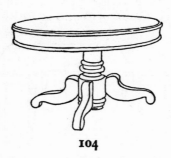

104

104. Pedestal Extension Table

Has circular or, less frequently, rectangular two-section top with rounded or molded edge. It is from 44 to 60 inches across closed and eight to 13 feet long when open, with four to six expansion leaves inserted. Has a plain conforming skirt about four inches deep, usually with molded lower edge, that conceals a telescopic bed. This is constructed of two parallel supports, each in four or five sections with matching grooves and tenons which slide from closed to open.

Table is supported by a baluster-shaped or octagon two-section column with four quadrangular, cyma-curved projecting feet, castered. This column is hollow and contains a single turned leg which serves as a support when table is extended.

Rosewood, black walnut or mahogany with crotch-grain veneered skirt; by cabinetmakers or early factories. Earlier examples rosewood or mahogany. *Ca. 1840–1870.* B to BBB

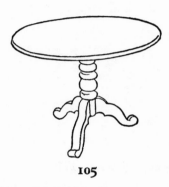

105

105. Transitional Tilt-top Table

Has either a circular top, 20 to 36 inches in diameter, or an oval one about 26 inches wide with rounded or molded rim. With circular top, the shaft is either baluster-turned or tapering vase-shaped, 16 to 18 inches tall, supported by a tripod of plain cyma-curved, scroll-cut legs terminating in either up-rolled or turned peg feet.

Shaft of oval-top table is three to four inches taller, is either baluster-turned, tapering and slender or heavier with inverted vase-shaping. It rests on a triangular or rectangular plinth base with concave sides and low feet. For a triangular base, the feet are turned and bun-shaped; for rectangular, concave brackets usually fitted with casters.

Mahogany, black walnut, butternut, maple stained brown, cherry, infrequently oak. *Ca. 1840–1850.* B to BBB

106

106. Pedestal-base Sewing Table

Slightly overhanging rectangular top, 18 to 22 inches wide by 16 to 18 inches deep. Skirt plain with pendent ball finials at corners. May contain single full-width drawer, three to four inches deep, or two full-width, the upper one about three inches deep and often fitted with baize-paneled writing flap and compartments for pens, ink bottle, and so on; the lower one, four to five inches deep divided for sewing supplies. Drawers have single or double mushroom-turned wooden knobs or brass rosette knobs, with or without brass keyhole surrounds.

Pedestal may be either baluster-turned or a plain tapering shaft. The former is supported by three S-curved scroll-cut legs terminating in incurved feet, frequently without casters. The tapering shaft type is supported by four cyma-curved, scroll-cut legs, castered.

Mahogany, veneered top and drawer fronts; black walnut; sometimes other native hardwoods. *Ca. 1840–1860.* B to BBB

107

107. Transitional Dressing Table

Survival of American Empire, with Victorian decorative details. About 30 inches wide, 16 inches deep and 30 inches tall. Plain rectangular overhanging top surmounted by either three-quarter gallery with scroll-cut downswept ends, or flat-arched or triangular-shaped rear gallery; the latter sometimes edged at the top with full-round spool-turned trim. Skirt plain containing full-width drawer about four inches deep, sometimes framed with wavy molding and fitted with small mushroom-turned wooden knobs. Simply turned tapering legs; small ball feet. About four inches from the floor there is a plain, full-width shelf, usually with front recessed about four to six inches. Table was sometimes used as a serving table or buffet.

Mahogany, rosewood, black walnut, butternut, maple or assorted hardwoods stained red or brown; chiefly by cabinetmakers and some early furniture factories. *Ca. 1840–1865.* B to BB

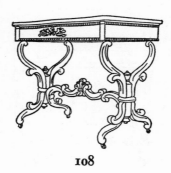

108

108. Lyre Trestle Table

Rectangular, slightly overhanging white marble or wooden top, 34 to 38 inches wide and 20 to 22 inches deep, with serpentined sides and rounded corners. Conforming bed about five inches deep, upper and lower edges finished in bands of wavy molding. At front, full-width drawer with either plain or serpentine front, edged with wavy molding and having a center medallion of conventionalized leafage scrolls carved in relief with an inset keyhole surround at the center.

Supported by a pair of lyre-like X-shape trestles, done in balancing carved cyma-curves, branches top and bottom, being scrolls terminating in volutes. The lower volutes form the feet of the trestles and are castered.

Trestles also have standing and pendent urn-shaped finials at the centers of top and bottom branches, respectively. Trestles are braced by a serpentine-arched carved stretcher, formed of double cyma-curved scrolls joined to a scrolled central finial.

Made by cabinetmakers of mahogany, with crotch-grain veneering, or of rosewood. With the latter, trestles and stretcher may be of other hardwood, stained and grained to simulate rosewood. Always a sophisticated piece and not numerous. If top is of marble, probably used as a serving table and if of wood, as a parlor or sofa table. *Ca. 1840–1860.* BB to BBB

109

109. Lyre Trestle Card Table

Has two-leaf, foldover top, 36 to 40 inches wide, slightly serpentined with rounded edges. Top rotates 180 degrees, resting on bed when open. Bed may contain traylike drawer. Skirt slightly serpentined, conforming to shaping of top; wavy molding on lower edge. Supported by lyre-shaped trestles like the preceding, but less elaborately shaped and carved. Urn-shaped standing finials at joining of top branching scrolls. Trestles braced by arched stretcher in balancing cyma-curves.

Made by cabinetmakers. Mahogany, with crotch-grain veneer skirt; or rosewood with trestles and stretcher of maple or other hardwood, stained and grained to simulate rosewood. *Ca. 1840–1850.* BB to BBB

110

110. Lyre Trestle Sofa Table

Rectangular top about 24 inches long by 18 inches wide, serpentined on all sides with rounded corners and edge. Plain skirt, about four inches deep, banded along lower edge with wavy molding. Usually contains a full-width drawer with hidden finger grips in place of handles.

Tall, lyre-shaped trestles supporting table rest on narrow shelf with sides cut in balancing cyma-curves. Two scroll-cut, cyma-curved bracket feet, castered.

By cabinetmakers. Mahogany, with skirt, drawer front and shelf crotch-grain veneered; less frequently, rosewood or black walnut. *Ca. 1840–1865.* B to BBB

Lyre Trestle Tea Table

Has rectangular or oval top, 28 to 36 inches wide and 36 to 42 inches long — a narrow fixed leaf (about 10 inches wide) and two very wide drop leaves. These may have a width twice that of the fixed leaf or nearly touch the floor when vertical. The rectangular top has plain or rounded edge, slightly rounded corners. (Oval top has rounded edge.)

Supported by a pair of trestles, usually scroll-cut in lyre shape, with frieze-like skirts above, one of which may be fitted with a long narrow drawer of medium depth. Trestles braced by molded or shaped stretcher placed about four inches from floor, with shaped bases and projecting down-curved scrolled feet, castered. Raised leaves have swinging legs, turned, slender and tapering, or shaped and molded. These may have plain stretchers at lower ends, pivot-joined to that of the trestle in the manner of the earlier gate-leg table. (This usually found when table has excessively wide drop leaves.)

By cabinetmakers of mahogany, rosewood, or, with later examples, of black walnut. Not numerous. *Ca. 1840–1865*. BB to BBB

111. Pembroke Table (A and B)

Has same design and construction as Transitional Drop-leaf Table (*see No. 102*), but top is smaller and leaves narrower. Top is from 34 to 40 inches wide and, with leaves raised, 36 to 42 inches long. The central fixed leaf is 16 to 18 inches across and the matching drop leaves are 12 to 14 inches across. When raised they are supported by pull or pivot brackets. The end skirts are plain and without a drawer.

Four turned legs, usually fitted with socket casters. These legs are tapering (A); slightly vase-shaped with some ring turnings and small peg feet; spool-turned, not tapered (B).

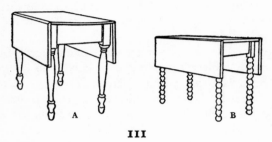

III

Some by country cabinetmakers; frequently by early factories in considerable quantity.

Black walnut, maple, cherry; rarely mahogany; very often assorted native hardwoods stained brown or red to simulate either black walnut or mahogany. Numerous, in demand as living room or small dining table. *Ca. 1840–1865.* B to BBB

112. Spool-turned Drop-leaf Table

Has an oval or rectangular top, 40 to 44 inches wide by 56 to 64 inches long. Fixed center leaf, 16 to 18 inches wide, and, if top is oval, ends usually have conforming bow. End skirts are plain, about four inches deep, generally without a drawer. Drop leaves have swinging legs. Six spool-turned legs either without feet or with small peg feet generally with socket casters.

112

By early factories of black walnut, assorted native hardwoods, stained to simulate it or, occasionally, of mahogany. *Ca. 1845–1865.* BB to BBB

113

113. Spool-turned Side Table

Made with fixed leaf only as side table, or with fold-over top as card table. Fixed leaf is 16 to 18 inches wide by 20 to 24 inches long with rounded edge and square corners. With double top, leaves have square edges and square or slightly rounded corners. When open, top rotates 180 degrees, leaves resting on table bed. Skirt plain, about four inches deep. Four spool-turned legs, small peg feet generally *not* castered.

Made by early factories of black walnut, assorted native hardwoods stained brown or, infrequently, mahogany. *Ca. 1845–1865.* B to BB

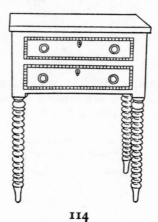

114

114. Spool-turned Sewing Table

Rectangular top, either wood or marble, 22 to 26 inches wide by 16 to 18 inches deep. Wooden top has plain edge and square corners; marble, slightly rounded edge and corners. Deep skirt with two full-width drawers of either equal or graduated depth. These may be plain and separated with bands of wavy molding or slightly recessed and framed with the same molding. Small mushroom-turned wooden knobs; usually inlaid shield-shaped brass keyhole escutcheons or inset keyhole surrounds. Top drawer may be fitted with writing flap and compartments for pen, ink bottle and paper; lower one divided for sewing materials. Four spool-turned legs; plain or small peg feet.

Made by early furniture factories of black walnut, maple stained brown or, less often, mahogany. *1845–1865*. B to BB

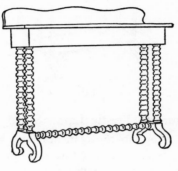

115

115. Spool-turned Dressing Table

Rectangular overhanging top, serpentined at front and sides, a rear gallery piece with conforming serpentined upper edge. Table is 28 to 34 inches wide, 14 to 16 inches deep, 30 to 32 inches tall. Skirt plain with full-width drawer about three inches deep; drawer front plain, usually without handles. A pair of supporting trestles made of spool-turned uprights, and scroll-cut open-arched foot brackets, are downcurved, voluted and braced by a matching spool-turned stretcher.

Black walnut, maple or assorted hardwoods, natural finish or stained brown; made by early furniture factories as separate pieces or as part of spool-turned bedroom set. *Ca. 1850–1870*. AAA to B

116

116. Spool-turned Trestle Lamp Stand

Rectangular top, 18 to 20 inches long and 14 to 16 inches deep, with square corners. Edge rounded or framed with a split spool-turned molding. The lower edge of the shallow skirt is valanced in balancing serpentine or cyma-curves. Trestles, each with two slender spool-turned uprights, rest on wide shelf-like stretcher with edge finished in split spool-turned molding matching top. Scroll-cut and arched foot brackets. A similar table, four to six inches longer and two inches deeper, was made as a sofa table.

Made by early factories of black walnut, mahogany or assorted hardwoods stained red or brown. *Ca. 1850–1865.* AAA to B

117. Nest of Tables

Three or four identical tables of diminishing size, nested. Largest has rectangular top about 16 inches wide by 22 inches long, with either square corners and straight rounded edge, or is slightly serpentine with molded edge. Skirtless top is supported by four slender spool-turned legs mounted on narrow scroll-cut block feet. Rear legs braced by a single flat stretcher.

Mahogany, rosewood or black walnut by cabinet-makers or some early factories. Complete sets not nu-

117

merous. Single table, usually the largest, found oftener. May have flat wide stretcher bracing block feet, probably a later addition to strengthen a delicate piece. *Ca. 1850–1865.* B to BB

LOUIS XV SUBSTYLE

118. Ornate Marble-top Center Table

Has oval or cartouche-shaped top, 28 to 36 inches wide by 20 to 24 inches deep with concave molded rim, usually of marble but sometimes wood. Conforming skirt plain or molded, generally with carved medallions, centered. Lower edge may be straight or serpentine-valanced, with or without conforming molding.

Is supported by (1) cabriole legs, incurved, shaped and carved or finger-molded; whorl feet, castered; or (2) pedestal-like base of colonnettes. The cabriole legs are braced

118

by a cyma-curved or scrolled and pierced X-shape stretcher with urn or vase-shaped central finial sometimes surmounted by carved flowers and foliage. The pedestal base consists of four slender baluster-turned colonnettes, supported by four low, cyma-curved scroll-carved legs that terminate in whorl feet, castered, and a central urn or bowl-shape finial.

Earliest examples are of mahogany with skirt crotchgrain veneered, most elaborate are of rosewood and late ones of black walnut. Some fine tables with carving matching that of sofa and chairs in a drawing-room set came from the Belter shop. *Ca. 1850–1865.* BB to C

119

119. Pedestal Table

A cartouche-shaped marble top about 39 by 27 inches, with out-rounded corners and a concave molded edge, rests on a conforming bed with unseen crosspiece on pedestal shaft. All sides are alike and form a skirt about four inches high that is valanced in balanced scrolls. It is edged with a bead molding branching from central leafage-carved medallions. Beneath the out-rounded corners are turned pendent finials terminating in teardrops.

The bulbous pedestal, square or octagonal and plain, rests on a shaped base with pendent finial that is supported by four cyma-curved and voluted legs placed diagonally. Leafage-carved knees, whorl feet.

Made by cabinetmakers and some early factories of pine, entirely faced with crotch-grain mahogany veneer or, less frequently, of rosewood veneer with applied carving and molding. *Ca. 1845–1865.* B to BB

120. Pier Table with Mirror Panel

Demi-cartouche-shaped top, wood or marble, four to five feet wide by 20 to 24 inches deep, with rounded or molded edge and out-rounded corners. Conforming skirt finger-molded, deeply valanced, with large pendent medallion of foliated flowers and fruits carved in medium or high relief at the center. Front legs cabriole, with foliated flower carving at knees. Carved whorl feet.

120

At the rear, large cabriole-shaped supports carved to match the front legs flank a large rectangular mirror panel. About three inches from the floor there is a full-size shelf, shaped to conform to the top, with concave molded edge.

An elaborate drawing-room piece, probably made to order in a large city cabinetmaking shop of rosewood or, less frequently, of mahogany. A gilt pier glass was generally hung above such a table (*see No. 245*). Unusual and rare. *Ca. 1855–1865.* C to CC

121. Drawing-room Side Table with Double-shelf Pediment

Five feet wide, 25 inches deep, and five feet five inches tall. Has a demi-cartouche-shaped wooden top surmounted by a whatnot-like pediment, with two shelves. The top shelf has an intricately pierced and carved gallery, at the center of which is an oval medallion containing a woman's head carved in high relief. This is flanked by intertwined foliated scrolls which join two pairs of matching brackets. One of each pair is placed at about a 60-degree angle; the other two serve as terminal exten-

121

sions of the gallery. Both shelves are supported by graduated brackets, pierced and carved, with lower ends nearly equal to the depth of the table top. Beneath the shelves are rectangular mirror panels.

Table top has half to three-quarter round projections above the legs, double bead-molded edge. Conforming skirt has straight lower edge finished with rounded molding, a central shallow drawer ornamented with a carved band of pendent grapes, leaves and tendrils and brass keyhole surround. Four ornate cabriole legs, with out-rounded and carved stiles above. Legs have foliated carved knees and ankles, and whorl feet. They are braced by a modified X-shaped stretcher, arched, pierced and carved at center in balancing scrolls.

A specially designed piece, of rosewood, and of New York provenance, made by Belter or one of his most skillful contemporaries. It is an existing example of some of the ornate pieces executed for expositions, such as the Crystal Palace, which have generally disappeared and are known only from contemporary illustrations. *Ca. 1855–1865.* CC to #

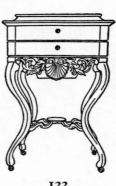

122

122. Shell-carved Sewing Table

Plain raised top, rounded edge and square corners, 16 inches square and hinged at the rear. When raised, it discloses a square mirror panel inset on the underside and gives access to a traylike compartment about two inches deep. Top is framed by a deep concave molded section slightly overhanging the table bed and hinged.

Beneath it is a well about three inches deep, with compartments for spools and other sewing accessories. Bed is 20 inches wide and contains two drawer fronts separated by a molded bearer strip. The upper one is fixed and masks the compartmented well. Single drawer beneath is frequently fitted with a baize-paneled writing flap and compartments for writing accessories. Both fronts are plain except for wooden keyhole rosettes.

Beneath the table bed is a shallow pendent drawer with front in form of an elaborately carved centered scallop shell, flanked by balancing foliated scrolls. Slender cabriole legs. Rudimentary feet, socket casters, braced by a serpentine H-shaped stretcher, surmounted at center either by a small circular shelf or urn-shaped finial.

Always a sophisticated piece, made of rosewood or black walnut. Example pictured is by Belter. Rare. *Ca. 1850–1865.* BB to BBB

Cabriole-leg Card Table

Double-leaf, fold-over top, 30 to 36 inches wide and 16 to 18 inches deep. Leaves serpentine-shaped at front and sides. Open top rotates 180 degrees and rests on table bed which has a straight or conforming skirt with lower edge scroll-molded. Four cabriole legs, sometimes scroll-carved at knees. Whorl or rudimentary feet, castered.

Rosewood, black walnut and, seldom, mahogany, by cabinet shops and early factories. *Ca. 1850–1870.* AAA to B

123. Cabriole-leg Pier Table

Like preceding in line and construction but with single fixed leaf, 34 to 40 inches wide. Slightly serpentined at front and sides, with concave molded edge; wood or marble. Skirt either straight or has conforming serpentine curve with lower edge valanced in balancing cyma-curves. Front often has a wide carved medallion or a cartouche, flanked by leafage done in relief.

Cabriole legs leafage-carved at knees. Rudimentary or whorl feet. Legs are frequently about two inches longer

123

than normal, making top 31 to 33 inches from the floor.

Rosewood or black walnut, by cabinet shops and early factories. Not as numerous as card table. *Ca. 1850–1865.* B to BB

124. Cabriole-leg Library Table

Rectangular top, 50 to 56 inches wide by 28 to 34 inches deep, with large leather or baize panel. Edge molded, corners slightly rounded. Plain skirt, four to six inches deep; either a single centered drawer or two half-width ones at front. Drawers plain, or molding-paneled; seldom fitted with handles, but have either circular wooden keyhole escutcheons or inset brass keyhole surrounds. Plain cabriole legs. Rudimentary or whorl feet.

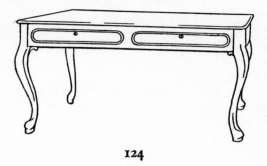

124

Mahogany, rosewood or black walnut, by cabinet shops or early factories. Black walnut ones more numerous. *Ca. 1850–1870.* AAA to B

RENAISSANCE SUBSTYLE

125. Renaissance Extension Table

A large table, with ornate carved and molded details matching those of a corresponding sideboard (*see No. 177*). Circular top 42 to 54 inches in diameter that extends to seven or eight feet. Edges of top and expansion leaves are molded or can be carved in low relief in a repeating motif. Skirt is about four inches deep with molded edge and face; may be ornamented by alternating medallions and strapwork cartouches carved in relief and placed about 16 inches apart. With an ornate table, leaves are likewise skirted.

The pedestal is generally octagonal, raised about two inches from the floor. Its faces form recessed panels that are carved and molding-framed. From alternate panels project large downswept bracket feet, castered. At the top, these have carved fruit and leafage swags and below ornamental blocking. On the sides there are conforming recessed molding-framed panels that terminate in boldly carved volutes.

Black walnut, incidental paneling burl-veneered, by furniture factories; elaborate examples, sometimes ban-

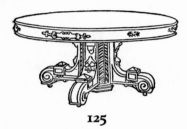

125

quet-size, made to order by cabinetmakers in the larger cities. In the dining room of the A. T. Stewart mansion in New York City, there was a table of this type that would seat 24 people. Many such tables were discarded because of size. Few dealers have examples in stock. *Ca. 1865–1875.* BB to C

126. Renaissance Center Table

Top of marble, veined, white or mottled, with molded edge. Shape may be circular, 26 to 34 inches in diameter; oval, 22 by 33 inches to 28 by 39 inches; rectangular, with slightly bowed ends, 26 to 36 inches long by 18 to 22 inches wide. Conforming shallow skirt boldly molded, with straight lower edge. With rectangular top, skirt has attached pieces, cut in balancing scroll and geometric outlines, at center of sides and ends.

Pedestal base consists of central baluster-turned column and four cyma-curved scrolled legs. Column has an octagon base with a pendent acorn or teardrop finial. Diagonally placed legs join it at its base. These may be orna-

126

mented with either turned rosettes or foliage-carved scrolls at knees or below.

Made by factories of black walnut, sometimes found with wooden top (probably replacement). *Ca. 1865–1880.* B to BB

Scrolled-leg and Column Pedestal Lamp Stand

Like preceding but with much smaller top. Can be circular, 18 to 20 inches in diameter; oval, 20 to 24 inches long by 14 to 16 inches wide; rectangular, 20 to 24 inches long by 14 to 18 inches wide, or square, measuring 16 to 20 inches.

By factories. Black walnut, or, when part of a bedroom set, ash, chestnut or maple, ebonized.

Top may be either of marble or wood. *Ca. 1865–1880.* AAA to B

127

127. Renaissance Trestle Table

Rectangular top, 32 to 36 inches long by 18 to 20 inches wide, with boldly bowed ends and molded edge. Plain conforming skirt about four inches deep with straight, cock-beaded lower edge. Sides and ends of skirt have flower and leaf-carved medallions, centered, one of which may serve as the handle for a full-width drawer of medium depth. Where bowed ends join the straight sides, there may be plain dies with urn-shaped pendent finials.

Table is supported by a pair of trestles, either cyma-curved and lyre-scrolled, with shaped block feet having pawlike carved ends, or lyre-shaped and pierced with balancing scrolled openings. With the former, block feet are braced by a balancing vase-shaped turned stretcher having small box-shaped plinth, centered, which supports urn-shaped finial. With the lyre-shaped type, trestles are braced by arched and scrolled stretcher pierced with balancing scrolled openings.

Generally black walnut, by factories. *Ca. 1870–1880.* B to BB

128

128. Renaissance Drop-leaf Table

Has an oval top about 40 inches long by 30 inches wide, with concave molded edge consisting of narrow fixed leaf and deeply curved drop leaves. When raised, leaves are supported by slender swinging and slightly shaped legs, with bead-molded edges. Beneath the fixed leaf the table bed contains a narrow drawer of medium depth which has a paneled front fitted with a small brass knob. Is supported by shaped trestles with large pierced rosettes below narrow vertical raised panels. These have molded plinths and rest on scroll-cut and arched foot brackets, castered. These have central raised rosettes and are braced by a single shaped stretcher.

Black walnut, by furniture factories. Not numerous. *Ca. 1870–1880.* AAA to B

129. Renaissance Vase or Lamp Stand

From 34 to 38 inches tall; circular top 16 to 18 inches in diameter, with heavily molded rim framing a marble or glass-covered needlework disc. Rim is about two inches wide with three applied valance brackets equi-spaced on lower edge. Top is supported by an elaborate baluster-turned column and three convex-concave, shaped and molded scrolled brackets joined to column halfway from

129

top to bottom. A trilateral base with concave shaping and molded edge supports them and rests on three down-curved, bracket feet.

Rim, column, brackets and feet are sometimes decorated with gilded incised beading. Brackets and feet may also have small turned wooden rosettes.

Made by factories of black walnut; occasionally of assorted native hardwoods, finished with black lacquer and gilt beading. *Ca. 1870–1880.* AAA to B

LOUIS XVI SUBSTYLE

130. Louis XVI Center Table

Rectangular top 34 to 38 inches long by 18 to 22 inches wide, with bowed ends and either straight or bowed sides.

A fine example, made by Daniel Pabst of Philadelphia or other urban contemporaries, generally has large inset marble panel of conforming shape framed by raised and molded rim. A simpler table may have either a marble

130

or wooden top of conforming shape with concave molded edge.

The molded skirt is about four inches deep with slightly valanced edge and has small foliage and scroll-carved medallions, centered. The dies above the legs have either carved rosettes or molded blocks. Four turned and tapering legs, either plain or fluted. Large vase or urn turnings finish upper ends and, below, blockings at stretcher level terminate in slender vase or urn-shaped feet, castered. Legs are braced by H-shaped stretcher with concave molded end-members, and turned or shaped and molded center-member, surmounted by urn-shaped, turned or foliage-carved cone-shaped finial.

Made by factories of black walnut or ebonized maple. *Ca. 1865–1875.* AAA to B

131

131. Louis XVI Sewing Table

Rectangular lid about 24 inches long by 16 inches wide, hinged at back, which gives access to a full-width fixed tray, divided for sewing accessories and contained within the ogee-molded skirt. Below is a pendent drawer of medium depth with sides and ends pierced in a balancing design of foliage and scrolls.

Four slender cylinder, ball or button-and-ring turned legs that rest on shaped block feet with cyma-curved ends. Feet braced by a stretcher turned to match legs. Open-work basket finial about 10 inches in diameter at stretcher center.

Made by factories of black walnut or, less frequently, maple ebonized. *Ca. 1870–1880.* B to BB

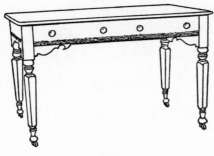

132

132. Turned-leg Writing Table

Designed for library or office use, it has a rectangular top 36 to 42 inches long by 20 to 24 inches wide, with molded or rounded edge and rounded or canted corners. Top may be plain but frequently has large rectangular baize or leather panel with a wood banding about two inches wide. The skirt is about four inches deep and is (1) plain with molded lower edge; (2) molded or (3) simulates a slightly sunk panel, with or without burl veneer, framed by convex molding. The front skirt generally contains a full-width or two half-width drawers fitted with (1) brass pendent ring and square plate handles and matching or wooden rosette keyhole escutcheons; (2) carved fruit and leafage handles and wooden rosette keyhole escutcheons; (3) mushroom-turned wooden knobs and inset brass or iron keyhole surrounds or (4) keyhole escutcheons only.

Ball or peg feet, castered. Four tapering legs baluster-turned and slender, or octagonal and heavier with elements of ring-and-ball turning at upper and lower ends.

Where legs join the skirt, they may be braced by flat, scroll-cut, cyma-curved brackets.

Made by factories of black walnut, sometimes with burl-veneered skirt and banding of top. *Ca. 1860–1880.* AAA to B

COTTAGE QUALITY

133

133. Circular Extension Table

Circular top, 42 to 48 inches in diameter. Extended, with four leaves, each 14 to 16 inches wide, is from six feet six inches to seven feet eight inches long. A plain skirt, about four inches deep, forms a square and conceals the telescopic bed (*see No. 104*).

Four turned legs. Ball feet, castered. Turnings may be (1) cylinder, slightly tapering with ring-and-ball elements, (2) vase-shape with ring-and-ball elements or (3) ring-turned combined with a square central section, molded or plain. Sometimes a matching fifth leg that serves as a medial support is present.

Made by furniture factories in quantity, usually of black walnut or of other native hardwoods; natural finish or brown stain. *Ca. 1870–1885.* AA to AAA

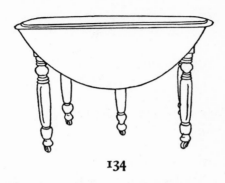

134

134. Oval Drop-leaf Extension Table

Like the preceding in construction and turned elements but has demilune drop leaves attached to a two-piece fixed leaf. Center separation, and ends bowed to conform to curve or drop leaves. With leaves raised, top is oval, has a molded or rounded edge and measures 42 to 46 inches wide, by four feet six inches to five feet six inches long. Is equipped with four to six removable rectangular leaves, making the extended top approximately seven to nine feet long.

Table is supported by four turned legs and a matching medial support.

Made by factories in large quantity. Black walnut or other native hardwoods, natural finish or stained to simulate black walnut. Late examples may be of oak, natural finish. *Ca. 1870–1885.* AA to AAA

135

135. Cottage Drop-leaf Pedestal Table

Has a circular top 30 to 34 inches in diameter or an oval one about 30 by 36 inches. The central fixed leaf is 18 to 20 inches wide and the drop leaves eight to 10 inches. When raised they are supported by pull or swinging brackets. The end skirts are plain, about four inches deep and joined to the side rails to form the table bed.

Pedestal consists of a bulbous baluster-turned shaft above a plain octagon section to which the flat scroll-cut legs are attached. These, placed diagonally, are cyma-curved and have socket casters.

Used as a center or tea table. By factories, in great numbers, generally black walnut, sometimes maple or other native woods. *Ca. 1870–1880.* AA to AAA

136. Cottage Bedroom Table

Rectangular or oval top, 22 to 26 inches long and 16 to 18 inches wide, with concave molded edge. If rectangular, corners canted or rounded. Table bed plain, about three inches deep. One side may serve as front for shallow drawer.

Supported by two trestles — slender, baluster-turned or spool-turned uprights mounted on scroll-cut foot brackets, braced by a single conforming stretcher.

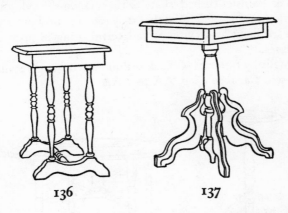

136   **137**

By factories. Pine, painted, or ash with black walnut turnings; black walnut; maple.

Frequently part of bedroom set. Numerous. *Ca. 1870– 1885.* A to AA

137. Cottage Pedestal Lamp Stand

A 16 to 18 inch square top, with concave molded or rounded edge, rounded corners, plain shallow skirt perhaps with full-width drawer. A simple, baluster-turned supporting shaft, with octagon-shaped lower section and pear-shaped finial sometimes touching floor, with four short, flat scroll-cut legs, cyma-curved.

By factories. Most frequently pine, painted, or of ash, black walnut or stained maple; usually part of bedroom set. *Ca. 1870–1885 or later.* A to AA

138. Circular-top Pedestal Stand

Circular top 14 to 18 inches in diameter with molded edge. Baluster-turned shaft with octagon-shaped lower section, and turned finial that may touch floor. Four short flat scroll-cut legs, cyma-curved, terminating in upcurved volutes.

Made by factories of black walnut, ash or maple stained brown. *Ca. 1870–1880.* AA to AAA

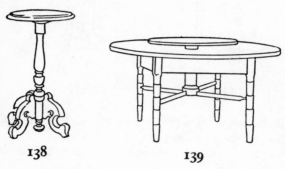

138   **139**

139. Lazy Susan Table

Takes its name from its circular revolving tray, which surmounts the circular top. Tray, usually 24 to 34 inches in diameter, is raised two to three inches above the table top. It revolves on (1) a central turned base, attached to the top, or (2) a postlike spindle, which goes through the top to a low, box-shaped plinth, supported by an X-shaped stretcher of turned members.

Table top from four feet to five feet six inches in diameter. With an unusually large example, where top is over six feet in diameter, it may consist of a fixed leaf a little wider than the diameter of the revolving tray and two demilune drop leaves.

Four legs that are (1) vase-shaped with ring turnings, terminating in ring-and-ball turned feet; (2) cylinder-and-ring turnings, terminating in ring-and-ball or peg feet or (3) plain square legs, with or without bead-molded or chamfered edges.

Made chiefly in rural sections from Pennsylvania south. Black walnut, maple and assorted native hardwoods with pine top, sometimes painted Amish blue or dark green. Very popular with collectors for use in country homes. Not numerous and therefore expensive. *Ca. 1840–1880.* BB to C

140

140. Hutch Table

A survival design, first made in Europe during the seventeenth century or earlier. Serves as settee when top is vertical and as table when horizontal. Rectangular top 34 to 42 inches long by 26 to 30 inches wide with slightly rounded corners. On underside two nearly full-width cleats with quarter-round ends bored for holes in which turned wooden pins on which it tilts are inserted.

Base has vertical board ends, 12 to 14 inches wide, shaped at top in a concave curve and at bottom in a Gothic arch. They are joined at seat level by a chestlike section, eight to ten inches deep, with hinged lid.

Made occasionally of black walnut; more frequently of maple, assorted native hardwoods with pine or other softwood top stained or painted in a solid color. Earlier handmade examples are usually of Pennsylvania provenance; later ones factory-produced. Still made and sold unfinished by department stores. *Ca. 1850–1880.* AAA to B

Desks and Secretaries

BEFORE 1780, the writing surface of a desk or secretary was formed by either a sloping lid or a slanting front. Then came the Hepplewhite and Sheraton years with their five variations: fall-front; fold-over writing flap; cylinder-front; pull-out writing shelf; tambour roll-top.

The Victorian style used all seven types in one form or another and added two others which had been made earlier on the Continent and in England: the French style drop-front secretary and the English library or "writing table" as it was known there.

The French drop-front secretary, the only one made in one piece, was copied from the *secrétaire à abattant* widely made during the Napoleonic period. Always a sophisticated, custom-made piece, it was naturally produced in limited numbers. But, as with other French models, the idea was later adapted to simpler, less costly pieces. From it came the drop-front desk made in two parts more or less like a secretary, with either a perpendicular or sloping drop-front and a base which might be table, bureau, cupboard or trestle in form. They ranged from simple utilitarian pieces to graceful lady desks, including the dual purpose "fire screen desk." The early ones were done by local cabinetmakers or small furniture factories. Late desks, especially those with Eastlake details, were entirely factory-made. Late or early, this drop-front type is among the most numerous of the Victorian desks available today.

The English library table — large flat top resting on pedestal-like tiers of drawers with a wide kneehole between — was popular there as early as 1750 but over a hundred years went by before Americans realized its real advantages, despite the fact that George Washington used one in New York when he was President of the United States. (It is now in the Governor's Room, City Hall, New York.)

About 1850, desks specially intended for office or library use began to be made in increasing numbers. Of these the library or writing table appeared in Victorian dress and was christened the "flat-top desk." Its base varied and its form might be rectangular or kidney-shaped but it always had a flat writing surface, usually with a panel of baize or leather. The kidney desk was the work of cabinetmakers in urban centers. The rectangular flat-top was eventually a factory product, and in the last years of the Victorian period added a large and coarsely executed tambour roll-top, this becoming the well-known "roll-top desk" of the late nineteenth and early twentieth centuries.

An economic reflection of the period is to be seen in the absence of secret drawers and compartments in the various types of secretaries and desks, due without doubt to the spread of banks and public safe-deposit vaults.

Special Comments on Desks and Secretaries

A sloping lid is derived from the much earlier "writing box." It is usually hinged at the top, has batten strips on the sides to prevent warping, and a slightly raised molded edge at bottom. Top of lid serves as the writing surface, and, when raised to give access to the well beneath, is braced by a pivoted wooden bar. A sloping-top desk surmounted by a recessed cabinet has a fixed instead of a hinged top.

A perpendicular drop-front is full-width, hinged at bottom, usually with concealed pivot hinges, and is supported when open by the top of the projecting base — except for the French-style, one-piece secretary. With this, the drop-front is also counterbalanced and supported by a pair of folding brass brackets. The inner surface is the writing area and has a large textile or leather panel framed by wood banding about two inches wide.

A sloping drop-front is usually stile-and-rail constructed with either a large rectangular, slightly sunk panel or two smaller ones. When closed it slopes backward at about an angle of 10 degrees, and when open, slopes downward at a five-degree angle. It is so pivot-hinged that about two inches press against the base of the divided interior. It is also further supported by a narrow shelf above the full-width drawer at the top of the base.

A writing flap, whether flat or sloping, is hinged on its outer side and usually supported by pull brackets, though occasionally by the drawer beneath. Sometimes it is part of a boxlike, fold-over shallow compartment, not requiring extra support (*see No. 152*). Its writing surface has a large textile or leather panel, usually framed by wooden banding.

A fall-front is drawerlike in construction, hinged at bottom, and may be supported by brass quadrant brackets. It pulls out to about half its depth. The writing surface has a textile or leather panel framed by banding and the space at the rear has pigeonholes and small drawers.

A slant-front is hinged at the bottom. It consists of transverse flush end pieces from two to four inches wide which are joined to the central one or two-piece section by glued joints. A slightly overhanging bevel or thumb molding usually finishes the top and side edges. The writing surface has the usual textile or leather panel with wood banding. Front when open is supported by pull brackets, hinged brass brackets, or rests on a narrow shelf above drawers or cupboard.

A cylinder-front is quarter-round and pivots on concealed brackets. It has a large curved panel, faced with burl veneer. When open it disappears behind the compartment of pigeonholes and small drawers of the interior. Below these is a pull-out writing shelf with baize or leather panel framed by wooden banding.

A tambour roll-top consists of a horizontal panel that slides or rolls back in curved grooves in the sides of the desk compartment. The tambour slide is made of strips of wood, about an inch wide, with fronts rounded. These are mounted on a heavy canvas backing and when assembled, the slide has a reeded appearance. The outer edge of the panel is finished with a heavy cross rail fitted with incised finger grips and a centered lock.

A flat-top is of tablelike proportions and usually has a large conforming panel of baize or leather surrounded by wooden banding about two inches wide.

With few exceptions, the writing surface of a desk or secretary, whatever its type, is from 30 to 34 inches from the floor.

Large drawers in desks and secretaries have the same

construction details as those of chests of drawers (see Section VI, page 134). Small drawers of writing compartment have sides, backs and bottoms of thin soft wood, generally about a quarter-inch thick. They are either joined by dove-tailing or are fastened by brad-size nails. Bottoms are flush and nailed to sides and backs.

Secretaries are generally constructed in two sections. The upper or bookcase part fits onto the desk base and is held in place by projecting dowels. The bookcase section usually has a separate lift-off cornice held in position by projecting dowels. Bookcase doors are fitted with panes of glass, either single ones or two separated by a central horizontal muntin. Some ornate examples have oval panes of either clear or mirror glass. The glazing is framed by applied moldings of conforming shape. The doors are hung with butt hinges and the right-hand one has an overlapping astragal molding and is fitted with a lock. Generally, both doors are fitted with matching wooden keyhole rosettes.

Lower or desk section may have drawers of equal depth, or a top one shallower than the others; a top drawer with cupboard beneath; or a cupboard only. Drawer fronts are fitted with mushroom-turned wooden knobs, brass handles or leafage-carved wooden handles. Cupboard has a single full-width fixed shelf; is enclosed by solid doors with large panels framed by applied molding, possibly trimmed with applied carved medallions and spandrels. There are butt hinges, and the inner edge of right-hand door has an overlapping astragal molding and lock and key.

With both desks and secretaries, all raised decorative details are executed separately and then glued in place.

Stiles and rails of doors with slightly sunk rectangular panels are dowel-joined and the molding which edges the paneling is glued, sometimes nailed, in place. If panels are oval or circular, the surrounding molding is generally raised and glued in position.

141

141. Schoolmaster's Desk

Narrow, slightly overhanging top, 24 to 36 inches wide, usually with a low gallery either of plain solid pieces or of spool-turned parts (as pictured). The hinged lid slopes at about a 30-degree angle, has square or slightly rounded sides and generally a slightly raised retaining strip at the lower edge. The well beneath is eight to 12 inches deep at rear and six to eight inches deep at the front. It may have four to six pigeonholes, sometimes with two shallow drawers beneath. It may have a single full-width drawer about four inches deep, fitted either with mushroom-turned wooden knobs and inset keyhole surround or a keyhole surround only.

Four turned legs, either (A) tapering, with baluster-and-ring turnings and peg feet, or (B) spool-turned. About 36 inches tall.

Black walnut, ash, butternut, or assorted native hardwoods and softwoods, painted. Once extensively used by businessmen and schoolteachers; later quantities were made in furniture factories in all sections. Some late examples for school use had cast-iron trestles in place of the turned legs. *Ca. 1840–1870.* AAA to BB

142

142. Sloping-lid Desk with Raised Compartment

Desk section is like the foregoing but is 40 to 48 inches wide and is surmounted at rear by a recessed compartment that is either open or fitted with a pair of doors. With open type, the compartment is about 24 inches tall and eight inches deep. It has a flat, slightly overhanging top with rounded edge and plain sides. The left-hand side of the interior has a large open space and the right, eight tall account-book pigeonholes separated by scroll-cut dividers.

The closed-front type may be 40 inches tall by 10 to 12 inches deep. The flat top has a cove-molded cornice and sides are either plain or have rectangular, slightly sunk panels. The front has a pair of rectangular doors, with plain sunk panels, small wooden knobs and an inset metal keyhole surround. The interior has either two full-width shelves or a central shelf flanked by tall and small pigeonholes. Beneath, one to three tiers of shallow drawers, usually of one-third width, fitted with matching wooden knobs.

This type may be made in two parts, the sloping lid of the desk section generally hinged at the rear or front or, infrequently, made as a fixed top when the full-width drawer beneath is omitted. The drawer, when present, is about six inches deep and fitted with an inset metal keyhole surround, with or without a pair of wooden knobs. Plain square legs or tapering and turned ones with ring-and-ball elements; peg feet.

Made by country cabinetmakers, chiefly in the Middle West, of black walnut, butternut, or assorted native hard-and-softwoods, painted a dark color. The desk pictured is of butternut and is one of those used by members of the first Legislature of the State of Wisconsin, in 1848. *Ca. 1840–1860.* AAA to BB

143. Sloping-top Library Desk

A further development and later design, related to the preceding. Larger, with a more elaborate recessed com-

partment and fixed sloping top. Made as library or office
desk, after 1850. Its design also reflects some of the larger
desks of the Louis XV Period. Is 46 to 54 inches wide
by 28 to 34 inches deep and 42 to 48 inches tall. Fixed,
slightly overhanging top with rounded corners and
molded edge. At rear nearly full-width raised cabinet,

143

12 to 20 inches high. In its simpler and earlier form this
cabinet has a flat, slightly overhanging top and contains
a central cupboard with double doors flanked by (1) narrow, single-door cupboards; (2) four tiers of shallow
drawers or (3) open spaces fitted with full-sized pigeonholes, either horizontal or vertical. Doors simply paneled;
drawer fronts plain; small mushroom-turned wooden
knobs, inset metal keyhole surrounds or surrounds only.

The later and more elaborate raised cabinet is architectural in design. The central two-door cupboard has
a flat, overhanging top with low arched pediment, nearly

twice as tall as flanking sections, that have two full-width shallow drawers each. Their tops are surmounted by low galleries, either plain or pierced. Doors and drawers molding-paneled, fitted with wooden keyhole rosettes.

With either type the cabinet is raised about two inches above the desk top, forming a full-width space open at front, ten to 12 inches deep. From it the desk top slopes downward at about a 20-degree angle, forming a writing surface which has a wide banding and large rectangular baize or leather panel.

Beneath there may be (1) four tall tapering turned legs, with or without an octagon section, and a skirt at front with central arch flanked by single drawers matching those above, or (2) a central kneehole flanked by cupboard or drawer sections and supported by short turned tapering legs.

Early examples mahogany with crotch-grain veneered doors and drawer fronts; less frequently, rosewood. Later examples in Renaissance substyle black walnut or ash, with black walnut trim. Made on order by cabinet-making shops and by some early factories. Not numerous. *Ca. 1850–1870*. B to BB

144. Drop-front Bureau Desk

An upper section, 18 to 22 inches tall, recessed about a third of the depth of lower or bureau section. Flat, slightly overhanging rectangular top 34 to 38 inches wide by about 12 inches deep, square or rounded edge. Beneath, a full-width drop front having either large rectangular panel or two nearly square ones, framed with wavy molding and fitted with a centered metal keyhole surround. Interior is divided, generally with centered small drawers flanked on one side by three tiers of small pigeonholes, the other by account-book pigeonholes.

Carcase of lower section has either plain or paneled ends and square front corners. It contains three full-width drawers fitted with mushroom-turned knobs and

144

inset metal keyhole surrounds. The four corner stiles extend to the floor to form plain legs about six inches tall that are braced at the front by flat scrolled brackets. Total height varies from 46 to 52 inches.

Made by cabinetmakers or early factories of mahogany, with crotch-grain veneered drop-front and drawer fronts, assorted native hardwoods, stained red, or, less often, of black walnut. *Ca. 1840–1860.* BB to BBB

145. Drop-front Bureau Secretary

Has a recessed upper section, 50 to 60 inches tall, which surmounts a lower section similar to that of the preceding bureau desk. Upper section has a flat, boldly cove-molded cornice top, 36 to 42 inches wide, above a plain frieze and contains a bookcase and desk compartment. Bookcase has two full-width shelves and is enclosed by a pair of plain glazed doors, fitted with an

145

inset metal keyhole surround. Below, a hinged, counterbalanced drop front, with rectangular, slightly sunk panel, fitted with an inset keyhole surround. Writing surface has large baize panel framed by wooden bands. Interior of desk is divided with either three centered open shelves or a tier of two drawers above an open space flanked on one side by three wide pigeonholes and on the other by three or four vertical ones.

Bureau section has a slightly overhanging top, rounded or molded edge. Ends usually paneled and the top-drawer level sometimes overhangs the rest by one or two inches. Has three full-width drawers of equal depth; the top one may be ogee-molded with finger grips on lower edge. Other drawers are fitted with mushroom-turned knobs and inset keyhole surrounds. The corner stiles form plain short legs, braced at front by flat scrolled brackets. Total height varies from over six to seven feet.

Made by early factories of mahogany, with drop front and drawer fronts crotch-grain veneered, of assorted native hardwoods stained red, or, less often, of black walnut. *Ca. 1850–1865.* B to BB

146. Drop-front Table Desk

Smallest and lightest of this type. A recessed section with drop front, tablelike base with single drawer. Has plain rectangular, slightly overhanging top with rounded or concave molded edge, 32 to 38 inches wide by eight to ten inches deep. The drop front is 18 to 20 inches high with large rectangular panel fitted with an inset metal keyhole surround or an applied wooden keyhole rosette. Writing surface has a green baize panel framed by wide wooden bands. Interior compartmented, small drawers below pigeonholes or a central open space with one or two drawers above, flanked on one side by three tiers of two square pigeonholes each and on the other by two account-book pigeonholes. A light-colored, fancy-grain wood, such as bird's-eye maple or satinwood, is sometimes used for this interior.

The projecting top of the tablelike base slopes slightly, has matching molded edge and supports the lowered drop front. Beneath, single full-width drawer of medium depth, mushroom-turned wooden knobs or leafage-carved wooden handles. Four turned tapering legs, ring-turned elements top and bottom; peg feet, castered.

Made by cabinetmakers or early factories of mahogany,

146

with drop front and drawer fronts crotch-grain veneered black walnut, sometimes with burl-veneer facings; or of assorted native hardwoods, stained red or brown. With some late examples there is an applied central ornament of carved fruit and leafage on the drop-front panel. *Ca. 1845–1865.* B to BB

147. Drop-front Secretary

Construction and general design copies the French *secrétaire à abattant* of the 18th and early 19th centuries. It is the only secretary built in one piece.

Flat, rectangular cove-molded cornice, 38 to 40 inches

wide, surmounting a plain frieze, sometimes ornamented with a centered applied carving of rose flanked by leafage. This and the carcase have rounded or chamfered front corners with carved or split-turned ornaments at top and bottom and sometimes at center. The hinged,

147

counterbalanced drop front is about 30 inches wide by 24 inches high. Writing surface is paneled with either green baize or leather framed by a wide wooden banding. The arrangement of the compartmented interior varies from a tier of half-width drawers above an open space, with central drawer beneath flanked by two shallower ones, to a double tier of small drawers below an open arcaded area flanked by two small lockers. This interior is frequently satinwood-veneered with rosewood banding. The small drawers are fitted with brass, ivory or rosewood knobs.

The lower part of the carcase contains a cupboard enclosed by a pair of solid doors, either plain or with large cartouche-shaped panels formed by applied carved and scrolled moldings that match the larger panel on the drop front. All are fitted with either scrolled brass keyhole escutcheons or inset keyhole surrounds. Secretary has a wide-banded base, slightly scrolled skirt above low, plain or scroll-carved bracket feet.

Rosewood veneer, interior satinwood; or mahogany with crotch-grain veneering and bird's-eye maple interior. Some later examples black walnut. With these three tiers of full-width drawers, fitted with carved leafage handles, may replace the cupboard.

This type of secretary was the work of cabinetmakers in the larger cities, such as Belter of New York, Henkels of Philadelphia, Galusha of Troy, New York and others who were French-trained. A considerable number made in New Orleans were shipped up the Mississippi as far as southern Wisconsin. Always a handsome and sophisticated piece. Not numerous. *Ca. 1840–1865.* BBB to CC

148. Transitional Secretary with Writing Flap

Recessed upper section with flat, slightly overhanging top, 38 to 42 inches wide. Beneath, low plain frieze and pair of nearly square solid doors with slightly sunk panels, inset metal keyhole surrounds. Interior is compartmented with an account-book pigeonhole at either end and space between an open area over a tier of shallow drawers and small pigeonholes, frequently made of a light-colored wood, such as maple, plain or bird's-eye, and drawers are fitted with small brass or wooden knobs.

On the top of the lower section, in front of this cabinet, is a fold-over, baize-paneled writing flap supported
by narrow pull brackets. Carcase has plain or single-
paneled ends and square front corners. It contains three
full-width drawers of equal depth, with mushroom-
turned wooden knobs and inset metal keyhole surrounds.

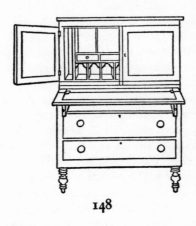

148

Four ring-and-ball turned legs, about eight inches tall,
terminating in peg feet. Total height varies from 52 to
56 inches and base is from 18 to 20 inches deep. Legs,
equal-depth drawers and arrangement of cabinet interior are the Victorian elements of its design.

Made by cabinetmakers or early factories of mahogany,
with crotch-grain veneered door panels, writing flap and
drawer fronts, or assorted native hardwoods stained red.
Ca. 1840–1860. BB to BBB

149. Gothic Secretary

Has recessed upper part, 36 to 42 inches wide by 40 to 48 inches tall and 10 inches deep, with a flat, beveled or cove-molded cornice, sometimes surmounted by low triangular pediment in silhouette, with plain or wavy-molded upper edge. Beneath a plain frieze and a pair of full-width, glazed doors fitted with inset metal keyhole surrounds. Inner edge of right-hand door has an overlapping molding, either half-round or wavy molding. With the latter, pierced and scroll-cut spandrels ornament the upper corners.

When there are two panes of glass in each door, a central horizontal muntin separates them. Less frequently there are six panes each, set in simply molded muntins. Below the doors, a tier of two half-width drawers with small mushroom wooden knobs and inset metal keyhole surrounds or keyhole surrounds only.

Lower section usually has paneled ends with square or slightly rounded front corners. At the top, in front of the bookcase, is a fold-over writing flap, either flat or with slight downward slope. Its writing surface is paneled with green baize and supported by pull brackets. Carcase contains three full-width drawers of equal depth, fitted with mushroom-turned wooden knobs and inset metal keyhole surrounds. Sometimes the top drawer is ogee-molded and has finger grips on the lower edge. The corner stiles extend to floor and are braced at front by a scroll-cut valanced skirt or by brackets. Total height is from five feet, eight inches to seven feet.

Made by cabinetmakers or some early factories of mahogany with cornice, writing flap and drawer fronts

crotch-grain veneered; rosewood; butternut; maple and
assorted native hardwoods stained red. Later examples
black walnut. Popular and widely made, with a number
of minor variations in design and decoration. Much liked
by collectors today for use as secretary or glass or china
cabinet. Numerous. *Ca. 1850–1870.* BB to BBB

149   **150**

150. Gothic Secretary with Cupboard Base

Like preceding in design and construction except for
height and cupboard base. Recessed bookcase top, 38 to
44 inches wide, beveled or cove-molded cornice, occasionally surmounted by a triangular pediment, above a
plain frieze with simply-molded lower edge. The glazed,
full-width doors may have (1) a large rectangular pane,
(2) two nearly square or (3) nine rectangular ones set
in plain molded muntins with single or triple arching
at top. Interior is fitted with three adjustable or fixed
shelves. Beneath doors are two shallow drawers with

mushroom-turned wooden knobs and, sometimes, inset metal keyhole surrounds.

Lower section has fold-over writing flap. Sides of carcase are usually paneled. Single full-width drawer, mushroom-turned wooden knob and inset metal keyhole surround, above full-width cupboard. This is enclosed by double doors with slightly sunk plain panels. On inner edge of the right-hand door, as well as the glazed one in the upper section, is a half-round or double bead astragal. Simple bracket feet. Total height varies from six feet eight inches to seven feet six inches.

By local cabinetmakers or some early factories. Rosewood, mahogany, with crotch-grain veneering, black walnut or sometimes maple and assorted native hardwoods stained brown or red. *Ca. 1840–1865.* BBB to CC

151. Scrolled-pediment Secretary

Similar structurally to the preceding but more elaborate. Bookcase section, 40 to 46 inches wide by about 10 inches deep, surmounted by arched pediment with upper edge scroll-cut in 16 balancing molded volutes flanking a central finial with pendent carved scrolls. Beneath, two tall rectangular doors with narrow stiles and rails, glazed with either one-piece panels or two nearly square ones separated by horizontal muntins. On inner edge of right-hand door is a wavy-molded astragal and an inset metal keyhole surround. Interior is fitted with three fixed or adjustable shelves. Below the doors is a low compartment fitted with a tier of six pigeonholes above two tiers of wide shallow drawers which flank an open central space with valanced top. This is enclosed by a pivoted panel which slides back above the pigeonholes.

Top of lower section has a fold-over writing flap about two inches thick, *not supported by pull brackets,* but fitted with strong butt hinges. Writing surface is either baize or leather, paneled, and banded with wood. Flap

151

has a mortised lock and upper surface has inset keyhole surround. When closed and locked, it secures both flap and the panel enclosing the pigeonhole compartment.

Carcase of lower section has paneled ends and slightly rounded front corners. It contains a full-width drawer of medium depth with an applied scroll-and-leaf carved decoration in relief immediately below the inset keyhole surround. Below, full-width cupboard enclosed by pair of solid doors; slightly sunk panels, arched at top by scroll-and-leaf carved spandrels, framed at sides and bottom with wavy molding. Right-hand door has astragal molding and keyhole surround, matching those of glazed door above. Interior has single shelf. Base low and plain, except for a centered carved ornament matching that on drawer front; it projects slightly and upper and lower edges are wavy-molded. Socket casters. Height varies from seven to eight feet.

Made mostly by local cabinetmakers, less often by early factories. Mahogany with crotch-grain veneering; rosewood; black walnut. *Ca. 1855–1865.* BB to BBB

152

152. Louis XV Secretary with Fold-over Compartment

Tall and elaborately decorated, with applied carving and shaped molded panels. Upper section has cove-molded, overhanging lift-off cornice, 38 to 44 inches wide, above low, plain frieze with simply molded lower edge. Pair of full-width bookcase doors, with tall, oval glazed panels framed with concave, double bead molding and applied scroll-and-leaf carved spandrels. Right-hand door has a wavy molding astragal and is fitted with an inset metal keyhole surround. The interior has three or four adjustable, full-width shelves.

Beneath bookcase two groups of four or six pigeon-holes above one full-width or two narrow shallow drawers which flank a central open area, frequently with arched top. Interior made of bird's-eye maple or satin-wood, drawers with rosewood or mahogany knobs. Enclosed by a pair of solid, full-width doors with horizontal oval molded panels and spandrels matching those above, also matching astragal and inset keyhole surround.

The lower section has solid ends and at the top of the front there is a projecting, fold-over writing compartment. When open it slopes forward slightly and the writing surface is formed by two hinged, baize-paneled and banded flaps with compartmented spaces for paper and other writing material beneath. A full-width cupboard below with single shelf is enclosed by a pair of solid, nearly square doors with quatre-foil molded panels and carved spandrels matching those above. Doors are flanked by flat, cyma-curved pilasters, partially disengaged from the carcase front. The base projects about half an inch, is plain and about two inches tall. Square, cyma-curved bracket feet at front; plain at rear. Total height is eight to nine feet.

Custom-made of mahogany, with crotch-grain veneering and sometimes rosewood moldings and spandrels, or of rosewood. Rare. *Ca. 1850–1860.* C to CCC

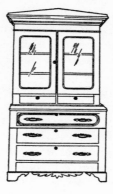

153

153. Late Gothic Secretary

Like the earlier Gothic secretary (*see No. 149*) except for the following which show its later date:

Large glass panels rectangular but with rounded corners. Applied moldings on upper and lower sections double-beaded, projecting instead of wavy. Lower section has rounded front corners, overhanging top drawer. Fronts of the three full-width drawers are panel-molded, with leaf-carved or strap-carved wooden handles and wooden keyhole rosettes. Carcase is supported by a slightly projecting base with conforming rounded front corners, simple bracket feet and valanced skirt. Total height is from six feet eight inches to seven feet six inches.

Factory-made; usually black walnut, sometimes ash with black walnut trim. Not as numerous as the earlier secretary. *Ca. 1865–1875.* B to BB

154

154. Transitional Fall-front Bureau Desk

Rectangular top, 34 to 38 inches wide by about 18 inches deep, with square corners and rounded or molded edge overhanging carcase about an inch. Four full-width drawers of equal depth; second one a fall-front writing compartment which pulls forward about half its depth. Its writing surface is paneled with baize framed by wood banding. Its rear is divided with a varied arrangement of pigeonholes and small drawers, frequently of plain or fancy maple or other light colored wood. The small drawers are fitted with knobs of the same wood or of brass.

All drawer fronts, including that of the fall-front, have mushroom-turned wooden knobs. Ends of carcase are more often plain than paneled. Base has plain bracket feet and a skirt with lower edge valanced in balanced cyma-curves, sometimes decorated with shaped or rounded central pendent finial. Height varies from 46 to 50 inches.

Mahogany, with crotch-grain veneered drawer fronts; maple, birch, butternut, walnut or assorted native hardwoods, stained red or brown by local cabinetmakers throughout the Eastern states and Middle West. Comparatively few examples have survived. *Ca. 1840–1850.* AAA to BB

155

155. Transitional Fall-front Bureau Secretary

Bookcase upper section surmounting fall-front desk section much like the foregoing. Upper section 40 to 46 inches wide by 46 to 52 inches tall and about 12 inches deep, surmounted by flat, lift-off cornice with wavy or spool-turned molding on lower edge. Below, a low frieze and a pair of full-width glazed doors with either single or double panes, frequently framed by wavy or spool-turned molding. Sometimes panes are mirrors. The astragal of the right-hand door may be wavy, spool-turned or half round. Inset metal keyhole surround. Interior has three or four adjustable shelves.

The lower section usually has paneled ends and contains four full-width drawers of which the top one is the fall-front feature. The writing flap is sometimes supported by quadrant sliding brackets. The rear of the interior is fitted with pigeonholes and one to four small drawers, with or without keyhole surrounds. Fall-front and drawers below are fitted with mushroom-turned wooden knobs and inset metal keyhole surrounds.

In place of the three lower drawers, there may be a full-width cupboard enclosed by a pair of solid doors with slightly sunk panels framed by molding matching that of the upper doors and with a like astragal and keyhole surround. The corner stiles form short rectangular feet, frequently fitted with socket casters and braced at front by scrolled brackets. Total height varies from seven to eight feet.

Made by local cabinetmakers or some early factories. Mahogany, with crotch-grain veneering; maple, birch, butternut, black walnut or assorted native hardwoods, stained red or brown in same sections as the corresponding fall-front desk. Secretary pictured was originally in the boyhood home of Samuel L. Clemens at Hannibal, Missouri. *Ca. 1840–1860.* BB to C

156. Renaissance-Eastlake Fall-front Secretary

Upper section has a low, cove-molded, lift-off cornice, 38 to 40 inches wide, above a pair of full-width glazed doors. Each has a one-piece glass panel with arched or semicircular top framed by a triple bead molding. With the semicircular top, there is a carved cartouche-shaped central detail flanked by applied burl spandrels. On the outer edges of the doors there are applied pilasters, generally with shaped brackets at upper ends and centered

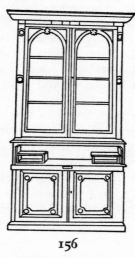

156

rosettes. Right door has a conforming astragal and inset keyhole surround or an applied keyhole rosette. Interior is fitted with three or four adjustable shelves with molded front edges.

The lower or desk part contains fall-front writing compartment above full-width cupboard. Face of fall-front ornamented with one or two molding-framed, burl-veneered panels, and inset metal keyhole surround or an applied wooden keyhole rosette. Interior has baize-paneled writing surface, and rear compartments with small drawers flanking an open space with or without pigeonholes. For this, bird's-eye maple or satinwood is sometimes used.

The cupboard beneath is enclosed by a pair of full-width solid doors with slightly raised burl-veneered panels having applied rosettes at their incurved corners. The right-hand door has an astragal and keyhole matching those above. Interior is fitted with a single shelf with molded front edge. Infrequently, three full-width drawers of nearly equal depth take the place of cupboard. They have conforming molding-paneled fronts and brass or plated bail or pendent ring handles with rectangular or square chased plates; keyhole surrounds, or applied wooden rosettes. Base is slightly projecting with molded upper edge; often fitted with socket casters.

Black walnut, burl-veneered spandrels and raised panels. *Ca. 1865–1880.* BB to BBB

157. Slant-front Bureau Desk

Similar desks made from 1700 on. Narrow, slightly overhanging top, 30 to 36 inches wide with molded, rounded or plain edge, sometimes surmounted by a low plain gallery. Front slants from a 45- to a nearly 60-degree angle; either plain or molded edges, either inset metal keyhole surround or an applied wooden keyhole rosette.

Interior compartments and open central space, sometimes with arched top, flanked by (1) 12 nearly square pigeonholes in two tiers, (2) six pigeonholes above four small shallow drawers fitted with small brass or wooden knobs or (3) six pigeonholes the full height of the interior. The pigeonhole dividers have rounded front edges and are sometimes of plain or fancy-grain maple or other light-colored native wood.

Carcase has plain ends with front corners square or slightly rounded, and generally contains three full-width drawers of equal depth with plain or slightly overlapping fronts. They are fitted with mushroom-turned wooden

157

knobs or leaf-carved handles and either metal keyhole surrounds or wooden keyhole rosettes. Either a low, slightly projecting base, cut to form plain scrolled bracket feet, or short ball-and-ring or spool-turned legs. Total height varies from 40 to 44 inches, depth from 17 to 20 inches.

By local cabinetmakers and later factories. Mahogany, with slant front and drawer fronts sometimes crotch-grain veneered; rosewood, black walnut, butternut, ash, or, occasionally, maple or assorted native hardwoods stained red or brown. With minor variations in detail and ornamentation was made throughout the Victorian Period. Some late examples are of oak or cherry surmounted by a gallery of brass rods and posts and with drawer fronts fitted with either brass pendent rings or bail handles and matching keyhole escutcheons.

In greatest demand of all desks by collectors. *Ca. 1840–1880.* B to C

158

158. Transitional Slant-front Secretary

Consists of two sections: an enclosed bookcase or cupboard top, and a slant-front bureau desk like the foregoing. Both are the same width, so sides of secretary form unbroken verticals.

Upper section is 34 to 38 inches wide by 44 to 56 inches tall and about 12 inches deep. It has either a flat, slightly overhanging top with wavy molded edge or a cove-molded cornice with front corners, either square or slightly rounded. The front has a pair of oblong doors fitted with either a metal keyhole surround or a wooden keyhole rosette, and either wood or glazed panels. If of glass, each panel may be a single or double pane, frequently framed by narrow wavy molding.

Interior usually has two shelves, sometimes a tier of four to six small pigeonholes, matching those in interior of desk, which are placed either at the bottom or immediately beneath the first shelf. Total height varies from six feet, eight inches to seven feet, six inches.

Chiefly by local cabinetmakers of mahogany, with drawer fronts and door panels crotch-grain veneered; black walnut, butternut or assorted native hardwoods stained red or brown. Not as numerous as the desk. *Ca. 1840–1860.* BB to C

Louis XV Slant-front Secretary

Made in two sections, a recessed bookcase top and a slant-front lower part with cupboard. Is seven to eight feet six inches tall, by 40 to 48 inches wide, with base about 22 inches deep. Bookcase section has an arched and scroll-carved pediment with central cartouche and voluted ends above a low cove-molded cornice. Sides plain, front has pair of glazed doors, flanked by scroll-carved stiles. Doors have large oval panels, either clear or mirror glass, framed by concave or wavy molding. Door corners ornamented by scroll-carved spandrels. Wooden keyhole rosettes on both doors. Overlapping astragal moldings on the right-hand one. Interior has three or four adjustable shelves.

Lower section has a slant front, decorated with a large medallion of balancing foliated scrolls carved in relief. Wooden keyhole rosette or inset metal keyhole surround.

Writing surface has large baize panel; is supported by folding brass brackets. Rear of interior has small drawers and pigeonholes sometimes flanking open central space.

Carcase beneath contains full-width cupboard, enclosed by a pair of solid doors which have circular molding-framed panels with central leafage medallions carved in relief, and scroll-carved spandrels. Low scroll-bracket feet.

Custom-made of mahogany or rosewood. *Ca. 1850–1865.* C to CCC

159. Architectural Three-part Secretary

Bookcase top; slant-front section; cupboard base. Height is from seven to eight feet, width 44 to 48 inches, depth of base about 24 inches.

Bold, overhanging cove-molded cornice, lunette-shaped pediment containing scrolls or special ornament carved in high relief. Plain frieze defined by a cock-bead molding. Sides have slightly sunk rectangular panels framed by concave molding. Glazed doors have molding-framed single panes, wooden keyhole rosettes. Inner edge of right-hand door has an overlapping triple bead molding. Interior has two or three adjustable shelves.

Molded base of bookcase rests on the top of the slant front's writing section, which has conforming paneling. That of slant front is decorated with a scroll and strapwork cartouche, carved in high relief. This may surround an engraved brass presentation plaque. Writing surface has large baize or leather panel, wood-banded. Rear of interior has pigeonholes and small drawers, central open space. Molded base overhangs cupboard base about four inches at front.

Cupboard has conforming paneled ends and flanking the pair of solid doors are scrolled and voluted carved pilaster brackets. Doors are paneled to match ends and

159

fitted with wooden keyhole rosettes. Molded base is supported by low block or bun feet.

Custom-made; rosewood, mahogany or black walnut, generally a presentation piece for a retiring officer of a bank, insurance company or the like. Unusual. *Ca. 1865–1875.* CC to CCC

Eastlake Slant-front Secretary

Similar to the preceding — sometimes with three full-width drawers in place of cupboard in lower section. Upper or bookcase section is 38 to 42 inches wide by

about 12 inches deep and has a flat, lift-off cornice that
is either beveled or cove-molded above a plain frieze,
generally burl-veneered. Doors have single rectangular
panes of glass framed with an overlapping and slightly
projecting molding. May also have central cartouche-
shaped details at the top. The right-hand door has molded
astragal. Both have wooden keyhole rosettes or inset
metal keyhole surrounds. Joining of bookcase and lower
section is masked by a slightly projecting molding at
front and sides.

The slant front is at a nearly 60-degree angle; its face
is decorated with a rectangular, slightly sunk panel with
inner edges of stiles and rails framing it, chamfered.
This panel has full-width centered band of burl veneer,
flanked top and bottom by narrow bands of reeding.
Mushroom-turned wooden knobs and an applied wooden
keyhole rosette or a keyhole rosette only. Desk interior
has central open area flanked at one side by four pigeonholes in two tiers above two tiers of shallow drawers and
on the other side by four account-book pigeonholes with
dividers scrolled in balancing cyma-curves. Writing area
has a rectangular baize panel banded with wood. The
slant front overhangs the three full-width drawers below,
and fronts of carcase sides are scroll-cut.

Drawers have either veneering and reeding matching
that of the slant front or two plain panels of burl veneer.
They are fitted with either carved wooden handles or
brass pendent rings with square plates set diagonally
and wooden keyhole rosettes. Piece has a plain, slightly
projecting base with molded upper edge; or corner stiles
may form short plain legs braced at front by scroll-cut
brackets. Socket casters.

Factory-made in quantity. Black walnut, trimmed with burl veneer; or, infrequently, butternut or other native hardwood, generally stained brown. *Ca. 1870–1880.* AAA to B

160

160. Eastlake Cylinder-front Desk

The design of its quarter-round solid cylinder front originated in the Louis XV Period and was used in America during the Hepplewhite, Sheraton and American Empire Periods.

Rectangular top, 30 to 34 inches wide, often surmounted by a shelf which is raised about 12 inches and has a low shaped gallery, generally with turned finials at ends. Shelf is supported at front by baluster-turned or scroll-shaped uprights, at rear by paneled back, sometimes faced with burl veneer. Low plain frieze beneath the desk top, with (1) wooden keyhole rosette, (2) inset metal keyhole surround, or (3) metal keyhole escutcheon for cylinder front. This front has rectangular panel, usually faced with burl veneer, framed by quadrant stiles and straight rails. Lower rail has (1) an incised, molded lower edge, (2) a pair of wooden knobs or (3) a centered metal escutcheon with rod handle.

Interior has two shallow drawers beneath small pigeonholes flanking either two or three large ones or a central open area. Drawers and pigeonhole dividers frequently bird's-eye maple, satinwood or other light-colored wood with knobs of black walnut. The pull-out writing shelf has a green baize panel banded with wood, and molded front with finger grips.

Carcase has paneled ends; usually contains three full-width drawers, either equal depth or with top one shallower and slightly overhanging. Drawer fronts have centered burl-veneered panels or half sunbursts. Wooden knobs, brass pendent-ring handles with square plates, or bar handles, with or without plates, and wooden keyhole rosettes. Inset metal keyhole surrounds or keyhole escutcheons. Plain shaped base, socket casters. Height varies from 56 inches to five feet.

Factory-made. Black walnut trimmed with burl veneer. *Ca. 1870–1880.* AA to AAA

161. Eastlake Cylinder-front Secretary

Has upper bookcase section, 38 to 42 inches wide by about 12 inches deep, surmounted by a cove-molded, lift-off cornice with low plain frieze below. A pair of full-width doors with single glass panes have narrow burl-veneered raised panels and applied wooden rosettes ornamenting their stiles and rails. The right-hand door has a double or triple bead astragal; keyhole rosette at center. Interior has three adjustable shelves with molded or rounded edges.

Lower section is like the preceding desk but a little larger. Top drawer is sometimes shallower than the two lower and may overhang them about an inch. With

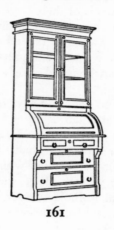

161

some, lower drawers are replaced by full-width cupboard with single shelf and pair of solid doors. Their raised panels are burl-veneered; ornamentation of stiles and rails like upper section.

Factory-made. Black walnut with burl trim. Numerous. *Ca. 1865–1875.* B to BB

162. Sloping Drop-front Desk with Enclosed Base

Top is usually surmounted by a raised shelf that is supported by flat uprights scroll-cut in cyma-curves. Often bottle-shaped or acorn finials at corners; both shelf

and top have low galleries at rear, with centered cresting
or scrolled upper edge, sometimes pierced.

Face of drop front has either slightly sunk rectangular

162

panel, molding-framed, or two smaller ones separated by
wide central stile.

Panel usually has applied carved central ornaments,
if single — a large lozenge-shaped ornament with con-
ventionally scrolled edge and central rosette; if two
smaller ones, each has vertical ornament done in leafage,
open-rose motif. Applied wooden keyhole rosette on
front.

Enclosed base has usual rectangular slightly overhanging top with molded edge; and (1) four full-width drawers with plain or paneled fronts, fitted with carved
wooden handles and wooden keyhole rosettes or brass
pendent-ring handles with either square chased plates

set on the diagonal, or rectangular ones and square, diagonally placed or circular keyhole escutcheons; (2) full-width, paneled-front drawer, fitted with carved wooden handles and wooden keyhole rosette, above full-width cupboard enclosed by paneled doors with centered carved ornaments corresponding to that of the drop-front; (3) full-width drawer above a half-width cupboard with single doors and two tiers of half-width drawers with ornamental details and fittings matching those above.

Base may be slightly projecting with molded upper edge or flush with slightly valanced or straight skirt. Socket casters fitted into concealed corner blocks. Height varies from 56 to 64 inches with shelf.

Factory-made; black walnut, with late examples oak or cherry. *Ca. 1860–1880.* B to BB

Sloping Drop-front Secretary

Like desk just described, with four full-width drawers in enclosed base, but has an enclosed bookcase section in place of raised shelf. Bookcase has flat, slightly overhanging cove-molded cornice. Sides plain, or paneled to conform to those of rest of secretary. The full-width doors have single clear glass panes framed with a slightly projecting applied molding. Joining of bookcase and desk is masked by a slightly projecting molding. Drawer fronts are plain with a centered band of burl veneer, flanked top and bottom with reeding, and are fitted with metal bail handles and oblong chased plates and circular keyhole escutcheons. Total height six feet four inches to seven feet; width 30 inches; depth 17 inches.

Factory-made. Black walnut with burl-veneer trimming. Not desirable as a collector's piece because of poor proportions. *Ca. 1870–1880.* AA to AAA

163

163. Sloping Drop-front Desk with Table Base

Rectangular, slightly overhanging top, 28 to 30 inches wide by about 10 inches deep, with either square corners and molded edges or rounded corners and edges. May be surmounted by a low gallery, usually with a molded flat cresting at back flanked by scroll-cut ends. The nearly full-width drop front is stile-and-rail constructed; has wooden keyhole rosette and large, rectangular, slightly sunk panel framed with convex molding. Panel is either plain or fielded with a slightly raised one of conforming shape. Sides of desk section may be plain or paneled.

Writing area has a large rectangular baize panel framed with wooden banding about two inches wide. Rear of interior has varied arrangement of small drawers and pigeonholes, with or without an open central area.

Table base has a rectangular, slightly overhanging top with concave molded or rounded edge, cut out at rear so that writing section fits within it. Table bed contains a full-width drawer, three to four inches deep, fitted with applied carved wooden handles, mushroom-turned wooden knobs and a wooden keyhole rosette or rosette only. Four tapering legs, round or octagon, with ring or ring-and-ball turned elements. Peg or button feet, castered. Total height 46 to 50 inches, depending on height of gallery and its cresting.

Factory-made of black walnut with interior sometimes of bird's-eye maple or other light-colored wood. Desk pictured went through the great Chicago fire of 1871 and subsequently was used in paying over $4,000,000 in insurance claims. *Ca. 1865–1875.* B to BB

164. Sloping Drop-front Desk with Trestle Base

The writing section is like the foregoing. Overhanging top frequently has low triangular gallery, with short urn or bottle-shaped turned finials at its four corners, or is surmounted by a raised shelf. This is the same size as the top and is supported by four baluster and ring-turned uprights about ten inches high. At rear of shelf is a molded pediment-shaped gallery with a central applied boss and at the four corners, short bottle-shaped finials.

Base contains single, full-width drawer about three inches deep. Either mushroom-turned wooden knobs or leaf-carved handles; wooden keyhole rosette. Trestles, each consisting of two slightly tapering turned uprights

with ring-turned elements. Low concave block feet
braced by centered turned and tapering stretcher with
conforming ring turning near each end; ball-turned element at the center. Total height with raised shelf is 56
to 64 inches.

Factory-made; black walnut; interior sometimes bird's-
eye maple or similar light-colored wood. *Ca. 1865–1875.*
AAA to B

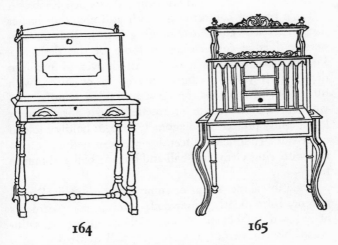

164   165

165. Louis XV Drop-front Lady Desk

Rectangular slightly overhanging top, 28 to 30 inches
wide, about eight inches deep; square, slightly rounded
or chamfered front corners; concave molded or rounded
edge. At rear, low pierced gallery in balancing S-scrolls.
Surmounting top is a conforming shelf, raised about
10 inches, with arched and scroll-pierced gallery at rear
and short urn-shaped finials at four corners. Shelf has

four tapering, ring-turned supports or flat, cyma-curved front supports and turned rear ones.

Sloping drop front has rectangular, slightly sunk panel, plain or burl-veneered, framed by applied triple bead molding and with a wooden keyhole rosette. Writing surface baize-paneled, wood-banded. Varied arrangement of pigeonholes flanking a central section composed of small pigeonholes, an open space and one or two tiers of shallow drawers fitted with turned wooden knobs.

Table base of conforming width and about 17 inches deep. Has a slightly overhanging top with front corners and edge conforming to those of the desk top. Bed of table contains a full-width drawer of medium depth with plain or burl-veneered front fitted with turned wooden knobs, or carved wooden handles and wooden keyhole rosette or rosette only. Cabriole front legs slightly projecting, diagonally placed; boldly molded outer sides, rudimentary feet. Rear legs turned and tapering with ring elements; ball-and-bun or ball-and-button feet.

Made in cabinet shops or some factories of black walnut or, infrequently, rosewood; interior compartments of grained light-color woods, such as maple or satinwood. Not numerous. *Ca. 1865–1875.* B to BBB

166. Lady Drop-front Desk with Mirror Panels

Indirectly derived from a European Renaissance drop-front chest with trestle base. Desk is 34 to 36 inches wide by six feet four inches tall, and about 18 inches deep. Rectangular top with straight front and square corners, surmounted by full-width shelf with serpentine front and molded edge. Low arched gallery at the back carved with flower and leafage motifs. Shelf supported by S-curved molded brackets, short urn-shaped finials. Beneath, at the back, a horizontal mirror panel.

The rectangular drop front is fitted with an inset metal keyhole surround, has a large, slightly sunk panel with central applied carved medallion of fruit and foli-

166

age motifs done in high relief; lower rail ornamented with applied balancing carved scrolls and leafage. Desk interior has a writing surface paneled with baize, wood-banded, and tier of three or four small shallow drawers, fitted with wooden knobs, below three tall pigeonholes flanked by open spaces.

Sometimes made of bird's-eye maple or other grained wood of light color.

Below the writing compartment is an area, open at

front and sides, that is nearly as tall as the paneled drop-front. It is defined at front corners by cyma-curved molded supports and at rear by a full-width mirror panel.

Boxlike base about three inches high with slightly overhanging top and molded lower edge, centered leaf and scroll-carved medallion. Short scrolled front legs; plain rear ones.

Factory-made. Black walnut or, less frequently, rose-wood; interior sometimes of bird's-eye maple, satinwood or other light-colored wood. Not numerous. *Ca. 1865–1875*. AAA to B

167. Shelf-top Lady Desk

Sloping lid type; shallow top surmounted by a two-shelf whatnot, 24 to 26 inches wide by about eight inches deep. Space between shelves about eight inches; lower one raised about 12 inches above desk. Shelves have square corners, molded edges and low three-quarter galleries; supported by scroll-cut, cyma-curved uprights at front, and at rear by square or turned ones; short shaped finials.

Hinged lid of desk 14 to 16 inches deep; slopes at about 10-degree angle, and has conforming overhang and molded edge. Writing surface has rectangular baize panel with wide wood banding. Well beneath sometimes compartmented at rear. Front and sides of desk paneled, lower edges valanced in simple scrolls. Slender flat legs, sometimes bead-molded, braced by box stretcher with recessed front on which rests full-width shelf.

Factory-made of black walnut, with or without burl-veneer trim. *Ca. 1870–1880*. AAA to B

167   **168**

168. Fire Screen Desk

A type of lady desk which appeared in England about 1800 and was produced in Sheraton and Regency Styles. Most American examples have Early Victorian stylistic details.

Because of its double purpose, front and back of enclosed upper part have same finish. Desk part is placed within the upper ends of the plain, quadrangular trestle supports and is surmounted by a beveled or cove-molded overhanging top, hinged rear. This gives access to a well within the plain frieze divided for writing accessories. The frieze is fitted with a scroll-carved keyhole medallion or a rosette and its lower edge is defined by a cock-bead molding.

The drop-front has a slightly sunk panel framed with narrow wavy molding with matching keyhole detail. Shallow interior, with two tiers of pigeonholes, open at top, with dividers of graduated height and sometimes arched. Baize or leather writing panel with wooden banding. Lower ends of trestles rest on small plinths, molded top and bottom and braced by a baluster-turned stretcher. Cyma-curved bracket feet, joined to trestle plinths and castered. Space between desk and stretcher is open in the fire screen manner.

By cabinetmakers. Mahogany, with crotch-grain veneer; rosewood; infrequently, black walnut. Pigeonholes sometimes satinwood or bird's-eye maple. Unusual. *Ca. 1840–1860.* B to BB

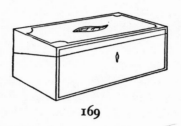

169

169. Lady Writing Box

Derived from traveling desk of the Sheraton Period but smaller, less elaborately fitted. Rectangular box, 12 to 14 inches wide eight to 10 inches deep, four to six inches high. Top and bottom are hinged at rear, and sides are cut on a diagonal so that when open the two provide a writing surface that slopes away from the user at about a 10-degree angle. Writing surface has two center-hinged flaps, with baize or velvet panels wood-banded at sides. Beneath are full-width wells, generally lined with colored paper, printed in small geometric patterns. Beyond the lower flap, a shallow section is fitted with square compartments for ink bottles. These flank a removable pen tray, with a semisecret well beneath. Sometimes the deeper well below the upper flap is fitted with compartments for needlework accessories.

Front of box has small keyhole fitted with an inset keyhole surround or centering a small stenciled gilt decoration of foliage and scrolls.

Pine, veneered with mahogany, rosewood or black walnut, usually with gilt striping to simulate brass trimming of earlier examples. By local cabinetmakers or toy and novelty shops. Numerous but often found in poor condition. A few oversize examples are supported by integral table legs. *Ca. 1840–1865.* A to AA

Davenport Desk

Practically a copy of an English desk of that name, popular in Great Britain during the Regency Period and imported in some numbers to the United States. English and American types can be distinguished by one feature: upper part of English-made desk is mounted on concealed grooves and can be pulled forward; American-made part is fixed.

Oblong top, 26 to 30 inches wide by six to eight inches deep, with square corners and convex, molded, overhanging edge at back and sides. Generally surmounted by a plain or pierced three-quarters gallery. Hinged lid slopes at about 20-degree angle; conforming overhang and molded edge; usually rectangular baize or leather panel, wood-banded. Beneath the lid a full-width well, about four inches deep at front and eight inches deep at rear, which is compartmented with pigeonholes only or pigeonholes and small shallow drawers.

Lower edge of well has an applied, slightly projecting molding at front and sides; overhangs pedestal-like base about ten inches. Overhang is supported by scroll-cut, sometimes pierced, brackets. Pedestal base paneled on all sides except the right. This contains shallow, full-width pencil drawer; either four equal-depth drawers or a cupboard beneath. Drawers have applied carved handles and keyhole rosettes. Cupboard has single shelf and paneled door fitted with a keyhole rosette. Plain molded base with conforming projections (about 20 inches long) beneath the brackets that support the overhang. Four turned feet, usually castered. Total height 32 to 34 inches.

Made by factories or cabinetshops. Black walnut, with or without burl-veneer banding; occasionally rosewood with pigeonhole compartments of satinwood. Sometimes called "pulpit desk" or misnamed "lady desk" because of small size. *Ca. 1860–1875.* B to BBB

170. Wooten's Patent Desk

Here is a complete office, even to letter slot and a 40-unit filing section. Closed, it resembles a cylinder-front desk with cupboard base; open, its fall-front writing flap and variety of compartments show the inventiveness of W. S. Wooten, granted a patent on October 4, 1874. The dimensions are 73 inches tall, 43 inches wide, 31 inches deep. It is constructed in three units — the main carcase and the pair of quadrant-topped hinged fronts which have the thickness (about 15 inches) of bank vault doors.

Carcase has rectangular, slightly overhanging top, about 15 inches deep, with a bevel-molded edge; it is surmounted by a low three-quarter gallery, with urn-shaped finials and a central cartouche of Renaissance details. Sides of carcase are paneled. The two hinged front sections are quadrant-rounded at top, with burl-veneered sunk panels, simulating a cylinder front. At

170

sides and center there is a conforming raised or reeded molding which joins a plain projecting cross-molding. Below it, the fronts of the units are vertical and each has a large rectangular panel with flatly arched top. These are faced with burl veneer, and molding-framed to match those above.

The stiles of these units have split finials and incidental raised panels. The center one overlaps and is fitted with an oxidized metal turn-handle and keyhole pierced plate. The left-hand unit has a decorative frame with flap marked LETTERS. Right-hand one has matching frame with plate reading WOOTEN DESK MANF. CO., INDIANAPOLIS, IND. W. S. WOOTEN'S PATENT. OCT. 4, 1874.

The right-hand unit when opened reveals 40 small filing sections. Within the left, there is a letterbox surrounded by pigeonholes and small shelves. The main carcase is fitted with a drop-front writing flap. When raised, it conceals the compartments; lowered, it is supported by pivoted metal brackets. Writing surface has large baize panel, wooden banding. Below the flap, five shallow drawers flanked by tall pigeonholes. Base plain, with molded upper edge. Pair of projecting foot brackets, castered.

Made by the Wooten Company of black or bleached walnut. Writing flap and small drawer fronts faced with curly maple; drawers have black walnut rosette knobs. An expensive, elaborate desk for a man of affairs. Several that belonged to important people are still extant; the list includes that of Joseph Pulitzer, founder of the *New York World,* whose desk is now at the Pulitzer School of Journalism, Columbia University. John D. Rockefeller's, at which he is believed to have planned the organization of the Standard Oil Company, is now in the Rockefeller Room at the Phillipse Castle Restoration, Tarrytown, New York. That of Professor Spencer F. Baird, Secretary of the Smithsonian Institution, is in the Director's office of the Smithsonian Institution, Washington, D. C. Sidney Lanier's is in the Lanier Room of

Johns Hopkins University and another example is in the museum of the Wisconsin State Historical Society at Madison.

Not numerous. *Ca. 1874–1880.* B to BBB

171

171. Double Pedestal Flat-top Desk

Similar to desk made in England during the Chippendale Period. Large rectangular top, four to five feet wide by 26 to 34 inches deep, with square corners, slightly overhanging molded edge and full-size baize or leather panel, wood-banded. Frieze beneath, four inches high with wavy or bead-molded lower edge, often contains central drawer flanked by narrower ones. Drawer fronts plain or paneled; mushroom turned wooden knobs or applied leaf-carved handles and inset metal keyhole surrounds or wooden keyhole rosettes. Sometimes shallower frieze, without drawers and paneled with wavy or bead molding.

Pedestals flanking the wide kneehole are paneled on

all sides with treatment of fronts, depending on whether drawers or cupboards are present. Sometimes pedestal on right has drawers and that on left a cupboard. Drawers have plain or molding-paneled fronts with knobs or handles, keyhole surrounds or rosettes. Cupboard doors paneled, to conform to the sides; keyhole surrounds or rosettes.

With an unusually large desk, drawers or cupboards extend only half the depth of the pedestals and are duplicated at rear, thus making front and rear exactly alike, even to the shallow frieze drawers. The pedestals usually have plinth bases with molded upper edges or low bracket feet with casters fitted into concealed corner blocks. Total height is 28 to 30 inches.

Mahogany, trimming crotch-grain veneer; rosewood; black walnut with burl-veneer details; ash or butternut trimmed with black walnut; and, less often, cherry, ebonized maple, sometimes trimmed with gilt striping, or white oak with quarter-sawed panels. Fine examples were custom-made; simpler ones factory-produced. *Ca. 1840–1880.* B to BBB

Roll-top Desk

Too well-known to require an illustration or detailed description. The flat top is surmounted by a sliding horizontal tambour front, the pedestals are narrower and contain drawers. Early examples are of black walnut; later ones mahogany, cherry or oak. Factory-made. *Ca. 1875 to after 1900.* A to AAA

172

172. Single Pedestal Flat-top Desk

Smaller, often simpler than the foregoing. One pedestal, generally the right-hand one, replaced by turned tapering legs.

Flat, slightly overhanging top, 30 to 38 inches wide by 20 to 24 inches deep, square or slightly rounded corners and molded edge. Surface of top usually plain, but may have baize panel, wood-banded. Plain frieze beneath is about four inches high with molded edge and usually contains two half-width drawers. These have plain or panel-molded fronts fitted with wooden knobs or leaf-carved wooden handles and inset metal keyhole surrounds or wooden keyhole rosettes. The paneled pedestal contains either drawers, with fronts and fittings matching those above, or a cupboard with paneled door which has either a keyhole surround or rosette. Pedestal has either a plinth base with molded upper edge or plain bracket feet, castered. Made for home or office or schoolroom use by teachers. For the latter, the flat top was sometimes surmounted by a low three-quarter gallery.

Factory-made. Black walnut; ash or butternut, black

walnut trimmed; cherry, maple or assorted native woods, usually painted to simulate black walnut. *Ca. 1860–1880* AAA to B

173

173. Kidney Desk

Made in England during the Sheraton Period but not in United States until late Victorian years.

Flat, kidney-shaped top, 36 to 48 inches wide, overhanging with deep molded edge, has conforming leather or baize panel with wood banding. Carcase is molding-paneled on all sides. Rounded ends, each with three or four drawers separated by molded bearer strips. Drawer fronts have molding-framed, slightly sunk panels, and wooden or brass knobs.

Between reeded front stiles is a paneled knee-hole, half the depth of the piece. It has a shallow drawer with concave front paneled to match the others and fitted with knobs and an oval molded keyhole trim of brass or wood. Its molded bearer strip serves also as the cornice of semi-circular paneled area. Lower edge of carcase is molded to match the bearer strips. Four tapering legs, ring-turned, carved at upper and lower ends. Small peg feet; sometimes cup casters. Height is 28 to 30 inches.

Mahogany, cherry, black walnut or, for late examples, oak. Fine examples, custom-made; simpler ones, factory-produced. Several made about 1875 are still in use in executive offices of Walter Baker & Company, Dorchester, Massachusetts. A small kidney desk with enclosed plain base in place of legs belonged to the late Don C. Seitz; at it he wrote several biographies. *Ca. 1870–1880 or later.* AAA to BBB

SECTION IX

Sideboards, Hunt Boards and Sugar Chests

THERE ARE four styles of sideboards. They are the Transitional, the Gothic, the Renaissance and the Eastlake. The first is a compact piece with enclosed base, adapted from the New England short sideboard of American Empire and earlier periods. Product of the cabinetmaker's shop, its general outline reflects the American Empire period but with Victorian decorative details, such as wavy molding and pierced and carved cresting. Not made after about 1850.

Contemporary with it, and continuing for ten to fifteen years longer, is the Gothic substyle, a design adapted from the earlier English pedestal sideboard. All decorative details are Gothic, such as pointed-arch panels, incised trefoils, crotchets and cusp finials. Some of these sideboards were especially designed by architects and made by cabinetmakers to order. Comparatively few examples are still extant.

The Renaissance style took the place of the Louis XV substyle in sideboard design, and, instead of such details as the cabriole leg and serpentine front, resulted in a completely enclosed base surmounted by an elaborate arched pediment. With this design came that beloved Victorian feature, the marble top, and such decorative details as carved flowers or fruits, and sporting trophies.

These sideboards ranged from large architectural examples, especially made, to the medium size, produced by factories making better grade furniture.

The Eastlake sideboard is generally more compact with decorative details limited to incised beading, burl-veneer panels and a pediment surmounted by a flat cornice molding, sometimes combined with simple arcading. The marble top is also found with this style.

Special Comments on Sideboards and Their Construction

The Transitional and Gothic sideboards, being made by cabinetmakers, have the same traces of handwork found on similar chests of drawers and bureaus, but moldings and carved details are consistently applied.

With the Renaissance style, the carcase is generally made of parts sawed and planed by machinery. Carved medallions, animal heads, swags of flowers or fruits are done separately and glued in place. With fine pieces the carving is handwork. For a less expensive sideboard the carving was roughed out with a power-driven fret or band saw and then hand-finished superficially with coarse carving chisels. Such work can be readily recognized. It is most often seen on wooden drawer handles. This style of sideboard often has a plinth base, usually fitted with concealed casters.

The Eastlake sideboard is factory-made and fitted with brass pendent-ring or bail handles. Its molded base is fitted with iron socket casters.

174

174. Small Transitional Sideboard

Such decorative details as oval panels, rounded pilasters and paw feet are survival designs of the American Empire and earlier periods, but height, compactness, construction of top with open central well and use of applied bands of wavy molding are Victorian.

This type has rectangular, slightly overhanging top with rounded front corners, broken into three units by a central well depressed about six inches. There is a plain gallery, also in three units, separated by short rounded pilasters. The central unit is taller and surmounted by a pierced, leafage-scroll carved and flatly arched cresting.

Carcase with either plain or paneled ends. Four rounded pilasters, dividing front into units conforming to those of the top, of which the wider one below the central well may be recessed about two inches. Each unit contains medium-depth drawer with cupboard beneath. Drawer fronts have horizontally placed oval panels

framed by wavy molding, stamped brass rosette knobs
or mushroom-turned wooden ones; central drawer has
either oval brass keyhole escutcheon or inset keyhole
surround. Drawer openings finished top and bottom with
bold bands of wavy molding. Cupboards have vertically
placed oval panels, framed with wavy molding, and
either oval brass keyhole escutcheon or inset brass keyhole surrounds. Each cupboard contains a fixed shelf
with rounded front edge. Door openings are banded at
bottom with wavy molding matching that above.

Plain conforming base with four rounded projections
serving as plinths for the pilasters. At front four short
paw or scrolled-bracket feet; at rear two plain bracket
feet. Dimensions are about four feet two inches tall, by
about the same length; 20 inches deep.

Made by cabinetmakers, probably for a special location,
of mahogany with liberal use of crotch-grain veneer. *Ca.
1840–1845.* B to C

175. Gothic Sideboard

Architectural quality suited to a city mansion or large
country residence. From six to seven feet long, from
42 to 50 inches tall, depending on the height of gallery;
about 22 inches deep.

Rectangular overhanging top, plain or molded edge
and square front corners. Front may be straight or have
a recessed central section.

Gallery has (1) low, triangular shape with conforming panel framed by applied bead molding, flanked
by rectangular plinths surmounted by small trefoil
finials, or (2) tall, sloping-arched central section flanked
by lower sections that are arcaded with small pointed

arches and surmounted by a conforming number of
finials. With this, the central section is ornamented with
a recessed ogee-arched panel, having central applied
medallion or foliated flowers or fruit carved in relief.

Top supported by end pedestals flanking central
medium-depth drawer, about half as wide as the total

175

length, with open space beneath. Drawer front has molding-framed panel with rounded ends or recessed one with
arched ends, inset metal keyhole surround and finger
grooves on the underside instead of handles.

With a more ornate example, the open space is spanned
by a flat pierced arch with pendent trefoil finials and incised trefoil spandrels.

Each pedestal contains either cupboard or a drawer
with cupboard beneath. Drawers match the central one
in depth, paneling and other details. The single cupboard
doors have (1) cusp-arched panels formed by applied
molding or (2) large recessed pointed-arch panels con-

taining smaller ones framed by applied molding and surmounted by trefoil finials and crotchets. Inset metal keyhole surrounds and butt or concealed pivot hinges on
doors. Pedestals low, plain plinth bases.

Custom-made by city cabinetmakers, most frequently
of mahogany, with gallery, drawers and doors generally
faced with crotch-grain veneer, or rosewood. Simple examples are sometimes known as "Carpenter Gothic"
furniture. Scarce. *Ca. 1840–1850.* BB to C

RENAISSANCE SUBSTYLE

176. Break-front Sideboard

Rectangular top, five feet six inches to six feet six inches
long, with central straight section that breaks forward
about three inches and is flanked by narrower ones having
a bold quarter-round convex curve. Top is surmounted
by a full-width shaped pediment, 24 to 30 inches tall, with
a flatly arched central section a little narrower than the
break front. This is flanked by downswept curves interrupted by short horizontals that are surmounted by
flaring flower-and-leaf carved finials. The edge of the
pediment has applied conforming concave molding, interrupted by and ending in downcurved volutes. Beneath
the arching front is ornamented with a large carved
festoon of foliated fruits or flowers done in high relief.

Below it and raised about 16 inches from the top of
the carcase, recessed full-width shelf with conforming
front edge is attached to the pediment and supported by
two slender baluster-turned posts. Below the shelf there

is a less boldly done central festoon of carved pendent bunches of grapes with leaves and tendrils.

The carcase is divided into three conforming sections, each having a shallow drawer with cupboard beneath. Drawers are of conforming shape and at the center of each is a large carved medallion, done in conventionalized

176

leafage scrolls, with an inset metal keyhole surround. The wide cupboard of the central section has flat double doors; those of the ends, single, quarter-curved ones. All are stile-and-rail constructed with rectangular sunk panels. Those of the central double doors have large medallions of foliated fruit carved in high relief and as corner decorations scrolled spandrels. The curved panels of the end doors are ornamented only with foliated fruit medallions. Doors are fitted with matching keyhole rosettes. Cupboards contain single fixed shelves with rounded or molded front edges.

Carcase rests on plain plinth base of conforming shape, about four inches high with projecting molded upper edge. May be fitted with concealed socket casters. Total height varies from five feet to five feet six inches. Custom-made of black walnut or, less frequently, mahogany or rosewood. *Ca. 1850–1865.* BBB to CC

177

177. Rounded-end Sideboard

Reflects design of a French *desserte* of the Louis XV and Louis XVI Periods. Like the preceding consists of a tall shaped pediment surmounting a three-section carcase.

Has rectangular top, six to seven feet long by about 20 inches deep, frequently of white marble. It has a straight front and quarter-circle rounded ends. The elaborately shaped pediment is from three feet, six inches to over four feet tall, and has semicircular arched top edged with a cove molding that sometimes terminates in short horizontal ends. The sides flare downward in a scrolled outline to the full width of the carcase. Scrolling starts with a cyma-curve followed by alternating concave and convex C-shaped curves, and is emphasized by boldly done moldings. These develop from large volutes which overlap onto the face of the pediment; they flank a large scrolled cartouche which surrounds a plain or foliated fruit-carved medallion. Below, two recessed, graduated shelves about 26 and 14 inches respectively above the marble top. They have conforming shape, scrolled and carved uprights. Beneath each shelf is a molding-framed oblong oval panel of either mirror glass or burl veneer.

The carcase has a wide straight section flanked by quarter-circle ends, and a tier of two shallow drawers with double-door cupboard beneath. Drawers and doors are separated by central panel-molded stile. Drawer fronts have oblong oval panels, bead-molded, and wooden rosette knobs and keyhole rosettes. Cupboard doors have molding-framed rectangular panels with shaped upper and rounded lower corners. At the center of each, a large swag carved in high relief of a foliated fruit above a pendent bunch of grapes. Knobs and keyhole rosettes matching those of drawers. Cupboard has one fixed shelf inside.

Drawers and doors of central section are separated from the end sections by stiles matching that at center.

Except for curved outline, drawers of end sections match others. Cupboards beneath may be either open or enclosed. Doors, when present, have single molding-framed panels with square corners and no ornament.

Base about four inches high and plain, except for molded upper edge. Either molded-edge block feet or is a plinth base fitted with concealed socket casters. Total height of piece varies from six feet six inches to nearly eight feet.

After President and Mrs. Hayes announced that they would not serve wines or like beverages during their stay in the White House, they were presented by teetotalers with a rounded-end sideboard. which was without space for decanters and wine bottles. It replaced one of earlier design and more liberal arrangement. With the end of the Hayes occupancy the gift stood for some years in a well-known Pennsylvania avenue restaurant serving both food and drink.

Custom-made, also produced by quality furniture factories. Black walnut with panels sometimes faced with burl veneer. *Ca. 1855–1870.* C to CC

178. Three-cupboard Sideboard

Has an arched pediment surmounting a carcase containing a tier of three shallow drawers with cupboards beneath. The rectangular top, either wood or marble, varies in length from six to seven feet; about 20 inches deep. It has rounded front corners and a molded or rounded edge. The pediment has a triple-arched, nearly full-width top, scrolled sides; is 22 to 30 inches tall. Its outline is accented by a bold cove molding which flanks a shell or leafage-carved finial. Immediately below is a large animal head trophy carved in high relief and mounted on an oval plaque, which is framed by branching foliated scrolls enhanced with fruits and pendent bunches of grapes. Under it, a full-width recessed shelf about eight inches deep with rounded corners and molded edge. It is raised about 16 inches from the carcase top and supported by scrolled uprights, hung with

178

foliated fruits carved in high relief. Below the shelf is a central high-relief festoon of foliated fruits.

Three drawers of the carcase are decorated with balancing carved scrolls done in high relief; leaf and fruit motifs. Lower edges of drawers form a continuous projecting molding with invisible finger grips. Center drawer nearly twice as wide as flanking ones. No keyhole rosettes. Cupboard doors are of the same width and have large rectangular sunk panels. The central one is flanked by narrow stiles with applied split baluster turnings, each panel ornamented with a large carved trophy swag, and small carved spandrels of foliated fruit. Wooden keyhole rosette. Cupboard interiors have single or double shelves, fixed or movable, with rounded front edges.

Base of carcase about four inches high with convex molded upper edge, conforming rounded corners. Either turned ball or square block feet about four inches high. Total height of piece varies from about six feet two inches to a little over seven feet, depending on pediment arching.

Custom-made of black walnut, sometimes with top of white, veined or mottled marble. Not numerous. *Ca. 1860–1870.* C to CCC

Single-cupboard Sideboard

Design and construction same as the foregoing but length reduced about a third for smaller dining room.

Rectangular top, generally marble, 42 to 54 inches long by 18 to 20 inches deep; rounded front corners and molded edge. Surmounting it a shaped pediment, 24 to 36 inches tall, with top a semicircular arch having a vase-shaped or shell-carved finial or a superimposed cartouche; or a serpentine curve interrupted by a superimposed cartouche; or a segmented curve without finial.

Top is edged by a projecting cove molding that may be overlapped by a central carved cartouche. Sometimes this molding has horizontal cornice extensions surmounted by urn-shaped finials, mounted on square molded plinths. More often, outline is downswept in cyma-curves, edged by a less pronounced but matching molding.

Beneath the arching, carved in high relief, may be the lower part of the cartouche, with pendent finial; branching foliated scrolls, with pendent fruit and leaves; a swag — horticultural or hunting motif. The recessed shelf is raised about 14 inches, with end or inset molded uprights. Below the shelf, a molding-framed oval or oblong panel, frequently of mirror glass.

The carcase has a straight front with corners boldly rounded and paneled, or slightly rounded and plain; they may be chamfered with carved and scrolled split finials top and bottom. A single tier of half-width shallow drawers is separated from a pair of cupboard doors below by a full-width projecting molding. Drawer fronts have molding-framed panels, or are edged by projecting concave molding and have carved leaf-and-fruit handles and keyhole rosettes.

Cupboard doors either square or rectangular with molding-framed or molding-decorated panels. Sometimes semicircular top with large central hunting trophy swag carved in high relief. Doors fitted with wooden keyhole rosettes.

Carcase ends have plain, rectangular and slightly sunk panels. Base is about four inches tall with molded upper edge. Lower edge either straight or valanced in balancing cyma-curves. Projecting rounded and molded block feet, about two inches high, castered; sometimes rests directly on floor. Total height of piece varies from five feet eight inches to seven feet three inches.

Factory made; black walnut; sometimes butternut.

Plentiful, but sometimes found with pediment missing
or arching sawed off to reduce height. *Ca. 1860–1875.*
BB to C

179

179. Eastlake Sideboard

Usually smaller than preceding. Has rectangular top,
often of mottled marble, 38 to 44 inches wide and about
18 inches deep, with square corners and plain or partially
beveled edge. It is surmounted by rectangular pediment,
24 to 36 inches tall with flat, cornice-molded top, sometimes combined with a simple pierced arcade. Sides of
pediment are straight, stepped with bracket-like projections. It contains two wide rectangular panels, burl-
veneered or mirror glass framed by beveling. Between
these a shallow shelf, with square or chamfered corners
and molded edge, supported by small quarter-circle or
scroll-cut brackets. A concave or bead-molded cross-

member finishes the joining of pediment and carcase top.

Carcase has a straight front, square corners and single panel ends, and pair of half-width drawers of medium depth above either a full-width cupboard with double doors or a half-width one flanked by two deep half-width drawers. Drawer fronts have burl-veneered panels flanked by vertical bands of reeding or framed by incised stringing. Brass pendent ring or ball handles, shaped and chased plates and matching keyhole escutcheons. Doors rectangular with large slightly sunk panels matching drawer fronts, and matching keyhole escutcheons. Extensions of the corner stiles serve as feet and are joined by a slightly projecting skirt with beveled upper edge and straight or simply valanced lower one. Small socket casters.

Factory-made. Black walnut; less often butternut or cherry; some late examples oak. Larger sideboards of like design custom-made. Small most frequently found today. *Ca. 1870–1880.* B to BB

180. Southern Sugar Chest

Originally used to keep sugar, coffee, tea, spices and other luxuries under lock and key in Southern plantation mansions. Has a rectangular, slightly overhanging lid. Beneath, a compartmented well about 14 to 16 inches deep. Front of well is plain. Inset keyhole surround at top. Below well, a full-width drawer about 10 inches deep, with mushroom-turned wooden knobs and inset metal keyhole surround. Carcase ends have large rectangular panels. Corner stiles terminate in short vase-turned legs with small peg feet. Height varies from 36 to 40 inches; depth is about 18 inches.

180

Made south of Mason-Dixon Line by plantation car-penter-cabinetmakers. Black walnut, butternut or other hardwoods stained brown. Not collected outside the South. *Ca. 1840–1860.* B to BBB

181. Southern Hunt Board

A specialized piece made and used chiefly in Virginia and Kentucky, beginning with the Hepplewhite Period. Victorian details are scrolled and voluted rear member of gallery, and tapering turned legs which may be baluster-shaped or reeded. From four feet six inches to six feet long, about 18 inches deep, and 36 to 42 inches tall. Has a slightly overhanging top with straight front, square corners and plain edge, surmounted by three-quarter gallery scroll-cut at rear with central, nearly circular finial, flanked by balancing cyma-curves terminating in volutes. Side members of gallery low and plain.

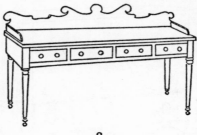

181

Skirt beneath is eight to 10 inches high and contains two to four drawers of equal width. Fronts are plain. Mushroom-turned wooden knobs. Four turned and tapering legs, either reeded or baluster-shaped. Small peg feet.

A simple plantation piece, made locally of black walnut. Unusual. *Ca. 1840–1860.* B to BBB

Whatnots, Étagères and Other Open Shelves

FOR SOME twenty-five years after 1850, no Victorian parlor was properly furnished unless it included a corner or side wall arrangement of shelves for the display of bric-a-brac, bibelots, delicate trifles and curiosities. Aptly christened "whatnot" because of the endless variety and number of articles which might be found on its graduated tiers of shelves, it had come into use in England nearly fifty years before it invaded the American home.

Its design is always that of a series of full-size graduated shelves supported by turned uprights or scroll-cut brackets. A kindred piece of display furniture, the étagère, has a large central mirror flanked by small graduated shelves and one or two full-size shelves beneath the mirror panel. This is a distinction without too much difference, since to the French any frame of open shelves is an *étagère*.

In its day, a whatnot was on the order of a miniature museum, installed out of harm's way in the seldom-used parlor. It was a useful conversation piece for adults and for small fry; and on decorous Sunday afternoons when the usual pleasures permitted were a walk to the cemetery or sitting down with an instructive book, examining its contents was an adventure.

There was the whatnot in my grandfather's parlor, for

example. The top shelf held a tall glass vase containing several peacock's feathers, a white Parian bust of a young woman with a band of rosebuds in her hair, and a lily-in-hand vase of Parian ware. On the shelf below were a purple overlay glass carafe, a polished pearl shell, a French cologne bottle tricked out with gilt and applied jewels, a Meissen saucer set in a tripod of gilt wire, an irregular block of polished petrified wood, a Staffordshire rustic figurine and a plush folding frame with photographs of Grandfather and Grandmother. The next shelf was well-filled with a similar assortment, such as a piece of pink spiny coral, a conch shell which recorded the roar of the sea when held to the ear, a Chinese ivory thimble case, a polished marble urn and more porcelains on display frames. The lowest shelf of all held the photograph albums of tooled leather with brass catches and a large half-folio volume of *Vues de Paris à Daguerreotypes* dated 1856.

Special Comments on Whatnots and Étagères

With a few elaborate exceptions, all whatnots are factory products. With both corner and flat-wall types, the graduated shelves are of the same design, with shaped and concave molded edges. They are supported by either baluster-turned uprights surmounted by small urn, acorn or steeple finials, or by cyma-curved brackets which are scroll-cut and pierced.

Small turned feet raise the lowest shelf three to four inches from the floor.

The shelves often have low gallery pieces at the rear, pierced in simple scroll-cut repeating geometric motifs. A corner whatnot sometimes has an enclosed cupboard base. A flat-wall whatnot may have various added details, such as a shallow drawer placed either beneath the bottom shelf or the table-high one, second from the bottom. Sometimes it has a cupboard base and occasionally a desk section is included. Whatnots with these variations are not numerous but should be considered as unusual rather than rare.

Black walnut is the favored wood but rosewood whatnots do exist. One with pierced and carved shelf supports of laminated wood is attributed to Belter.

An étagère is also factory-made. Surmounting the base is a shaped pediment back which frames the large mirror panel of pier-glass proportions. If the base is low, it often has a marble top with a shallow drawer beneath. Flanking the mirror are small graduated shelves, supported by triangular pierced brackets or turned or shaped uprights. Feet are either turned or shaped. Decorative carving surmounting the pediment back, the incidental panels and moldings are all applied work.

182. Spool-turned Corner Whatnot

From four to six triangular shelves, which increase in size from top to bottom by approximately two-inch steps and are equidistant from each other. Four feet six inches to six feet high, by 14 to 20 inches deep. Shelves have matching quarter-circle, cyma-curved or serpentined fronts, with either concave-molded or rounded edges.

Top shelf is galleried with two scroll-outlined and pierced strips about two inches high flanked by steeple or ball-turned finials. Lower shelves may be plain or have matching gallery pieces. Shelves, except for the bottom one, are supported by three slender spindles, either baluster or spool-turned, recessed to conform to shelf size and with front finials matching those of the top. Bottom shelf raised from floor about three inches; three spool or ball-and-ring turned feet.

Black walnut, by furniture factories in large quantities. Mahogany or rosewood used for finer examples; inexpensive ones made with spindles, finials and legs of assorted hardwoods, shelves of pine or other softwoods, stained to simulate black walnut. Plentiful. *Ca. 1855–1870.* AAA to BB

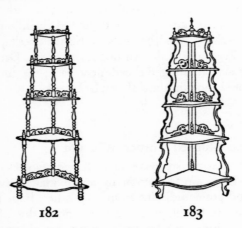

182   183

183. Scroll-bracket Corner Whatnot

Like the preceding but in place of spindles shelves are supported at front by cyma-curved uprights, pierced or solid, and ending in short, steeple-turned finials and at rear by a plain, straight-edged upright that is continuous from floor to top shelf, where it terminates in a tall steeple-turned finial. Split steeple-turned finials are attached to face between the shelves.

Top shelf has scrolled and pierced gallery, lower shelves frequently matching galleries or may be plain. Short, scroll-outlined legs.

Black walnut. Cheapest examples of assorted hardwoods with softwood shelves stained to simulate black walnut. Plentiful. *Ca. 1860–1875.* AAA to BB

184

184. Cupboard-base Corner Whatnot

Lower shelves enclosed as cupboard, 28 to 30 inches tall by 18 to 20 inches deep. Quarter-circle rounded front; either double, nearly full-width doors or single door, flanked by paneled stiles about four inches wide. Doors curved with rectangular, slightly sunk panels, framed with bead molding or wavy. Wooden keyhole rosettes. Interior single fixed shelf with rounded edge.

Cupboard top slightly overhanging, rounded or bead-molded edge; surmounted by three conforming graduated shelves with matching edges, supported by (1) slender turned spindles; (2) scroll-cut, cyma-curved, pierced uprights; (3) two tracery-like flaring backpieces, set at a right angle and pierced in ornate pattern of cyma-curved scrolls. Top shelf galleried, between steeple-turned finials; lower shelves have either gallery strips or pierced back.

Total height five to six feet. Either plinth base or short turned peg or shaped bracket feet, castered.

Black walnut or, less frequently, rosewood or mahogany, by cabinet shops and some furniture factories. Not as numerous as preceding whatnots. *Ca. 1855–1870.* B to BB

185. Spindle or Bracket Flat-wall Whatnot

Similar to corner whatnot in construction and decorative detail but larger, designed to stand against wall. Four feet six inches to six feet tall, by 32 to 42 inches wide, 14 to 18 inches deep. Four to six graduated rectangular shelves, with fronts and ends bowed, or serpentined, with molded edge, or straight with rounded edge. The top shelf usually has rear gallery which may be repeated with lower shelves. These galleries, two to four inches high, are either scrolled and pierced in a balancing or repeating cyma-curve pattern or are solid and arched. With some examples, the top gallery is taller, elaborately pierced in a lyre or similar motif and surmounted by an arched cresting.

Shelves are supported by either four slender spindles or scrolled and pierced shelf stumps. Spindles may be

baluster, spool or, less frequently, spiral-turned. They
are recessed; front ones have short steeple-turned finials.
Shelf stumps have receding cyma-curved silhouette with
conforming piercing, and molded outer sides. Front ones
are placed diagonally and rear ones flat, flanking gal-

185

leries. With both types of supports, steeple-turned finials
surmount the four corners of the top shelf.

A single, full-width shallow drawer may be present,
either in the base or table-high below the second from
the bottom shelf. Drawer front either straight or curved
to shape of the shelf; finger grips on lower edge, or
turned wooden knobs and wooden keyhole rosette, or
inset surround.

If there is no base, whatnot has short turned legs corresponding to the spindles above, or scroll-outlined feet

matching shelf stumps. A whatnot with enclosed base is supported by (1) ball-turned feet, (2) scrolled-bracket feet or (3) extensions of the corner stiles.

Black walnut; finer examples sometimes mahogany or rosewood. Cheap examples made of maple or other hardwood with softwood shelves, stained to simulate black walnut. Sometimes sold in pairs. May be found with one or more galleries missing or replaced by plain strips. Plentiful. *Ca. 1855–1875.* AAA to B

186

186. Pierced-side Flat-wall Whatnot

Is similar to preceding but has five graduated shelves with straight fronts and rounded edge supported by scroll outline and pierced sidepieces that conform to the graduated width of shelves. Their design combines cyma, C-shaped and conventionalized leafage scrolls. Galleries at rear of shelves scrolled and pierced to match.

Gallery of top shelf usually taller with arched top, and more ornate. Enclosed base six to eight inches high, with plain paneled ends, and two half-width drawers or one full-width. Drawer fronts are plain and fitted with brass pendent rings with square plates set diagonally or with turned wooden knobs and inset keyhole surrounds. Low scrolled and molded bracket feet.

Black walnut or rosewood. *Ca. 1855–1865.* B to BBB

Whatnot Desk

A combination of a flat-wall whatnot and a chestlike drop-front desk, designed for a parlor or boudoir. Has an open shelf at top, 26 to 30 inches wide by about 12 inches deep, with front straight or serpentined and square or rounded corners surmounted by spool-turned finials. Edge of shelf is faced with wavy or spool-turned molding. Uprights supporting shelf are spiral- or spool-turned and rest on the conforming top of desk section, which has low gallery at rear pierced in delicate S and C scrolls.

Ends and drop front of desk cabinet have slightly sunk panels. Keyhole of drop front has applied scroll-carved cartouche or rosette, and flanking stiles are decorated with applied split-spool turnings. Writing surface has baize panel, wood-banded. Interior is pigeon-holed; drawers; open inkwell space.

Beneath desk cabinet an open shelf of conforming shape with low pierced gallery at rear and sides. Turned uprights, matching those above, support shelf and desk and rest on a base about two inches high, with top serving as bottom shelf of whatnot. It has a straight or serpentined skirt, conforming lower edges, and spool-turned feet. Height 54 to 58 inches.

Black walnut or, infrequently, rosewood. Because of perishable nature of turned uprights, comparatively few examples have survived. *Ca. 1860–1870.* B to BB

187. Whatnot Desk with Cupboard Base

Is 30 to 36 inches wide, by 50 to 54 inches tall, and 16 to 18 inches deep. Upper section: two open shelves of graduated depth, mounted on a recessed cabinet containing tier of shallow drawers. Shelves have straight fronts and square corners, top one surmounted at back by low gallery with balancing scroll-cut upper edge and ball-and-steeple turned finials at four corners. They are supported at front by flat uprights, scroll-cut in cyma-curves, and at the back by plain ones. The recessed cabinet has rectangular slightly overhanging top, with rounded edge and front corners. Tier of three shallow drawers of equal width. Inset metal keyhole surrounds.

Lower section: On top, in front of the drawers, is a fold-over writing flap, baize-paneled, with wooden banding. Carcase has large rectangular, slightly sunk panels, a full-width drawer of medium depth with incised finger grips on lower edge, and inset metal keyhole surround. It overhangs cupboard about one inch. Cupboard has single shelf and is enclosed by a pair of solid, full-width doors with rectangular, slightly sunk panels that have small scrolled spandrels. Right-hand door has wavy molded or half-round astragal, inset metal keyhole surround. Low plain base with rounded front corners, projecting about half an inch, is supported by block feet with conforming corners.

Black walnut, mahogany with crotch-grain veneer, or rosewood. Not numerous. *Ca. 1860–1870.* B to BBB

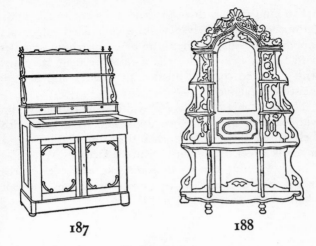

187   188

188. Short Mirror Étagère

Of French origin, this tall architectural elaboration of the whatnot has a mirror flanked by tiers of small shelves combined with an open table-like base. Dimensions are six to seven feet tall, by 46 to 50 inches wide, and about 16 inches deep. Pediment back has arched and scrolled top carved and pierced, generally with pendent bunches of grapes and leaves in high relief, and is surmounted by shell-carved or cartouche-shaped finial.

Sides consist either of uprights shaped in repeating cyma-curves with conforming piercings, or of three pairs of baluster-turned spindles with vase-shaped finials. These flank but are separate from two interior uprights, either scroll-cut or baluster-turned. Between them is the mirror, about 30 inches tall by 18 inches wide, with wide molding-edged frame, generally ogee-arched at top.

Flanking mirror, three graduated tiers of small, demi-cartouche-shaped shelves with cove-molded edges are supported by shaped shelf-stumps or matching spindles with finials. Below mirror is a raised-rectangular panel with incurved corners, fitted with rosettes and a large incised central oval.

The pier-table base has full-width demi-cartouche top with concave molded edge, duplicated by a full-width shelf raised about three inches from the floor. Turned or scrolled feet. By quality furniture factories.

Black walnut; rosewood; some late examples of ebonized hardwoods. Not as numerous as the flat-wall whatnot. *Ca. 1860–1870.* B to BB

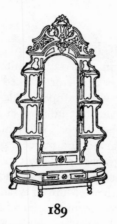

189

189. Long Mirror Étagère

Taller than the preceding, has a mirror of pier-glass proportions surmounting low enclosed base. Dimensions are seven to eight feet tall, 48 to 54 inches wide, 16 to 18 inches deep. Back has an arched, molding-edged top, triangular or curved, surmounted by a cartouche finial with carved detail. Flanking base are either raised rectangular panels or corresponding foliated fretwork. Below this is a secondary cornice with bold, semicircular arching and short horizontal extensions, with or without spool-turned finials.

Sides flare downward in four graduated units, partially or entirely cyma-curved. The pier-glass mirror has an arched top and is sometimes framed by a projecting molding. It is four to nearly six feet tall by 24 to 28 inches wide. Set into the flanking sides, three tiers of graduated mirror panels, rectangular with curved ends and placed vertically. Below, small, demi-cartouche shelves with molded edges, supported by scrolled and pierced triangular brackets or baluster-turned spindles. Beneath the bottom tier of shelves the conforming panels are solid and raised.

Base has a white marble top with concave molded edge; is either demi-cartouche and full-width, or slightly over half-width with serpentine front; is flanked by drop shelves. Enclosed base contains half-width shallow drawer. Front has either small raised panels flanking a leaf-carved handle or balancing foliated scrolls, carved in relief, with a finger grip on under edge. Lower edge of base is usually formed by projecting concave molding. Square or turned feet.

By quality furniture factories. Black walnut, with or without burl-veneer trim. Some fine examples, custom-made, rosewood. *Ca. 1860–1870.* B to BB

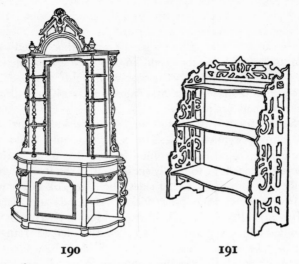

190   191

190. Étagère with Cupboard Base

A rococo version of preceding. Seven feet six inches to eight feet six inches tall, 48 to 54 inches wide, 18 to 20 inches deep. Top of back projects and overhangs the shelves that flank the central mirror. Has arched pediment, triangular or curved, with projecting molded edge; is surmounted by cartouche finial with carved detail. Beneath this, a hemispherical recessed dome flanked by turned, urn-shaped finials.

Back has straight sides edged with flat-carved scrolls. In the center, rectangular mirror with arched top, molding-framed, flanked by three tiers of uniform, small shaped shelves supported by baluster-turned spindles. At rear of shelves, slightly sunk panels.

Base about 26 inches tall, with slightly overhanging marble top which has straight front flanked by quarter-circle rounded ends. Beneath is a low frieze, molding-edged top and bottom, containing a shallow half-width drawer. Drawer has molding-edged front, leaf-carved handles and keyhole rosette. Below this drawer is a cupboard with single door, which has a molding-framed panel arched at top to match the mirror above. Enclosed cupboard is flanked by open ones with curved fronts, each fitted with a single quadrant-shaped shelf with rounded edge. Conforming plinth base with four out-rounded pilasters.

Black walnut, panels and dome burl-veneered, by cabinetmaker, probably on order. Could be of English origin. *Ca. 1860–1870.* BBB to C

191. Openwork Hanging Shelves

Light framework, about 36 inches tall by 22 to 26 inches wide and eight inches deep, containing three graduated shelves with either serpentined or straight fronts and rounded edges. At rear of top shelf, usually an arched, pierced gallery done in design of joined horizontal and curved elements. Supporting sides, pierced in matching patterns, have scrolled front edges increasing in depth to conform to the shelves, and extending about four inches below the bottom shelf in semicircular archings. Thus the piece may either be hung on wall or rest on top of a stand or chest of drawers.

By local cabinetmakers, factories or novelty shops. Black walnut; sometimes mahogany or rosewood. Late examples may be of maple or birch ebonized. Frequently

found with small parts missing or loose. Plentiful. *Ca.*
1852–1880. AA to AAA

192

192. Standing Shelves

Like the preceding but not as light and delicate. Gallery at rear of top shelf is generally plain with straight upper edge. Sides are scroll-cut and flare downward to conform to the width of the three shelves, which are graduated in depth from about six to 10 inches. Bottom shelf is usually raised eight to 12 inches from floor, and has a skirt of medium depth valanced in balancing cyma-curves.

In place of feet, the lower ends of the sidepieces are cut in curves that form semicircular arched openings.

By local cabinetmakers, factories and novelty shops. Black walnut, occasionally mahogany. Plainer examples maple, birch or softwood, stained to simulate black walnut or painted dark color. Generally found in good condition. Similar hanging shelves for plates also made later (now in demand for usefulness). Plentiful. *Ca. 1850–1880.* AA to AAA

193

193. Miniature Hanging Étagère

Shaped back, arched at top and balanced at bottom, with intricate allover pierced design done in flowers, leaves and birds, or as an arabesque surrounding a rectangular mirror. This is flanked by recessed pierced side-pieces, which project about six inches with concave front edges. They may be joined above the mirror by a shaped pediment, forming a hood over it. They also support three small, quarter-round open shelves, the top pair slightly below the mirror top, the middle ones at mirror center, the lower pair placed on either side of a central straight-front shelf, of the same depth, immediately below the mirror base.

Black walnut; less frequently mahogany; sometimes maple or birch, ebonized. Probably factory-made as decorative novelty. Unusual, but not rare. *Ca. 1865–1880.* AA to AAA

194

194. Hanging Shelf Bracket

Shield-shaped top about eight inches wide, with bowed front and incurved sides having continuous flat edge. Top attached at right angle to a triangular back about 18 inches high, which tapers in balancing concave curves to a small cone or acorn finial.

Shelf supports are a pair of triangular, scroll-cut brackets, either pierced or solid, which flank a miniature stag's head, carved in full relief and mounted, trophy-like, on a small shield-shaped panel. The back is usually further decorated with conforming incised lines of gilding. The stag-head motif corresponds to that of some sideboard pediments (*see No. 178*).

Black walnut. May have been copied from similar brackets of Swiss or Black Forest origin. Originally sold in pairs. Antlers of deer are apt to be broken or missing in those found today. Unusual rather than rare. *Ca. 1860–1870.* A to AA

Rustic Bracket

Of like design and construction, back edged with molding carved to simulate short lengths of branches; supporting brackets carved in like manner. In place of stag's head, a swag of pine cones, twigs and fern leaves carved in high relief. Black walnut by local carvers, factories or novelty shops. Not numerous. *Ca. 1860–1870.* A to AA

Bookcases, Wardrobes, Hatracks, Cupboards and Kitchen Pieces

ALMOST from the start of the Victorian Period, there were few homes without a bookcase of some sort. From a simple arrangement of open shelves, bookcase design rapidly shifted to more elaborate ones with large glazed doors, made in Gothic, Louis XV, Renaissance and Eastlake substyles. Produced in increasing numbers throughout the period, they were in direct ratio to the growing number of books published annually in the United States.

With houses large enough to include a separate room as library, the break-front bookcase was popular. It and similar ones of large size were consistently made in sections. Some have a low base with a tier of drawers; with others, the base is taller and contains a capacious cupboard with solid doors. Some of the simple open and Gothic bookcases are handwork; the rest are usually factory-made.

The wardrobe was a development of the much earlier European *armoire* which started out as an enclosed cupboard for arms and armor and by the eighteenth century became the standard clothespress for the French home. Consequently it was first made in the United States as a companion piece to a matching bedroom set of the Louis XV substyle. Since built-in clothes closets were few and small at the time, the wardrobe was a necessary piece of furniture for storing the voluminous hoop-skirted dresses then in fashion.

These useful and practical wardrobes continued as standard furniture well into the 1880's, and because of size served the same purpose as the modern built-in closet.

The wardrobe is always six feet or more tall; and depending on its width, has either a single or double door. Full-size mirror panels appear on the doors of some fine examples; the base often contains a large medium-depth drawer. A few are the work of cabinetmakers, but the majority are factory products. Because of their large size, many are put together with screws and may be taken apart for ease in moving. Some of the best examples are of New Orleans provenance and are still found in the handsome houses of the Mississippi Valley. The East-lake wardrobes are usually of poorer workmanship, obviously mass-produced.

The hatrack is of Victorian origin. Called variously a "hatstand," "hat tree" or "hall stand," what circumstances brought it into being is lost information though the most obvious and plausible suggestion is that city-block houses, with their narrow entrance halls, required a special piece of furniture to accommodate the outer wraps of visitors. From such specialized urban use in the early years of the period, its popularity as a nicety in household furnishings spread to the larger villages. By the 1860's it was considered necessary equipment for the hall of any well-furnished home, except a farmhouse, where wooden cross-strips fitted with turned pegs or metal hooks and nailed to the wall beside the front door, were adequate.

Most hatracks were tall pieces of furniture with retaining arms for canes and umbrellas. They ranged from simple to ornate. There was also a hanging type, designed for the cottage home — of fanciful shape with small central mirror and six or eight garment pegs.

The hatrack continued to be made for some years after the close of the Victorian Period, then went out of favor about thirty years ago. Now, because of its practical use, it has been rescued from oblivion and returned to its original place in the entrance hall.

The dish cupboard is really a survival of the American Empire and earlier periods. It is the work of cabinet-makers, and is of two kinds: the triangular corner cupboard, and the rectangular one known as a "dresser." After 1850 changing styles in dining room furnishings sent both into eclipse, except for a few corner cupboards produced in the Eastlake substyle. These have a recessed upper section, either open or enclosed with glazed doors.

Kitchen cupboards, mostly of Pennsylvania Dutch origin, are fairly plentiful. They are the product of small local furniture factories, which also made such related pieces as the water bench and dry sink, now promoted and used as living or dining room furniture.

195. Open-front Bookcase

This is 28 to 40 inches wide by 10 to 12 inches deep, and 54 to 58 inches tall. Has either a plain flat top with molded front edge, or a three-quarter gallery about eight inches tall, formed by the continuation of sides and back, arched with carved scrolls, or flat with convex molding. The slightly lower sides are usually down-curved.

Carcase sides are plain, with molded front edges. Interior contains three or four shelves with molded front edges, either fixed and graduated eight to 14 inches apart or adjustable. Has an enclosed slightly projecting

195

base with plain or simply valanced skirt and low bracket feet.

Mahogany with crotch-grain veneer; rosewood; black walnut; other native hardwoods stained brown or with natural finish; assorted softwoods stained to simulate black walnut or painted dark colors. Occasionally a rosewood or black walnut bookcase with gallery top has a facing of bird's-eye maple behind the shelves. Some plain without gallery vary in width and height because made by local cabinetmakers or carpenters to fit specific locations. *Ca. 1840–1880.* AA to AAA

196

196. Enclosed-front Bookcase

General construction and size like preceding. Flat, slightly overhanging top with plain or convex molded edges may be surmounted by a shaped three-quarter gallery arched at back, with down-curved sides. Is fitted with either one or two glazed doors, depending on width of piece. Inset metal keyhole surrounds or applied keyhole rosettes. Single pane or two separated by a centered horizontal muntin, sometimes arched at top in semicircular or cusp shape. Corners above the arch may have plain or pierced spandrels. Stiles and rails of frame may also be ornamented by narrow, panel-like burl strips, with applied wooden rosettes at corners, if bookcase is black walnut.

Enclosed base projects about two inches, is from eight to 12 inches high. Skirt has straight or slightly valanced lower edge. Sometimes base contains drawers, one full-width for single-door type; two half-width if double doors. Drawers are medium-depth, plain, with mushroom-turned wooden knobs, for mahogany piece; leaf-carved wooden or brass pendent-ring handles for black walnut.

Custom-made of mahogany, with crotch-grain veneer; rosewood; factory-made of black walnut, cherry or other native hardwoods, stained or ebonized; assorted softwoods stained to simulate black walnut. *Ca. 1840–1880.* BB to BBB

197

197. Ornamental Bookcase

Is 44 to 56 inches wide by about 14 inches deep; seven feet eight inches to nine feet tall. Slightly serpentine, arched top; ornate carved and pierced silhouette pediment in Gothic motifs or conventionalized leafage scrolls flanking a taller C-scrolled central finial. Corner finials carved in a conventionalized acanthus leaf motif. The arched top also has applied conforming scrolls. The double doors beneath are flanked by narrow stiles carved in an incised chain or Gothic detail; full-size rectangular glass panes behind a carved and applied wooden tracery of either Gothic arch or double oval design, with cusp and trefoil, or leafage scroll-and-ribbon details combined with wavy or split-ball moldings. Below these tracery-filled panels there may be low horizontal wooden ones, with carved medallions of conforming leafage scrolls, framed by wavy or split-ball molding. Inner stiles of both doors are fitted with inset metal keyhole surrounds or keyhole rosettes.

Interior contains five or six fixed or adjustable shelves with molded or slightly rounded front edges. Sides of carcase usually plain, but may be paneled with two or three tiers of rectangular, slightly sunk panels.

Base contains two drawers, eight to 10 inches deep, same width as doors. Fronts have panels with wavy or split-ball molding, and centered medallions with carved leafage scrolls like those above.

Slightly projecting block feet, with fronts carved to conform to corner stiles, are connected by a low skirt with molding and valanced lower edge in Gothic or scroll detail.

Custom-made; most frequently mahogany but sometimes rosewood. Not numerous. *Ca. 1840–1850.* BBB to CC

198. Gothic Bookcase with Cupboard Base

Two parts. Upper recessed book section: 42 to 50 inches wide by about 10 inches deep, surmounted by (1) arched pediment with central medallion of applied carving in conventionalized leafage scrolls, flanked by turned tapering finials mounted on shaped and scroll-carved plinths or (2) flat, slightly flaring carved and pierced cornice, done in repeating trefoil or cusp motifs. The low frieze beneath is plain or carved with a repeat-

198

ing incised quatre-foil motif. Sides plain or have rectangular, slightly sunk panels. Enclosed by a pair of double, full-width glazed doors, sometimes flanked by mock stiles two or three inches wide, with two or three tiers of incised Gothic panels. Glass of doors may be in form of (1) large rectangular panes, cusp-arched at top, (2) three or four tiers of three rectangular panes set in bead-molded muntins with top tier Gothic-arched or (3) large rectangular panes back of a scroll-cut and carved wooden tracery of two tiers each of three Gothic arches separated by a tier of interlacing vertical ellipses. Inner stiles of doors have inset metal keyhole surrounds; the right-hand one a wavy or bead-molded astragal. Interior contains four or five fixed or adjustable shelves with molded or slightly rounded edges.

Lower section: Projects eight to 10 inches; in front of bookcase a wooden or marble top with square corners and plain or slightly rounded edge. Carcase has plain or paneled ends, conforming to those above, and the matching front stiles flank a wide drawer of medium depth fitted with mushroom-turned knobs and inset metal keyhole surround. Front may be ogee-molded with finger grips on lower edge.

Beneath drawer is a full-width cupboard with single shelf enclosed by a pair of solid doors fitted with keyhole surrounds matching those above. Doors have slightly sunk square panels which are either plain with cusp-arched tops, or decorated centered oval panels framed by spandrel-like applied carvings of intertwining S and C scrolls with conventionalized leafage.

Low block feet, bevel-molded and decorated with incised conventional rosettes. Valanced skirt with molded lower edge, and centered medallion of applied carving of balanced scrolls. Total height seven feet, six inches to eight feet eight inches. Custom-made of mahogany, rosewood or black walnut. Not numerous. *Ca. 1840–1850.* C to CCC

Louis XV Break-front Bookcase

Central section varies in width from about six to over eight feet; may be the same height as those flanking it, or six to 12 inches taller. Piece has two parts or, with a larger example, the upper and lower parts may be further sectionalized for convenience in moving. Sometimes central and side sections form separate units.

Flat cornice-molded top, with projecting central section, frequently surmounted by carved, scrolled and pierced cartouche; or stepped broken pediment ornamented with scroll carving, and balanced at corners by urn-shaped finials. Frieze beneath plain, or paneled with bead molding. Glazed bookcase doors with rectangular single panes, frequently Roman-arched tops framed by concave bead or wavy molding. Doors have wooden keyhole rosettes and are sometimes flanked by narrow mock stiles panel-molded to resemble pilasters. Interiors have three to five tiers of shelves with molded or rounded front edges, generally adjustable. Sides of carcase usually plain; may have rectangular slightly sunk panels.

Lower part conforms to the upper part in general design. Usually contains tier of three drawers of medium depth and conforming width. Fronts usually molding-paneled, with wooden rosette knobs and keyhole rosettes or surrounds matching those above, or surrounds only. (With some examples, drawers are omitted; always cupboard space, enclosed by wooden paneled doors molding-paneled to conform to the glazed ones above). May also be ornamented with centered applied carving. Each interior has single shelf with molded or rounded front edge. Molded plinth base, sometimes castered; or low block feet with slightly valanced skirt. Total height from seven feet six inches to over nine feet.

Nearly always custom-made for a special location. Mahogany, rosewood, black walnut, cherry or, infrequently, oak. Not numerous. *Ca. 1850–1870.* CC to #

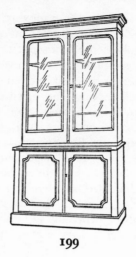

199

199. Simple Renaissance Bookcase

Two sections: recessed bookcase top, projecting cupboard base.

Upper part about 10 inches deep by 42 to 46 inches wide; flat, slightly projecting cove-molded or beveled cornice. Below, low plain frieze with lower edge defined by raised triple beaded molding. Pair of glazed doors beneath with large rectangular panes framed by molding matching that of frieze. Inner stile of right-hand door has astragal of matching molding, and applied wooden keyhole rosette. Interior has four shelves, fixed or adjustable.

Lower section: same width as upper, less than half as tall, nearly twice as deep. Slightly overhanging top, with concave molded edge and rounded front corners.

Carcase has either plain or paneled ends; contains full-width cupboard, fitted with single shelf, enclosed by a pair of solid doors with nearly square panels formed by applied molding. Right-hand door has astragal and keyhole rosette, matching bookcase door.

Low plinth base, concealed socket casters; or plain bracket feet, castered. Total height from six to seven feet.

Black walnut, sometimes maple or birch ebonized. Factory-produced. Quite plentiful. *Ca. 1865–1875.* B to BBB

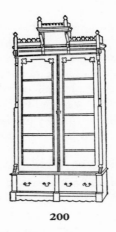

200

200. Eastlake Bookcase

Two or three doors with rectangular panes of glass, sometimes with modified arched tops. Four feet six inches to a little over seven feet tall, by 36 to 54 inches wide and about 12 inches deep. The shorter type has a flat slightly overhanging top surmounted by a rear gallery, four to six inches high and either molded or arcaded.

The taller type has a cove-molded cornice overlapping at center by rectangular pediment with plaquette of burl veneer flanked by scrolled brackets. For both, corners are short molded stiles surmounted by ball-turned finials.

Front corner stiles of carcase are plain, reeded or may have inset partial or full-length pilasters. Doorframes are plain, the edges surrounding the glazing molded or beveled. They have inset metal keyhole surrounds or wooden keyhole rosettes. Five to seven adjustable shelves inside, with plain or molded front edges. Beneath, an enclosed base about 12 inches high projects about two inches and contains two or three drawers six to eight inches deep. Drawer fronts are burl-veneered, with incised stringing, brass bail handles and keyhole surrounds or rosettes. Base has simple scalloped skirt, socket casters.

Factory-made; black walnut. Fairly plentiful, but in demand by collectors for display of glass, china and such. *Ca. 1870–1880.* B to BBB

201. Early Double-door Wardrobe

An enclosed cupboard seven to nine feet tall by four to five feet wide and 18 to 22 inches deep. Flat top with rounded front corners and either a projecting cornice consisting of a bold convex-concave element or a wide overhanging beveled cornice with square corners. Beneath, a plain frieze, about six inches high, defined top and bottom by a narrow band of either bead or wavy molding.

Front enclosed by a pair of full-width doors with large rectangular panels of wood or, occasionally, of mirror glass. These may have (1) square or quarter-circle segmented corners and be framed by a wavy or triple bead molding or (2) Gothic-arched tops and be framed by a narrow bevel. Doors overlap the ends, are hung with three pairs of butt hinges and fitted with either wooden keyhole rosettes or inset brass keyhole surrounds.

Interior usually has full-width, full-depth shelf at top and is fitted with wooden pegs or metal clothing hooks.

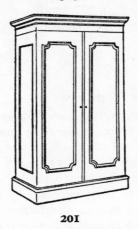

201

Ends of wardrobe are either plain or have rectangular, slightly sunk panels. Has a plinth base about six inches tall, molded at top.

Mahogany with crotch-grain veneering; rosewood; satinwood trimmed with rosewood (rare); black walnut, for late examples. A separate piece of furniture or part of bedroom set, by cabinetmakers and early factories. Sometimes found with doors removed, shelves added and converted into an extra-deep dish cupboard or bookcase. *Ca. 1840–1865.* B to BB

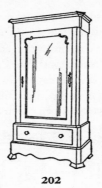

202

202. Single-door Wardrobe

Like the preceding in general design but narrower with one door. Dimensions seven to under nine feet tall, by three feet eight inches to four feet six inches wide, and 18 to 22 inches deep. Flat top with square, rounded or chamfered corners, surmounted by a projecting cornice with plain or wavy-molded edge. Frieze beneath projects about an inch, has conforming corners and is either plain or ornamented with a central shaped medallion of conventionalized leafage carved in medium relief.

The single door below has a large rectangular panel of either wood or mirror glass with scrolled upper corners, and is flanked by flat stiles about six inches wide with outer edges beveled to correspond to the chamfered corners of top. Door stiles plain or ornamented at center with medallions corresponding to that of frieze; left-hand one has wooden keyhole rosette. Sides of wardrobe plain or paneled.

Base about 10 inches tall, matches cornice in trim and shaping, contains single full-width deep drawer fitted with a pair of mushroom-turned wooden knobs and either a wooden keyhole rosette or an inset brass keyhole surround. Plain block feet, or rests on low projecting frame with upper edge finished in a band of plain or wavy molding and lower edge valanced in balancing cyma-curves ending in beveled block feet.

Mahogany, liberal use of crotch-grain veneer; rosewood; later examples black walnut; by cabinetmakers or early furniture factories. Known to have been made by a number of New Orleans cabinetmakers like Seignouret. Many were shipped up the Mississippi River to Natchez, St. Louis and as far north as Wisconsin. *Ca. 1840–1860.* BB to C

Eastlake Wardrobe

Either double or single doors. Seven feet six inches to eight feet ten inches tall, by three feet 10 inches to five feet wide, by about 18 inches deep. Its projecting concave, convex or bevel-molded cornice is generally surmounted by a low shaped pediment in silhouette, with frieze beneath about four inches high. Front may have a pair of nearly full-width doors separated by a narrow central stile or a single door flanked by plain stiles or by elaborately carved and molded column pilasters. Doors usually have burl-veneered panels framed by incised molding, sometimes further veneer ornamentation at center. With elaborate examples the panels are tall and mirror glass. Doors have wooden keyhole rosettes or brass keyhole escutcheons. Base may have molded block feet or rest directly on floor.

Factory-made. Black walnut; maple stained brown or natural; ash, plain or trimmed with black walnut; oak, cherry or mahogany. Simple examples are of pine or other softwoods, painted and grained. *Ca. 1870–1880.* AA to AAA

203

203. Cottage Hatrack

Five to six feet tall. A single tapering upright, about four inches wide, attached to a rectangular base. Two or three plain cross-arms fitted with turned spindle or spool pegs, about four to six inches long.

Another design places these cross-arms diagonally, like the spokes of a wheel, and adds a horizontal cross-arm for canes or umbrellas. The rectangular base is three or four inches tall, usually fitted with a sheet-metal dripping pan. Four knob feet.

Black walnut or, less frequently, mahogany; by cabinetmakers or early furniture factories. Two mahogany hatracks of this type were in the home of Duncan Phyfe at the time of his death in 1854, valued at a dollar each. *Ca. 1840–1860.* AA to AAA

204

204. Pierced and Scrolled Hatrack

Six to over seven feet tall, 30 to 36 inches wide and about 10 inches deep. Tall, scroll-outlined and pierced back, in front an attached tablelike top placed about 30 inches from floor.

Back is boldly scrolled and pierced in balancing S-shaped, C-shaped and cyma-curves and has either a serpentine cresting or a cartouche-shaped finial. A small central mirror with scrolled and molded frame is either fixed or tilting. Surrounding it is a balanced arrangement of eight to 10 baluster-turned garment pegs with rosette or button ends.

The table top is flanked by wooden or metal umbrella-arms in form of loops or open scrolls. Top may have conforming skirt deep enough to contain a shallow drawer.

Shape of base matches that of tabletop; metal dripping pans beneath umbrella-arms. Turned feet about two inches tall.

Made by some cabinetmakers of mahogany or rose-wood; more frequently by factories of black walnut. *Ca. 1850–1880*. AA to AAA

Hatrack Étagère

Is a variant of Long Mirror Étagère (*see No. 189*) with tiers of small shelves replaced by large wooden garment pegs. The marble top of base is about 14 inches from the floor with straight or serpentined front. Below, a shallow drawer over an open area. On either side scrolled or looped arms for holding canes and umbrellas with shell-shape cast-iron dripping pans inset into base. Made of black walnut by local furniture factories. One of this type is supposed to have belonged to the Reverend Henry Ward Beecher in Brooklyn. Unusual. *Ca. 1860–1875*. B to BB

205. Wall Hatrack

A late design of the Cottage type. Screwed to the wall like a large mirror; found in a number of shapes including rectangular, shield, lozenge, anchor or star.

Frame plain with beveled edge and small central mirror surrounded by six to eight baluster-turned garment pegs or ornamental metal hooks. The rectangular type has a wide frame with beveled or molded edge and a larger mirror flanked by decoratively scrolled metal hooks. Its dimensions are about 24 inches tall by 36 inches wide. Other forms are 36 inches tall by 24 inches wide.

Factory-made of black walnut or pine stained brown; rectangular type, black walnut, cherry or oak. *Ca. 1870–1880*. A to AA

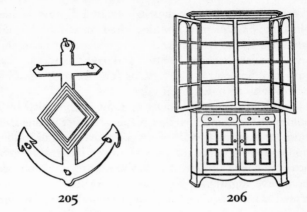

205   206

206. Transitional Corner Cupboard

Construction and lines much the same as those of the American Empire cupboard. Identifying Victorian characteristics are (1) front is full-width, not flanked by returns; (2) use of wavy molding for framing inset door panels, or as astragals or for cornice edging; (3) Gothic arches and such related details as trefoils, quatrefoils and spandrels.

Two parts, both of same depth. Seven to a little over eight feet tall, by 26 to 32 inches deep, by 37 to 45 inches wide at front. Upper section has either cove-molded or plain concave cornice with rounded corners and wavy molding edging. The cove-molded cornice may be surmounted by a standing frieze, about four to six inches high, pierced in leaf or Gothic motif or arcaded in a series of small pointed Gothic arches, with or without short trefoil finials at ends. Cupboard is enclosed by rectangular glazed doors, either full-width or flanked by narrow stiles, sometimes decorated with small incised Gothic arches. Glazing is frequently Gothic-arched at top and small panes are set in vertical and horizontal muntins. Doors have wooden keyhole rosettes and right-hand one has wavy molding astragal. Three or four fixed or movable shelves with rounded front edges.

Joining of upper and lower sections is concealed by a molding band. Lower section may have a tier of one full-width or two half-width drawers above a double-door cupboard or a cupboard only. Drawer has mushroom-turned wooden knobs and keyhole rosette. Cupboard doors have slightly sunk panels that are rectangular and framed with wavy molding or are Gothic-arched and have spandrels in the upper corners. Their fittings match those above. Interior has one or two fixed shelves with rounded front edges.

Has either a plinth base or is supported by turned or molded feet with valanced skirt. Mahogany, with liberal use of crotch-grain veneer; rosewood; late examples black walnut. By cabinetmakers. Not numerous. *Ca. 1840–1865.* BB to C

207. Eastlake Corner Cupboard

Two parts with upper section recessed five to seven inches. Dimensions seven feet six inches to nearly nine feet tall, by 32 to 36 inches deep, by 45 to 51 inches wide at front. Flat top with simple molded cornice, perhaps a molded top rail supported by eight to 12 short ball-turned spindles and flanked by ball-turned finials. Upper section enclosed by pair of tall rectangular single-pane glazed doors with inner edges of stiles and rails beveled. Right-hand door has crossbar handle with circular plate, or pendent-ring handle with square plate and matching keyhole escutcheon. Projecting molded blocks ornament upper ends of plain narrow stiles flanking doors. Four adjustable shelves with plain front edges.

Lower section has top with fold-over flap which forms full-width serving shelf. Beneath, a centered single

207

drawer about 16 inches wide by five inches deep, separated from flanking panels by narrow stiles. A brass bail handle with shaped plate, or pendent ring with square plate set diagonally, and a keyhole escutcheon matching that above. Below a pair of square doors flanked by stiles matching those above. Each has two rectangular raised panels placed vertically and separated by a plain central stile. The right-hand door has brass handle and keyhole escutcheons like upper section's. Single full-size shelf with plain front. Plinth base about four inches tall with beveled upper edge, flanked by molded blocks at base of corner stiles.

Made of ash, cherry or other native hardwood, seldom of black walnut or mahogany; occasionally of pine or other softwoods, painted and grained, by local carpenter-cabinetmakers. Unusual but not a rarity. *Ca. 1870–1880.* B to BB

Transitional Dresser

Two sections, upper one recessed nearly half the depth of lower part. Six feet six inches to seven feet eight inches tall by 40 to 50 inches wide, and 18 to 20 inches deep for lower section.

Has projecting cornice, cove-molded or double convex-molded, above plain frieze four to six inches high. Front of upper part is enclosed by a pair of glazed doors, full-width or flanked by plain narrow stiles. Each has six rectangular panes of glass arranged in three tiers and separated by straight molded muntins. Interior contains two full-width and full-depth shelves with plain or rounded front edges. Sides of section are raised four to six inches above counter top of lower part, and lower edge of front is rounded, with down-curved ends. Space between sections is open at front and enclosed at sides and back. Counter top of lower section is rectangular and slightly overhanging; square front corners, rounded edge. Below, three shallow drawers, either equal width or with center drawer about half as wide. Beneath a pair of doors with rectangular, slightly sunk panel; doors either full width or flanked by stiles matching those above. All doors fitted with mushroom-turned knobs. Base plain. Short turned feet or extensions of corner stiles scrolled to resemble bracket feet.

Black walnut or pine and other softwoods painted, by

country cabinetmakers. Many dressers available today are of Pennsylvania Dutch provenance. *Ca. 1840–1860.* BB to BBB

208

208. Kitchen Cupboard with High Counter Top

Average dimensions 46 inches tall by 40 inches wide and 18 inches deep. Slightly overhanging top, with or without simple three-quarter gallery three to five inches tall with quarter-round ends. Carcase contains tier of half-width, medium-depth drawers above a tall, full-width cupboard. Drawer fronts separated by a narrow central stile and fitted with wooden or glazed-earthen-ware knobs.

Cupboard enclosed by pair of paneled doors, full-width or flanked at outer sides and center by plain stiles. Doors have single plain panels or pair of narrow ones separated by stile, knobs match those above and may be closed by small turn buttons screwed to central stile. If no central stile, right-hand door has rounded astragal molding and keyhole, with or without an inset metal keyhole surround.

Sometimes there is a simple skirt with slightly curved lower edge. Instead of feet, cupboard ends are cut in shallow curves that form flat arches six to eight inches tall.

Pine or other softwoods, painted Amish blue, cypress-green, brown, gray or left natural by Pennsylvania Dutch carpenter-cabinetmakers. Plentiful. *Ca. 1840–1870.* AA to B

Pantry Cupboard

Plain utilitarian, one-piece cupboard made of wide, full-height boards, tongue-and-grooved, butt-joined and secured by cut nails. About five feet six inches tall, by 36 inches wide, by 20 inches deep and has flat, slightly overhanging top with either plain or rounded edge. Front is composed of two wide sidepieces flanking two single doors, with or without a cross member above upper, taller door. Both either paneled or made of two boards with batten strips on inner side. Small wooden or earthenware knobs; small turn buttons. If locks are present, keyholes are without escutcheons or surrounds. Upper cupboard is fitted with two full-size fixed shelves; lower one with single shelf. Rests directly on floor or is raised about six inches by corner extensions, cut and shaped to simulate bracket feet.

Pine or other softwoods, painted. Of southern New England provenance but may have been made elsewhere by local carpenter-cabinetmakers. Plentiful. *Ca. 1840–1865.* AAA to BB

209

209. Tin-paneled Food Safe

Wooden framework with three tiers of inset pierced tin panels at front, back and sides. Is 48 to 52 inches tall, by 36 to 40 inches wide; about 20 inches deep. Has a slightly overhanging wood top with plain edges supported by a wooden skeleton carcase constructed of light stiles and rails. Rectangular tin panels are pierced in identical designs, including rising sun, cathedral and sunburst. Front has pair of doors fitted with wood or glazed-earthenware knobs and a small turn button. Interior has three full-width, full-depth fixed shelves.

Plain base, simply turned legs, ball feet.

Maple or similar hardwood painted a dark color, with

tin panels left natural. Chiefly of Middle Western provenance, probably produced by small factories, with local-
ized distribution. A similar piece made in New England
has wire screening instead of pierced panels. Both types
used for keeping pastries and other foods screened from
insects and safe from mice or rats. *Ca. 1840–1870.* AAA
to BB

210

210. Water Bench

So named because pails of fresh water were kept on
its broad counter shelf; milk pails and other buckets were
stored in the cupboard below, and dipper, small basins
and mugs were put on narrow upper shelf. Often used
today as buffet.

It is 48 to 56 inches tall, by 44 to 56 inches wide; depth
of base 20 to 22 inches and that of top shelf six to 10

inches. The recessed, slightly overhanging shelf is surmounted either at back or at back and sides by a gallery three to five inches tall with cyma-curved outline and rounded ends. Shelf supported by scroll-cut end-pieces.

Beneath, a compartment containing either full-width shallow drawer or three narrow matching ones with plain or convex fronts and wooden or glazed earthenware knobs. Compartment is 18 to 20 inches above a full-width counter top that is open at the back or may have a gallery about six inches high, cut in balancing cyma-curves. Front of counter top is slightly overhanging, with plain or rounded edge and square corners.

Full-width cupboard below, 16 to 20 inches tall and enclosed by plain or paneled doors. Panels are rectangular, slightly sunk and either plain or shaped in balancing cyma-curves. Doors have knobs matching those above; may be separated by central stile to which small turn buttons are attached. Ends of bench extend to floor with lower edges cut to form flat arched and front corner stiles simulating bracket feet, sometimes connected by narrow cyma-curved skirt.

Pine or pine combined with other softwoods painted, by Pennsylvania Dutch cabinetmakers. Plentiful. *Ca. 1840–1870.* AAA to BB

211. Dough Tray

Also known as a "Kneading Table," this kitchen piece of European origin was brought to America by the Pennsylvania Dutch about 1700 and made and used by them throughout the Victorian period. Is still used by some Amish households. Bread dough was set to rise in the trough and then kneaded on its flat removable top.

It is 27 to 31 inches tall, by 36 to 44 inches long, and 20 to 28 inches wide. Top rectangular, made in one or two pieces with cleated ends, either slightly larger than trough or overhanging it six to 10 inches at ends and

211

four to six inches on the sides. Small-sized top has grooved cleats on its underside that secure it to the trough; larger one lifts off.

The trough is 10 to 14 inches deep with flaring sides and ends. Four canted, baluster-turned legs with simple ring turnings about four inches from the floor simulate peg feet. Legs are connected by a deeply valanced skirt. With larger top, was also used as ordinary table.

Maple; early examples of walnut, sometimes with top of pine. Those dating after 1820 are generally of maple and plentiful. *Ca. 1840–1880.* AAA to B

212. Dry Sink

Used in farmhouse kitchen without plumbing connections, it is a simple rectangular cabinet with some variations in size. Average dimensions 33 to 35 inches tall, by

44 inches wide, and 18 to 20 inches deep. Inset top, depressed five or six inches. Beneath it, a full-width cupboard with single or double doors, plain or paneled, with

212

wooden knobs and turn buttons. Instead of feet, the ends extend to floor with lower edges cut to form low flat arches.

Made of pine or other softwoods with exterior left natural or painted Amish blue, cypress-green, brown or gray. Plentiful; inexpensive; chiefly used today as plant stands, magazine tables or home bars. *1840–1880.* A to B

Section XII

Beds

According to their original cost, Victorian beds fall into three groups — elaborate, simple and in-between. In the first are the imposing architectural examples, made of the most costly hardwoods for handsomely appointed residences. Chiefly the work of cabinetmakers, often on special order, they were intended for large rooms with 14 to 16 foot ceilings. Consequently they are mostly of oversize proportions, and because of the difficulty in moving them when the contents of mansions were dispersed, the number that have survived is limited.

At the other end of the price range are the cottage beds, spool-turned or painted. Mass-produced of maple or pine for modest village and farmhouses, they are practical in size for modern use and of considerable variation in details of design. When replaced because out of fashion, many were relegated to lesser bedrooms or tucked away in attics or storerooms. As a result they are still plentiful, relatively inexpensive. They form a large proportion of the beds found in shops or at country auctions.

The in-between group is somewhat more ambitious of design but standard size. They were factory-produced, chiefly of black walnut or ash trimmed with black walnut; later other woods were used, such as cherry or mahogany. Their design details tend to become too involved, especially those with towering headboards; consequently fewer are found in dealers' shops.

Special Notes on Beds and Their Construction

Victorian beds are of two types — frame beds and bedsteads.

A bed frame consists of four posts, two side rails, two end rails, a headboard and either a turned "blanket rail," with or without a rudimentary footboard below, or a footboard that matches the headboard. With tall posts there is generally a tester frame, often in the form of a cove-molded cornice. Posts were turned from lumber three to five inches square with square sections where the rails join.

There are mortises on the inner sides of each post, about half its thickness, for the tenons on the rail ends. Mortise-and-tenon joints also hold head and footboards in place. Assembled posts and rails are made fast by countersunk bedscrews, which pass through the posts and thread into nuts mortised into the rails. A variant of this construction is found with some of the later frames, where side- and endpieces replace rails and are fastened with iron bed latches.

Head and footboards may be one piece, plain or paneled, or in two parts with a row of spindles between.

A bedstead has a head and footboard connected by sidepieces; it is fitted with concealed cast-iron bed latches. The decorative carvings and moldings are always fashioned separately and glued to the surface. This is also true of raised panels and cartouche-shaped central finials. Edges of slightly sunk panels are set into mortises cut in the supporting rails and stiles of a unit and then glued.

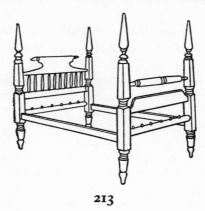

213

213. Transitional Three-quarter High-post Bed

Is without tester; all posts are alike. Turned from
pieces about four inches square, posts are from four feet
eight inches to five feet six inches tall. They combine
square and turned or square, octagon and turned sections.
Steeple finials surmount boldly done ring turnings. Below,
rails are simply turned, ending in peg or inverted vase
feet. Rails may be square or round.

Headboard, 16 to 20 inches high, may be (1) plain or
paneled, with flat upper edge, surmounted by a rounded
molding and quarter-circle cutouts at ends; or (2) a combination of ten short spool or baluster-turned spindles,
shaped top rail, and plain crossbar. A matching footboard
is present with the first type; with the spindle type the
foot posts are connected by a vase-and-ring turned blanket
rail which is usually placed above a low plain footboard
with down-turned ends.

Made by cabinetmakers along the Eastern Seaboard

and as far west as Wisconsin. Mahogany, maple, birch, butternut or black walnut, with head and footboards of pine. Many such beds found today in dealers' shops, especially those of maple, are of Pennsylvania Dutch provenance. *Ca. 1840–1865.* B to BBB

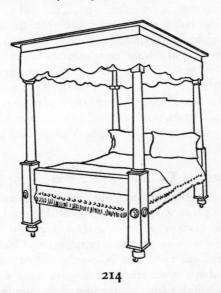

214

214. Transitional High-post Bed with Cornice Tester

Massive posts, eight to nine feet tall, surmounted by a full-size tester cornice 10 to 14 inches high. This has a boldly done projecting cove or beveled molding, above a frieze either plain or with incomplete Gothic arches. The four posts are alike, have Doric capitals, plain or clustered columns surmounting square sections about three feet tall, with or without chamfered edges. Projecting block feet about 10 inches tall, with plain or chamfered vertical edges.

The paneled headboard, 28 to 36 inches tall, has either a flat top with raised central oblong or an arched and molded top with three vertical panels below. The foot posts are connected by either a plain flat rail or by a rail-and-spool or ball-turned blanket rail with space between filled by eight to ten spindles with conforming turnings. Sidepieces and matching endpieces are about 12 inches high by an inch thick and fitted with iron bed latches.

Custom-made by cabinetmakers. Mahogany, with square sections of posts, tester frieze and parts of headboard crotch-grain veneered; or black walnut. More often found in the lower Mississippi Valley. *Ca. 1840–1865.* BB to C

215. Clustered Column Tester Bed

Is like foregoing in size and general construction but tester has plain wood parts, concealed by valance and full-length curtains at head of bed. Has four identical posts, eight to nine feet tall, tapering, and either plain or clustered columns. Just below the valance, each post has a double convex molding, simulating a small conforming capital, which is repeated at the joining of side and end boards and at the castered end.

Headboard is 36 to 40 inches tall with arched top ornately carved in high relief in rose and other flower and foliage motifs combined with scrolls. Paneling beneath may be either single intaglio rectangle or three smaller ones placed vertically. The sidepieces and footboard are of matching design; upper edges cut in bal-

ancing cyma-curves and ornamented with conforming
scrolled molding and small central medallion. Length
of bed varies from six feet six inches to a little over seven
feet, and width from five to five feet six inches. During

215

summer months sometimes completely enclosed with fly
netting.

Custom-made of mahogany, with posts, headboard,
foot- and sideboards crotch-grain veneered, or less often,
of rosewood. Generally considered of New Orleans origin, but may also have been work of St. Louis cabinetmakers. Produced chiefly for plantation and city mansions of lower Mississippi Valley. Typical examples in
some Natchez mansions open annually to the public.
Ca. 1840–1860. C to CCC

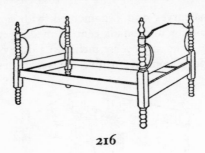

216

216. Transitional Low-post Bed

Posts are turned from pieces about three inches square
and are 36 to 44 inches tall. They end in stout vase-
shaped finials above ball or spool turning, and have a
square section at rail level, with ball or spool turnings
below. Head and footboards, from 16 to 18 inches high,
are identical, with upper edges either straight or sloping slightly from a central peak. Sides are cut in a concave curve; lower edges flat.

Made of maple or birch, with head and footboards
softwood stained red or painted a dark color. Black
walnut or butternut was used with later examples. Originally produced by local cabinetmakers but later became a quantity product of some furniture factories.
Ca. 1840–1860. AAA to B

217. Spool Bed (A, B and C)

Headboard 36 to 42 inches high, footboard either of
equal height or four to six inches lower. Plain side pieces
held in place by either bedscrews or bed latches. Made
in three typical designs.

(A) Both head and footboard have spool-turned posts with squared sections and small ball-and-ring or vase-turned finials. Connecting the posts are two spool-turned

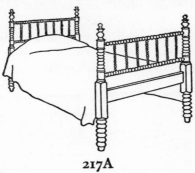

217A

cross rails which support seven to 11 slender spool-turned spindles about 12 inches tall.

(B) The spool-turned posts are short, surmounted by quarter-round turned segments which join the spool-turned top rail. The lower cross-rail is either spool-

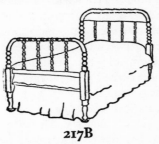

217B

turned or flat and space between two has from four to six spool-turned spindles. With this design the headboard is frequently taller than the footboard and immediately below the turned top rail is a plain crosspiece about four inches high surmounting the spindles. Also the sidepieces may have low cyma-curved brackets at their upper edges where they join the head and foot posts.

(C) The spool-turned posts are surmounted by tapering ball or button-turned finials and in place of spindles, the head section has a plain onepiece board, 18 to 20

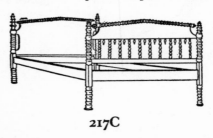

217C

inches high, with upper edge either flat or triangularly arched, surmounted by a spool-turned cresting with ends matching the finials. Headboard is joined to the posts by tenon-like extensions at top and bottom. Footboard has a matching cresting surmounting a crosspiece about six inches high. Between this and a lower cross-rail there are eight to ten spool-turned spindles, sometimes alternating with short turned pendent finials.

All three types are fitted with socket casters. Dimensions are from six feet four inches, to six feet eight inches long, by four feet six inches wide. Factory made of maple, birch or other native hardwoods, with solid type of headboard pine or other softwood stained brown or painted. Some examples made of black walnut. Occasionally referred to, now, as a "Jenny Lind" bed, because

it was in fashion at the time of her American concert
tours. Plentiful, especially those of maple or similar
woods. *Ca. 1850–1870.* AA to B

218

218. High-post Spool Bed

Spool-turned posts about two and a half inches in
diameter and from five feet six inches to seven feet tall
with either ball-turned finials or a full-size flat or arched
tester frame. Head and footboard may consist of spool-
turned top rails and plain bottom rails which support
seven spool-turned spindles, or headboard may have a
triangularly arched top rail with spool-turned cresting
above eight to ten spool-turned spindles. With the latter, the footboard is much lower, has a spool-turned
top rail and eight to 10 spool-turned spindles. Sidepieces plain, six to eight inches tall, secured by bed-

screws or iron bed latches. From six feet six inches to seven feet long and from four feet six inches to five feet wide.

Black walnut or, infrequently, maple stained brown by local cabinetmakers and some factories. Chiefly found in Ohio, Indiana and Illinois. Scarce. *Ca. 1850–1865.* BBB to C

219

219. Spool-turned Crib

Has four baluster- or spool-turned posts four to five feet six inches tall. Sides and ends are fencelike, plain turned top rail and flat bottom rail about three inches high. Space between is filled with either plain upright strips or slender, spool-turned spindles. One side is generally hinged along its lower edge.

A late example with tall spool-turned posts has arched and shaped top rails at head and foot. Body of crib is generally 24 to 26 inches from the floor. Length varies from three feet six inches to about four feet and width from 28 to 32 inches. Occasionally a crib was made double width for twins.

Made of mahogany when sides have vertical strips or simply turned spindles; of black walnut with spool-turned posts and spindles. Mahogany examples date *ca. 1840–1860;* those of black walnut, *ca. 1850–1875.* AA to AAA

220

220. Louis XV Tester Bed

Has tall headposts, eight to nine feet tall with full-width recessed tester 24 to 36 inches deep, and low footposts connected by a footboard of either equal height or conforming to that of the sidepieces. Bed is found in two general types.

(1) Tester consists of exposed molded cornice, with straight front surmounted by a pierced pediment boldly

silhouetted in intertwined scrolls flanking central cartouche. It rests on cluster-column headposts, and is connected to them by diagonally placed brackets cut in cyma-curved scrolls extending upward to the sides at about a 45-degree angle. The space within the tester frame was originally filled with quilted or pleated silk or satin.

Low headboard, usually surmounted by carved and pierced cresting which slopes slightly from a central cartouche. Beneath, one rectangular intaglio panel or two smaller ones. Footposts are clustered columns about three feet tall. Projecting bead-molded feet match those of headposts. They are connected by a paneled footboard of equal height, with straight flat top and valanced skirt.

The sidepieces are elaborately shaped and ornamented, with upper edges cut in balancing cyma-curves and lower edges scroll-valanced. Further ornamented with applied carving done in cyma-curves and leafage scrolls, which may flank central projecting semicircular brackets that surmount rose-carved supports.

(2) A plain exposed tester with serpentine front rests on turned headposts and is fastened to the high headboard by cyma-curved, scrolled brackets. The headboard, frequently over four feet high, has a triple-arched top surmounted by a carved and pierced cresting of conventionalized leafage scrolls. Beneath it are three parallel intaglio panels with semicircular or cusp-arched tops.

Footposts octagonal with button-and-ball finials. Short vase-and-ring turned feet, connected by a low footboard with upper edge cut in balancing cyma-curves that flank

a central pediment-like section. The sidepieces are plain
with balancing cyma-curved upper edges.

Custom-made of mahogany, with liberal use of crotch-
grain veneer; mahogany and rosewood; less frequently,
all of rosewood. Many produced for mansions of lower
Mississippi Valley by New Orleans cabinetmakers.
Ca. 1840–1860. CC to CCC

221

221. Louis XV Architectural Bed

Massive octagon posts surmounted by large gadrooned
finials. Headposts six to seven feet tall and joined to
ornate headboard, 14 to 18 inches taller, by tenons or
short horizontal spindles. Headboard serpentine, arched;
surmounted by gadrooned finial. Face ornamented with
conforming scroll carving, done in conventionalized
leafage motif. Beneath, three vertical arched panels, the

central one widest. All are framed by a plain beveling or a convex molding.

Footposts match headposts but are low, three feet six inches to four feet tall, surmounted by gadrooned finials. Foot and sidepieces are from 14 to 16 inches high; upper edges straight with scroll-shaped brackets. Bed usually fitted with large socket casters. Length varies from six feet six inches to seven feet, width from four feet six inches to five feet.

Custom-made of mahogany, with crotch-grain veneering, or, rarely, of rosewood. Not numerous. *Ca. 1850–1865.* BBB to C

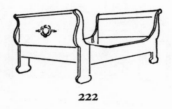

222

222. Transitional Sleigh Bed

Resemblance to horse-drawn cutter or sleigh less marked than with earlier American Empire bed. Head and footboards equal height, 36 to 44 inches, with out-curved top rails. Uprights above sideboard level have flaring cyma-curved outline, but are plain below and terminate in block feet fitted with socket casters.

Headboard and footboard each have large rectangular panel, sometimes ornamented with a central applied carved cartouche, done in flower and leafage or conventionalized scroll motifs. Below each panel is a plain

cross-member, 12 to 14 inches high, placed at same level
as sidepieces, which are plain with slightly concave upper
and lower edges. Bed parts held in place by iron bed
latches. Length of bed varies from six feet four inches
to six feet eight inches and is from four feet six inches
to four feet ten inches wide.

Made by cabinetmakers or early factories of mahogany, panels and sidepieces crotch-grain veneered; less
often rosewood. Also pine and assorted softwoods,
painted. *Ca. 1840–1850*. AA to B

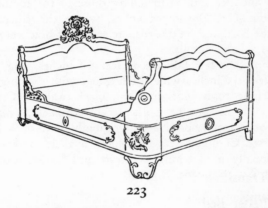

223

223. Louis XV Low Bed

Has arched and paneled head and footboards of nearly
the same height, and deep sidepieces. The serpentine-
arched top rail of the headboard is surmounted by a
large central finial, cartouche shaped, carved in high
relief in either flower or fruit motifs, surrounded by
leafage scrolls. Beneath the shaped cross-member supporting top rail is a full-width, slightly sunk plain panel.

Headboard uprights scroll-cut, with carved scrolls above small rectangular molded panels. Conforming bracket feet. Matching footboard is without central finial; has quarter-circle rounded ends. Its lower cross-member is ornamented with a large rectangular molded panel with scrolled ends and central rosette. The rounded ends are downswept in balancing cyma-curves to meet the side-pieces. Large rosettes, above carved leafage scrolls, match those of the headboard finial. Conforming bracket feet. Sidepieces about 12 inches high with straight molded edges and decorations matching those of the footboard cross-member. On upper edges, where the sidepieces join the head and footboards, are scroll-cut brackets with carved foliated scrolls.

About four feet tall, by six feet six inches long, and four feet six inches wide. Mahogany, with crotch-grain veneering; rosewood; or, later, black walnut. Ornate early examples are the work of cabinetmakers; simpler, later ones factory-produced. Originally part of a bedroom set. Complete sets are seldom available today but occasionally a matching bedstead and bureau can be found. *Ca. 1850–1865.* B to BB

224. Belter Bed

Headboard about five feet six inches tall, surmounted by a boldly arched, carved and pierced cresting, done in leaf-and-tendril motif with central cartouche carved in high relief. Ends of cresting are down-curved to meet the cyma-curved outline of the quarter-round corners. Matching footboard about 34 inches tall, less boldly arched, somewhat serpentined with lower edge close to the floor. Both headboard and footboards supported

by low, quarter-round block feet, generally castered.
Wide, out-bowed sidepieces with concave upper edges.
Lower ones straight, with flat, slightly projecting band

224

about three inches high. The same banding appears on
the bottom of the footboard.

Bed is from six feet eight inches to seven feet four
inches long, by five feet four inches wide. Made only
of laminated rosewood by John Henry Belter of New
York. Not numerous. *Ca. 1845–1863.* BBB to CC

225. Gothic Paneled Bed

Has structural lines common to all beds of sleigh type.
Head and footboards alike and about 40 inches high,
flanked by paneled octagon posts about six inches across,
surmounted by carved, three-tier cusp finials. Concave
molded feet fitted with socket casters. Headboard and
footboard each has flat top rail with boldly rounded
edge which overhangs a frieze-like cross rail. Beneath it
three tall, slightly sunk panels of equal width and lancet-
arched tops. They are separated by plain narrow stiles

and rest on a plain cross-rail which surmounts a slightly projecting secondary rail with molded edges.

Sidepieces have conforming molded edges and are from 12 to 14 inches high. They have incised horizontal panels with multiform cusp-arched ends nearly full

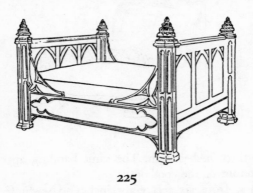

225

length and height. At joining of posts and upper edges, large triangular-shaped brackets with small carved crotchet ends are paneled in an incised design of three triangularly placed pointed arches. Smaller triangular incised brackets at joining of posts and lower edges. Paneling on posts consists of two tiers of slender, incised cusp-arched panels. Bed parts are held in place by cast-iron bed latches. Length of bed is from six feet six inches to seven feet; width four feet eight inches to five feet.

Custom-made. Mahogany with panels and sidepieces crotch-grain veneered; or black walnut with burl veneer. A bed of this type was shown at the Centennial Exposition of 1876 in Philadelphia. *Ca. 1840–1875.* C to CC

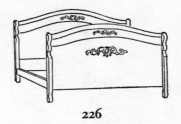

226

226. Louis XV Serpentine Arched Bed

Has headboard, 42 to 44 inches tall, with arched molded top rail connected by flat uprights with rounded upper ends and cyma-curved sides. Ornamentation below top rail consists of small central cartouche flanked by balancing leafage scrolls and a full-width applied arched molding. Matching footboard is six to eight inches lower than headboard, and has a larger central cartouche halfway between the arched molding and that of a full-width rectangular panel at the bottom. This second cartouche is sometimes present on the headboard also. Sidepieces of bed have straight edges and are either plain or molding-paneled.

A later bed of this design had a headboard about 16 inches taller, and top rail is surmounted by a conforming cresting carved in high relief in grape, plum and leafage motifs. Sidepieces have bead-molded upper edges with triangular scroll-cut and scroll-carved brackets at ends and applied plain banding on lower edges.

Length varies from six feet six inches to just under seven feet. Factory-made of mahogany, rosewood or black walnut. Often part of a bedroom set. *Ca. 1855–1870*. AA to AAA

227

227. Mid-Victorian Bed

Headboard with molded arched top, five feet to five feet eight inches tall. Shaping may be (1) a slightly flat arched curve, with sweep interrupted by balancing subsidiary concave or convex curves; (2) central semicircular arch flanked by downswept cyma-curves; (3) central serpentine arching flanked by a combination of concave C-scrolls and cyma-curves. Beneath arching is either a medallion carved in high relief with fruit and grapeleaf motifs, sometimes combined with scrolls, or a central boss surmounted by carved shell. Below the top member are two full-width panels, about six or eight inches high, separated by plain cross-rails. Upper panel sometimes decorated with an applied molding panel with semicircular ends. Headboard supported by flat uprights, with upper ends arch-cut and sides cut in balancing cyma-curves.

The footboard is 32 to 36 inches tall with molded top either a full-width serpentine arch or a central semicircular arch flanked by downswept cyma-curves. Has a carved central decoration, either duplicating that of the headboard or carved in related motif, such as three bunches of grapes surrounded by tendrils and leafage. Beneath top member is a plain slightly sunk panel with upper edge either straight or of conforming shape to arched top. With the latter, the carved medallion is at the center of this panel. The panel with straight edge is decorated with an applied molding panel matching that of the headboard. Footboard is supported by quarter-circle uprights. Rectangular sidepieces are six to eight inches high with triangular, scroll-shaped brackets at upper edges where they join head and footboards. Sidepieces sometimes decorated with applied molding panels matching head and footboard. Length of bed is six feet four inches to six feet eight inches, with width 54 inches.

Factory-made of black walnut or ash, with carvings and moldings of black walnut. Originally part of bedroom set. *Ca. 1865–1875.* AA to AAA

Painted Cottage Bed

Simplified version of the foregoing with same construction and dimensions. Painted landscape or floral vignettes in naturalistic colors take place of carved medallions or cartouches in center of head and footboard. Molding of shaped panels simulated by striping. Factory-made as part of bedroom set.

Pine, painted a yellowish brown with graining and striping in dark brown approximating that of black walnut. Plentiful. *Ca. 1865–1875.* A to AA

228

228. Renaissance Bed

Its design elements, adapted from those of Renaissance architecture, are complicated and its ornamentation is exceedingly heavy.

Headboard is eight to nine feet tall and usually has a semicircular, boldly cove-molded arch surmounted by a heavily molded and paneled pediment, which has a central cartouche done in conventional architectural form and carved in high relief, with scroll-carved and molded triple-arched finial. Face ornamented by three vertically placed panels with tops conforming to cornice. All have beveled edges and are framed by applied molding. Headboard is supported by straight uprights surmounted by quadilateral urn-shaped finials.

Footboard, 36 to 42 inches tall, has central continuous arch flanked by concave curves and molded top rail sur-

mounted by scroll-carved and voluted cartouche matching headboard's. Face is paneled to correspond to that of
the headboard; in addition, there is a large central
carved and applied rosette, flanked by raised panels with
beveled edges, at level of sidepieces. Above it, a full-
length applied molding; on footboard's lower edge a
projecting cove-like molding reversed. Quarter-circle convex uprights with upper ends either flat or cut in downswept curves and lower ones either plain or scrolled to
form bracket feet. Faces of uprights paneled and molded
to match footboard.

Head and foot sections connected by straight sidepieces 10 or 12 inches high with molded edges and plain
or molding-paneled faces. At joining of sections, upper
edges have triangular scroll-cut brackets.

A bed like this once belonged to Ole Bull, famous
Norwegian violinist who married Sara C. Thorpe of
Madison, Wisconsin, in 1870. Bed and matching bureau
are now owned by the Wisconsin State Historical Society. A similar bed was made for A. T. Stewart, merchant
prince of New York.

Length varies from six feet four inches to seven feet,
and width from four feet four inches to five feet. Made
by cabinetmakers and factories producing quality furniture. Black walnut, with raised panels burl-veneered.
Ca. 1865–1880. B to BB

229. Renaissance-Eastlake Painted Bed

Design similar to foregoing but less ornate and with
Eastlake details. Painted and grained in tones of yellow
and brown. Head and footboard panels decorated with
landscape or floral vignettes. Further painted decoration

consists of hairline striping in lighter color. Height of headboard seven feet to seven and a half feet. Length of bed is about six feet four inches, and width four feet six inches.

229

Pine, sometimes combined with other softwoods; some maple by factories producing less expensive furniture. *Ca. 1870–1880.* AA to AAA

230. Eastlake Paneled Bed

Headboard five and a half to six and a half feet tall, with molded cornice which may be (1) flat and slightly overhanging; (2) surmounted by low shaped pediment with arched and scroll-carved central finial and bead-molded upper edge terminating in slightly voluted ends; (3) surmounted by half-width arcaded pediment flanked by plain or molded pilaster with ball finials and triangular brackets.

With first two there is a low frieze, carved in relief
in scroll, floral or ribbon motifs. It may be broken into
three units by block capitals of two engaged columns
which divide the paneled area below. This may consist
of a single horizontal, molding framed panel or four

230

vertical ones. Straight uprights, frequently ornamented
with incised beading or fluting. With third type of headboard, uprights are surmounted by tapering urn-shaped
finials.

Footboard, 30 to 36 inches tall, has a flat, overhanging
top rail and decorative details matching those of headboard. Its lower edge has a projecting convex molding,
raised six to eight inches from floor by boldly shaped
bracket feet that sometimes have scrolled wings. Sidepieces are from eight to 12 inches high with projecting
molding top and bottom. Length varies from six feet
four inches to six feet eight inches; width four feet four

inches. Three-quarter size, about 46 inches wide; single, 36 inches wide.

Factory-made. Contemporary catalogues, such as that of Paine's Furniture Manufactory of Boston, illustrated this type, an ornate version of it standing on a dais provided with separate drapery-hung canopy. The list price, including matching bureau, was $575 with silk draperies and $475 without hangings. Comparatively few of these Royal Suite beds appear to have been made.

Mahogany, cherry, black walnut or oak with less expensive ones of maple, birch (finish natural or mahoganized), ash, or chestnut. *Ca. 1870–1890*. AA to AAA

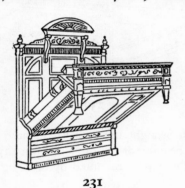

231

231. Eastlake Folding Bed

Hinged front fitted with either counterbalancing weights or pair of steel coil-tension springs. Headboard to which it is attached has arched or pedimented top seven or eight feet tall, sometimes with urn-shaped finials at ends. Below are simple rectangular or shaped panels, concealed when the hinged front is raised.

Front is surmounted by a hinged frieze with a pendent pilaster at each end. When lowered, frieze becomes the footboard and the pilasters its supporting legs. Front has a large oval mirror (or rectangular frequently with semicircular top), which may be flanked by narrow, molding-framed wooden panels. Bottom of front has a full-width slightly projecting molding, a plain horizontal panel or two full-width mock drawer fronts with pendent brass bail handles and keyhole escutcheons below. Simply molded base fitted with socket casters. Width usually four feet six inches and depth 20 to 26 inches. Length when lowered is six feet to six feet four inches. When closed resembles a wardrobe.

Other Eastlake folding beds simulated a tall chest of drawers, a cabinet with a pair of mirrored false doors, an upright piano, a cabinet organ. Demand for this type coincided with the appearance of apartment houses in the larger cities, which began about 1875.

Elaborate examples mahogany; simpler ones cherry, black walnut, oak, ash and other native hardwoods. Factory-produced. *Ca. 1875–1890.* A to AA

Section XIII

Washstands, Commodes, Bedside Tables and Towel Racks

In the Victorian or pre-plumbing period, the washstand was a standard piece of bedroom furniture. Both simple and elaborate sets included either an open or enclosed one. The first is like a bedside table but with towel bars and a low shelf added. Usually the enclosed type, often miscalled a "commode," resembles a chest of drawers of reduced size but has a single full-width drawer above a double-door cupboard, and its top always has a gallery piece at the rear. There is also the enclosed washstand with hinged top and slightly recessed cupboard base with single door, which now frequently does duty as a home bar.

Still another enclosed type occurred with some of the finer bedroom sets. This was a rectangular bedside stand with a drawer above a tall single-door cupboard, decorated with carving and other details matching those of the rest of the set. A further toilet adjunct was the towel rack. The more ambitious sets had one of the trestle type with plain or baluster-turned uprights. For the cottage sets, there was the spool-turned towel rack.

All these pieces, with the exception of a few early examples of cabinetwork, are factory products with the same characteristics of workmanship as other machine-made furniture.

232

232. Open Washstand

Is 32 to 34 inches tall with square or rectangular top which is slightly overhanging and has a rounded or molded edge. Square top measures 18 to 20 inches, and the rectangular one is 28 to 30 inches wide by 16 to 18 inches deep. At rear a plain or simply arched gallery with straight or slightly projecting scroll-cut ends. When scrolled they are rear supports for a pair of raised and slightly projecting towel bars, supported at the front by short scrolled brackets attached to the sides of the stand.

Beneath is a plain skirt which may contain a shallow full-width drawer. Its plain front is fitted with one or two pulls, either mushroom-turned wooden knobs or brass pendent-ring handles with square plates. Stand is supported by four plain or baluster-turned legs, partially ring-turned, with square sections at top and at shelf level. Small ball or peg feet. About 10 inches from the floor, legs are braced by a full-size shelf with plain or rounded edge. Beneath it may be a plain skirt deep enough to contain a shallow full-width drawer, fitted as above.

Made at first of maple, birch or similar hardwood and, infrequently, of mahogany or pine and painted, by local cabinetmakers or small furniture factories. Later made in quantity of black walnut, maple or ash by larger factories producing popular priced furniture. Sold as separate piece, seldom as part of a matching bedroom set. *Ca. 1840–1880.* A to AA

233

233. Early Commode Washstand

Is about 34 inches tall and has rectangular, slightly overhanging top about 30 inches wide by 16 inches deep. Rear gallery four inches high with top arched in balancing cyma curves. Gallery may be continued at sides by raised and slightly projecting towel bars. Front supports short, flaring scroll-cut brackets.

Carcase contains full-width drawer four or five inches

deep, above full-size cupboard enclosed by double doors. Ends either plain or paneled. Drawer front plain with mushroom-turned wooden knobs or, if placed in a slightly overhanging frieze, is boldly ogee-molded with finger grips on lower edge and with inset metal keyhole surround. Cupboard doors beneath are either plain and fitted with wooden knobs or have slightly sunk rectangular panels, sometimes with Gothic-arched tops. The right-hand one has a wavy molding astragal and is fitted with an inset metal keyhole surround. Cupboard interior may be equipped with a single, full-width, full-depth shelf. Base has a plain shallow skirt. Low bracket feet or supported by extensions of corner stiles.

By cabinetmakers or small early furniture factories of maple, birch or painted pine for simple examples and of mahogany, with crotch-grain veneering, rosewood or, less frequently of black walnut for more sophisticated examples, usually part of a matching bedroom set. *Ca. 1840–1860.* AA to AAA

234. Marble-top Commode Washstand

Like preceding in design, construction and size but lacks towel-bar ends and has white marble top slightly overhanging with rounded front corners and concave molded edge. Rear generally has simply arched marble gallery, with a pair of small marble bracket shelves about six inches wide, semioval in shape with molded edge, supported by cyma-curved brackets.

Drawer front usually has either one large molded panel with semicircular ends or two smaller ones, flanking a molded rosette, with leafage handles. Cupboard doors also have molded panels, either rectangular with semicircular top or semicircular top and bottom, with or without carved medallions of pendent fruits with leafage in medium relief.

Base has molded upper edge and is slightly projecting. Conforming block feet about an inch high. Part of a

234

bedroom set. Made in quantity by furniture factories, generally of black walnut but sometimes of ash with black walnut trim. Marble gallery often missing. Some examples found with wooden top, possibly replacement. Plentiful. *Ca. 1860–1870.* AAA to B

235. Cottage Commode Washstand

Like the preceding but painted and grained. Body color is usually light brown with darker graining. Panel moldings are simulated by striping in a dark brown and medallions are either darker graining with floral bou-

quets in bright colors or landscape vignettes in simple
contrasting colors.

Drawer front has turned wooden mushroom knobs or
leafage-carved handles. Right-hand cupboard door has
mushroom knob or inset metal keyhole surround. Skirt

235

valanced in balancing cyma-curves, lower edge has conforming line or striping. Originally part of a painted
cottage bedroom set.

Pine. Plentiful but not often found with original
painting in good condition. *Ca. 1860–1875.* AA to AAA

236. Hinged-top Washstand

Has rectangular, overhanging lid with concave molded
edge that is hinged at rear and surmounts plain enclosed
carcase. This contains full-size well about 14 inches deep
and a cupboard below with recessed front. The well projects about an inch at front.

There are two sizes of this washstand. The smaller

and more usual is about 30 inches wide, has one drawer, inset in the well, and single cupboard door. The larger is about 38 inches wide, has two well drawers and a pair of doors. Both sizes are about 32 inches tall by 18 inches deep.

The well interior of the smaller washstand has a built-in washbowl platform; at left is raised about four

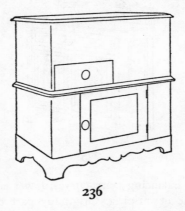

236

inches, and contains a drawer fitted with a mushroom turned wooden knob. Larger washstand has built-in platform at each end with drawer in each. Recessed cupboard. Low plain base, with skirt simply valanced in balancing cyma-curves. Both bowl and pitcher of water were kept in the well compartment, and on below-zero nights the closed lid kept the water from freezing.

Black walnut, ash or pine, painted, grained and decorated like other cottage furniture. Less plentiful than the painted commode washstand. *Ca. 1860–1875.* AA to AAA

237

237. Bedside Pedestal Stand

Has enclosed pedestal-like carcase about 32 inches tall, generally rectangular with overhanging molded-edge top, 16 inches square. Contains full-width drawer of medium depth above single-door cupboard, 20 inches tall. Ends of carcase are paneled or plain. Top may be of white marble or wood with square or rounded corners.

Drawer front is (1) plain with wooden or brass knob; (2) edged with a raised molding, with leafage-carved handle; (3) ogee-molded, faced with crotch-grain veneer, with finger grip on lower edge; (4) outlined with incised beading with brass pendent-ring handle. The single cupboard door may be (1) with slightly sunk rectangular panel, framed by raised molding, plain or ornamented with a carved pendent medallion of fruit with leafage in medium relief and wooden keyhole rosette; (2) plain, faced with crotch-grain veneer, fitted with a simple brass knob and framed by wide bands of ogee molding; (3) with slightly sunk panel, decorated by vertical bands of incised beading and rectangular or circular keyhole escutcheon.

Plain base, molded upper edge, small socket casters. An unusual variant of the bedside stand is in the form of a circular pedestal with round marble top. It usually is without drawer but has a tall cupboard with molding-paneled curved door and brass knob or inset brass keyhole surround.

Early examples made chiefly by cabinetmakers of mahogany, with crotch-grain veneering, or of rosewood, sometimes in pairs. Others of black walnut produced by quality furniture factories, also in pairs as part of matching bedroom sets. *Ca. 1860–1880.* AA to B

238. Shaving Stand

Maximum height six feet. Consists of oval or rectangular tilting mirror surmounting a cabinet mounted on a tall baluster-turned shaft. Tripod or quadrant base; either cabriole legs or cyma-curved brackets.

The mirror, about 12 inches high by eight inches wide, has either plain conforming frame with carved cresting or one of elaborate shaping, pierced and carved. Swivel mountings attach it to U-shaped standard over cabinet.

Cabinet usually has marble top about 18 inches square; contains a single shallow drawer with small wooden knob. Lower edge of the cabinet is either plain or with pierced and carved valance. Supporting shaft baluster-turned with vase-and-ring elements or boldly turned and partially carved, ending in carved vase-shaped pendent finial. Base has three short cabriole legs with leafage-carved knees and upcurved whorl feet, castered, or four cyma-curved bracket feet which may end in upcurved volutes, castered. With some examples the mirror is adjustable. Black walnut with drawer front plain or burl-veneered. *Ca. 1860–1880.* AA to AAA

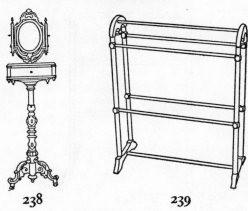

238   **239**

239. Trestle Towel Rack

Framework, about 28 to 32 inches tall by about the same width, consists of two open trestle ends which support five horizontal rods. Each trestle has two slender uprights, plain or baluster-turned, spaced about six inches apart and surmounted by a shaped top-piece generally arched and molded. Uprights supported by low shaped block feet, with lower edge cut to form a flat or arched opening. Top-pieces connected by three rods, each pair of uprights by one about halfway to the floor. Feet braced by a central stretcher matching the rods.

Generally black walnut as part of a factory-produced bedroom set. Early ones mahogany or rosewood; late examples black walnut, ash combined with black walnut, maple, birch or cherry stained brown or with natural finish. In demand today for guest towels or as drying racks. *Ca. 1860–1880.* A to AA

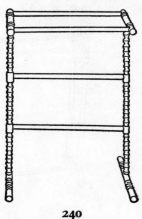

240

240. Spool-turned Towel Rack

Like preceding in size but of simplified construction with only four towel rods. Made entirely of slender turned parts. Each end has a single spool-turned upright surmounted by conforming top rail about six inches long, and is supported by a spool-turned base about two inches long which has small ball or knob-turned feet.

Top rails are connected by two plain rods and there are two others, equi-spaced, connecting the uprights. Maple and other native hardwoods, painted and grained to match bedroom set pieces; also maple, birch or black walnut in natural finish. Made a little later than the preceding but much in demand today for the same uses. *Ca. 1860–1880.* A to AA

Section XIV

Mirrors

Since ornate elegance was the theme of the more formal Victorian furniture, mirrors designed for use with such pieces generally had elaborate gilded frames. They are of three types: the oval wall mirror, the overmantel mirror, and the tall pier glass, generally with a low marble-topped base. Frames consistently have raised decoration of applied flower or fruit motifs with foliage and scrolls and pierced cresting. Grapes are favorites; some frames are so heavily decorated with pendent bunches as to resemble a formalized trellis.

Less ambitious frames simulate rosewood combined with bead molding in gilt. But whether ornate or simple, the frames are pine coated with gesso and either finished in gold leaf or painted and grained to resemble rosewood. The latter is most often found with the rectangular general-purpose mirror in a bold concave molded frame.

In the Eastlake substyle both pier glass and overmantel mirrors occur with walnut frames.

For the simple cottage home there is the molded frame with low arched top and rounded lower corners, and the rustic mirror with carving which resembles branches and twigs.

All of these Victorian mirrors were the work of specialized frame makers whose establishments were at least partially factorized. They were in the larger cities, as Boston, New York and Philadelphia, whence the ornate oval wall, overmantel and pier glasses were shipped.

Special Comments on Mirrors and Their Construction

The mirror glass, in all but a few of the later examples, is plain single-paned. Much of it is French plate from a quarter to three eighths of an inch thick. A beveled edge about two inches wide is an indication of a late example.

The method of gilding all frames, partially or wholly, was the same. The portion to be gilded was first coated with gesso (whiting and glue mixed with water) to make the surface smooth. When dry, a light coat of "tack" varnish was applied to make the gold leaf adhere readily. The gold leaf was prepared in sheets about two by three inches in size. (Made of 23-carat gold, it was beaten tissue-thin between leather skins by heavy mallets.) After leafing, the frame was rubbed with small bats of lamb's wool which tightened the bond of gold leaf and tack and removed loose, overlapping fringes of the metal. Finally, the parts intended for a bright finish were burnished.

Many of the larger gilded mirrors are found in poor condition with parts of the applied composition scrolls, flowers or fruit details loose or missing. Such a frame can be restored and regilded, but it is always an expensive undertaking which must be done by a specialist. Proper regilding can only be done with *gold leaf*. Those who suggest the use of one of the liquid "gilding preparations" are unskilled tinkers.

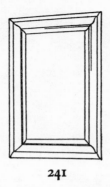

241

241. All-purpose Rectangular Mirror

Has a single panel of mirror glass contained in an oblong molded frame with mitered corners. Size varies from a small mirror, about 22 by 14 inches, frequently hung above a chest of drawers, to one about 58 by 36 inches for use in a parlor or as a large dressing glass.

Frame is from two to five inches wide and is cove-molded in a combination of concave cyma and convex curves. Made of pine coated with gesso, and gilded with gold leaf or painted to resemble rosewood or black walnut. Early examples are faced with crotch-grain mahogany and either ogee-molded or beveled. With a frame of natural finish, the mirror panel is often surrounded by a narrow gilt molding, either beaded or concave.

Generally manufactured in quantity by frame makers and sold wholesale to furniture dealers. Some with rosewood, black walnut or mahogany frames were made locally by cabinetmakers or small furniture factories. *Ca. 1840–1865.* AA to AAA

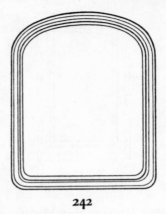

242

242. Cottage Mirror

Has convex, simply molded rectangular frame with flat arched top and rounded lower corners, 15 to 30 inches tall by 12 to 24 inches wide. The conforming mirror panel is frequently surrounded by a narrow concave gilded bead molding.

Pine coated with gesso painted to simulate black walnut, rosewood or, less frequently, mahogany. Also painted black or other dark color. Later examples black walnut. Produced in large quantities by frame manufacturers. Probably the least expensive mirror of the period, it was widely used with painted cottage bedroom sets and later was the ever-present mirror for kitchen, servant's bedroom and summer boardinghouse guest rooms. Frequently found today refinished in white enamel or other colors. Plentiful. *Ca. 1860–1880.* A to AA

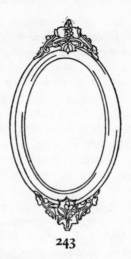

243

243. Oval Gilded Mirror

Widely popular throughout the early and middle years of the period for use in parlor, dining room or master bedroom, where it was usually hung vertically between windows. Frame design has many variations and elaborations. Three typical ones are:

(1) Unornamented convex frame, three to four inches wide, with or without a surrounding bead.

Dimensions of mirror are about 40 inches tall by 26 inches wide.

(2) Convex or convex-concave frame, usually with beading bands surrounding glass and outer edge. There is restrained cresting at top and matching pendent finial at bottom. These consist of foliated scrolls, often pierced, and may be elaborated by bunches of grapes with leafage in relief, done with applied composition to simulate

carving. Over-all dimensions are four feet to four feet six inches tall, by 28 to 32 inches wide.

(3) Shaped frame with tall cresting of intertwining pierced and raised scrolls, sometimes combined with an urn-shaped finial and a corresponding finial of pierced foliate scrolls at the bottom. Surrounding the mirror glass there is usually an oval band of raised flowers or bunches of grapes with leafage. Sides of frame may be further elaborated by foliated scrolls conforming to those of the cresting and pendent finial. Over-all dimensions are five to six feet tall by three to three feet six inches wide.

Frame is pine, coated with gesso; scrolls, leafage, flowers and fruits are of applied composition; the whole gilded with gold leaf, and portions brightly burnished. Made only by frame makers, who produced them in quantity by factory methods. Ornate examples were made chiefly in Philadelphia, New York and Boston and shipped to all sections. *Ca. 1840–1870.* AAA to BBB

Small Oval Mirrors

Simply ornamented convex or cove-molded frames with small mirrors, oval, are to be found today. They measure about 13 to 18 inches tall by 11 to 16 inches wide. Most of them are of gilt but some are black walnut with a simple inner gilt bead molding. Originally picture frames, they have been adapted to present-day use by substituting mirror glass for the former portraits. *Ca. 1865–1875.* A to AA

244

244. Gilded Overmantel Mirror

Has rectangular frame with flatly arched top surmounted by a pierced and carved cresting, either centered or full-width. Is either wide enough to cover a
standard chimney breast, 52 to 54 inches, or is about 20
inches narrower. Height varies from three to over six
feet.

With the simpler and shorter example, the convex
molded frame has a centered pierced and carved cresting which consists of a cartouche ornamented with
flowers or fruits or a pendent bunch of grapes with foliage done in relief and flanked by conventionalized leafage scrolls. There are also overlaid brackets of similar
leafage scrolls in the lower corners.

The taller and more ornate type has a wider frame
with a convex molded detail along its inner edge. The
cresting is full width and consists of intertwined flowers
or grapes in relief flanking a central scrolled cartouche.
Sides of frame may be molded or ornamented with leafage scrolls, flowers and, sometimes, pendent bunches of

grapes or other fruits. The lower corners usually flare slightly to form foliated scrolled brackets. This rococo type was designed chiefly for city mansions or similar country villas. There is one of this sort which nearly reaches the ceiling in the parlor of the Henry Clay home, Ashland, near Lexington, Kentucky.

Pine, coated with gesso and finished with gold leaf or, less frequently, painted to simulate rosewood or black walnut, usually with one or two lines of gilt beading added. *Ca. 1840–1870.* AAA to BBB

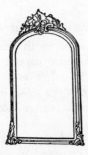

245

245. Pier Table Glass

Is like simple example of the preceding and so named because it was designed to be hung over a pier table. Dimensions are three feet, six inches to four feet tall by 22 to 25 inches wide. Convex molded frame, about three inches wide with flat arched top, may be plain or surmounted at center by pierced and carved cresting — a cartouche in silhouette flanked by balancing downswept foliated scrolls. Bottom corners may be overlaid by bracket-like leafage scrolls.

Pine, gesso-coated and gilded or painted to simulate rosewood; or black walnut. A rosewood-finished or black walnut frame usually has narrow gilt beading around mirror panel. Much less expensive than the tall pier glass, and very popular. Produced in quantities by a growing number of frame factories. Plentiful. *Ca. 1855–1875.* AAA to BB

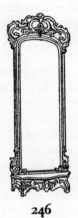

246

246. Tall Pier Glass

Like overmantel mirror in design, but much taller and narrower, measuring seven to nine feet tall by 30 to 42 inches wide. The one-piece panel of mirror glass is usually flat-arched at top and surrounded by a convex molding, plain or overlaid with foliated scrolls. Frame has elaborate top scroll-outlined pediment, 18 to 20 inches high, pierced and edged with intertwining foliated scrolls done in relief. At center there is either raised cartouche or a silhouetted panache. With some still more ornate examples a similarly decorated cresting takes the place of this pediment and is extended to include the valance cornices above the flanking windows as a single unit. At lower corners usually large overlaid S-shaped foliated scrolls, matching upper decorative details.

Frame rests on either a low projecting base with white marble top of demi-cartouche shape, or on a marble shelf of similar shape supported by ornamented brackets. Base about 16 inches tall. Molded cabriole front legs; deeply valanced and pierced skirt edged with raised foliated scrolls.

The drawing room of a handsomely furnished city mansion frequently has a matching pier glass and over-mantel mirror. Because of towering height, there is restricted demand for this type today.

A smaller and simpler pier glass, designed for less pretentious country homes and very usable today, has unornamented convex molded frame about three inches wide with flat arched top, made of pine gilded or of black walnut. Five to six feet tall, by 24 to 26 inches wide. *Ca. 1850–1870.* B to C

247. Eastlake Pier Glass

Six feet, six inches to eight feet tall by 30 to 36 inches wide. Rectangular flat frame surmounted by architectural molded cornice with small raised panels interrupted by central cartouche with raised panel and scroll-carved pendent finial. The top of this usually overlaps the serpentine, arched mirror panel slightly. Sides of frame have short molded and scrolled pilaster blocks at top and bottom, rest is faced with raised panels of burl veneer which may be ornamented with fine incised lines

of gilded scrolling. Mirror either has a low base molded
to match cornice or stands directly on floor.

Black walnut with burl-veneer trim or of maple ebon-

247

ized and ornamented with gilded incised scrolling and
small geometric details. Produced by furniture factories,
sometimes to match an Eastlake parlor set. *Ca. 1875–
1885.*

Eastlake Table Mirror

Design is same as preceding but about half as tall.
Mirror panel has either a flat arched or straight top.
Average size is three feet, six inches to four feet, six
inches tall by 24 to 26 inches wide. Made of black wal-
nut with burl-veneer trim and, sometimes, gilt scrolling.
Plentiful. *Ca. 1870–1885.* AAA to B

248. Rustic Mirror

Has rectangular frame, generally with a semicircular
arched top, naturalistically carved to simulate branches.

Top has silhouetted cresting of leaves flanked by curved twigs which continue down sides and terminate in pairs of matching pendent leaves. About 20 inches high by 14 inches wide.

248

Made in large quantities by furniture factories of black walnut, or other hardwoods stained to simulate it; used in homes furnished with cottage furniture. Plentiful. *Ca. 1865–1875.* A to AA

Melodeons and Early Pianos

DURING the nineteenth century, music invaded the American home to such an extent that ability to play some sort of keyboard instrument was considered an essential part of cultural training for a young woman. Consequently a parlor was not considered properly furnished if it lacked an instrument on which the daughter of the house could perform light classical pieces, Stephen Foster melodies or hymn tunes to entertain the family of an evening, during those years before the advent of phonograph, player piano or radio.

Victorians were partial to simplified organs known as "melodeons" or to the square piano, which at first was of spinet form.

Many of these keyboard instruments have survived, mostly in unplayable condition, and are used now as tables or decorative furniture. Sometimes one is found that has been converted into a desk by replacing keyboard and movement with compartments. With or without such alterations, their present-day use is primarily that of pieces of furniture and as such they are treated here. Construction of movement is outside the scope of this guide.

249. Early Melodeon

Is 28 to 32 inches tall, its case 34 to 40 inches wide by 20 to 24 inches deep and six to 10 inches high; has a slightly overhanging fold-over top. Also hinged at the rear; square corners, plain edge. At front a fixed flap, concealing keyboard. Sides of case are plain or have a slightly projecting banding at bottom, about two inches high, with upper edge beveled or trimmed with wavy molding.

Case usually supported by a pair of openwork trestles, scroll-cut and lyre-shaped and braced by a cyma-curved

249

stretcher. Pedals were attached at center. If supported by legs, these are octagon-shaped and tapering, having low turned collars at upper ends and circular molded feet, castered. Pedals were placed at the base of an openwork lyre-shaped frame.

Produced with four- to six-octave keyboard, infrequently double, by a considerable number of organ manufacturers such as Price & Company, Buffalo, New York; Prescott Brothers, Concord, New Hampshire; C. W. Fisk, Ansonia, Connecticut; and Estey of Brattleboro, Vermont. Rosewood veneered on pine, with lyre trestles and stretcher of maple painted and grained to simulate rosewood. Numerous to plentiful. *Ca. 1840–1870.* Case only, AA to B. Playable, B to BB

250

250. Spinet Piano

Popularly called a "spinet" to distinguish it from the larger square piano made later, this type was made in the United States some 20 years before the beginning of the Victorian Period. Characteristic details after 1840 include bands of wavy molding, lyre-shaped pedal frame and scrolled openwork music support. Is 30 to 34 inches tall with case four feet six inches to five feet wide by 24 to 26 inches deep and 10 to 12 inches high. Design and construction like that of the preceding melodion except that the keyboard flap is deeper and hinged. Slender, tapering, octagon legs; recessed lyre-shaped pedal frame.

Produced with five-octave keyboard by a number of early and little-known piano manufacturers who worked for brief periods in the larger cities of the Eastern Seaboard. Some examples of English origin.

Mahogany or of rosewood, veneered on pine. Not numerous. *Ca. 1840–1855.* Case only, AAA to BB. Playable, CC to CCC

251

251. Early Square Piano

Like the preceding in design and construction but notably larger, with heavier legs. Is 36 to 38 inches tall with case, five feet two inches to five feet 10 inches wide by 36 to 38 inches deep and 14 to 16 inches tall. Has same rectangular, fold-over top, with square or rounded front corners, plain or partially beveled edge and somewhat deeper keyboard flap. Base slightly projecting, about four inches high with upper edge beveled or banded with a convex or convex-concave molding. Tapering, octagon legs having turned collars at upper ends ending in low circular molded feet, castered, or by cabriole legs with carved cartouches at knees. Whorl feet that rest on octagon pads, castered. Increase in size of legs resulted from use of a cast-iron frame in the movement, which increased the weight of case materially.

Made with six-octave keyboard by a growing number of piano manufacturers, of whom Jonas Chickering of Boston was chief. Case more often rosewood than mahogany. Both veneered on pine; cabriole legs are of light softwood, painted and grained to simulate rosewood. A piano similar to the one pictured was in the White House during Abraham Lincoln's administration and he is said to have played it occasionally. *Ca. 1850–1875.* Case only, B to BB. Playable CC to #

252

252. Lyre-shaped Music Rack

Also called a "Canterbury" and so named for the English archbishop who first ordered a similar piece of furniture to be used for carrying plates, silver platters and the like. Is about 22 inches tall by 18 inches wide and 14 inches deep. An enclosed base is surmounted by a three-division rack with scroll-cut, lyre-shaped ends connected by baluster-turned cross-members and plain dividers. The enclosed base has a slightly overhanging top with outrounded corners and plain edge. At corners are spool-turned pilasters forming short baluster-turned legs ending in peg feet, or base may have plain corners and small block feet, castered.

Base contains full-width drawer about four inches deep that has a plain front fitted with mushroom-turned knobs.

Custom-made or produced by some factories. Considerable variation in details of design and construction. Some factory-made examples of the easel type that are all of turned parts.

Rosewood or black walnut or, less often, mahogany. Easel type black walnut or other native hardwoods in natural finish or stained brown or red. Numerous. *Ca. 1840–1880*. A to B

Section XVI

Papier-mâché and Lacquer Furniture

GREAT INTEREST in innovations in furniture and decorative household accessories was characteristic of the first ten or fifteen years of the Victorian Period both in England and in America. From various European and Oriental countries came new ideas, especially a vogue for black lacquer furniture ornately decorated with gilt stenciling, with flowers or landscapes done in naturalistic colors and with mother-of-pearl inlays.

This furniture was made of two materials, papier-mâché and wood of a close-grained kind such as maple or beech. Both were finished with fine black lacquer and then decorated. Designed chiefly for parlor or boudoir, these pieces remained in high favor from about 1840 to 1870.

Although it is known that the Litchfield Manufacturing Company of Connecticut made some tilt-top tables and pedestal work tables of this sort between 1850 and 1855, most papier-mâché furniture was imported from Birmingham, England, where Jennens & Bettridge were the leading makers. Pieces with a wood base were also imported, from England or France. In England such factories seem to have been mostly in Birmingham and Wolverhampton. In the United States lacquer furniture was the work of men trained abroad, who worked in the larger Eastern Seaboard cities.

Although papier-mâché and lacquer pieces are colorful furniture novelties they do not seem to appeal to many collectors. Hence there is little demand for such pieces and prices for them are consistently lower than average.

Special Comments on Papier-mâché Furniture

This substitute for wood is of Chinese origin and, as the name indicates, consists of chewed paper. Oriental boxes, trays, plates and the like were always in great demand in Europe and as early as 1750 such decorative accessories were produced and decorated in the Chinese manner at Birmingham, England. Here, in 1772, Henry Clay, a japanner by trade, patented a new process for making this material stronger and more resistant to heat and moisture.

Instead of chewed, water-soaked paper, pressed and dried in molds, the Clay process called for sheets of soft porous paper pasted together over a metal mold, oven-baked at over 100 degrees and then smoothed by files and rubbing with pumice stone. Other layers were added, and the process repeated until a usable thickness was reached. Then the shaped form was removed from the mold, immersed in a mixture of oil and spirits of tar, and rebaked at twice the earlier temperature. After a final smoothing with files and pumice, this piece of hard tough papier-mâché was japanned, usually a dense black, and was ready for decoration.

Through the ensuing years, some refinements and improvements were made, such as mother-of-pearl inlays, patented in 1825, and methods for forming larger structural parts. By about 1830, English manufacturers were making papier-mâché pieces of occasional furniture.

Decorating with gilt scrolls and strapwork was done by teams of girls; painting of flowers, birds, landscape vignettes and copies of genre art by professional artists.

Pedestals of tilt-top and work tables are of baluster-turned wood, finished with the same japanned ground color. The lower end of such a shaft is threaded, and screws into a nutlike block of wood embedded in the papier-mâché base, which usually has three or four cast-iron projecting feet screwed to its underside.

Chair legs may be of either papier-mâché or wood. Seat rails are consistently of wood except for the valanced front rail of some armchairs, which are of papier-mâché with mother-of-pearl inlays. Chair parts are joined by glued mortise-and-tenon joints.

Special Comments on Lacquer Furniture

Made to fill the same decorative needs as papier-mâché furniture, the superficial appearance of lacquer pieces is so close that it is doubtful whether the Victorian purchaser knew or cared whether he was getting one or the other.

In addition to the material, the difference is mainly one of weight. Papier-mâché pieces are lighter, more fragile. A tilt-top table top is noticeably thinner, about half an inch thick where a lacquer table is three-quarters to a full inch thick. Feet of lacquer tables are either turned or shaped brackets, never cast-iron.

Lacquer furniture is factory-made of wood and then finished in the same dense black ground coat as the papier-mâché. The decoration is gilt, generally stencil-done, combined with painted flowers or birds. With some pieces, notably chess tables, mother-of-pearl inlays are present.

Furniture pieces made of lacquered wood include small or large tables, sideboards, cabinets, beds, chairs.

253. Papier-mâché Side Chair

Two types of back: pierced and flaring; solid concave. Otherwise of similar design, finished in black with gilt and painted decoration and irregularly shaped mother-of-pearl inlays.

(1) Has a balloon-shaped back, with either large scroll-outlined piercings or a wreathlike grouping of small piercings, framing central panel generally painted with a landscape vignette.

(2) Has a solid, semicircular arched and concave back with scalloped edge, decorated with ornate gilt and painted scrolls that frame a central urn surmounted by exotic birds in bright colors.

Both have U-shaped seat, with slightly serpentined front, caned or upholstered. Front seat rail has valanced skirt connecting cabriole legs, with or without whorl feet. Skirt and knees are decorated with leafage scrolls, sometimes combined with small flowers in naturalistic colors. Rear legs square, tapering and canted.

Many such chairs of English provenance, the most elaborate being by Jennens & Bettridge. Probably made as a decorative occasional chair in pairs or sets of six for parlor or drawing room. Generally found today as single chair. Not numerous. *Ca. 1840–1865.* AA to AAA

253   **254**

254. Papier-mâché Armchair

About 40 inches tall by 24 inches wide and has semi-circular arched concave back rounded into scrolled sides. Decorated with gilt leafage scrolls, small flowers and trailing vines, including large central floral bouquet painted in naturalistic colors. Arm supports cyma-curved, have molded scrolls and terminate in leafage volutes.

Deep U-shaped upholstered seat with serpentine front. Conforming front seat rail has semicircular pendent finial. Boldly shaped cabriole front legs, whorl feet. Arm supports, seat rail and legs decorated with gilt stenciling in floral and leafage motifs enhanced by mother-of-pearl inlays. Rear legs plain, square and canted.

Probably of English or French provenance since American papier-mâché manufacturers did not attempt such large pieces in this medium. Not numerous. *Ca. 1845–1865.* AAA to B

255

255. Papier-mâché Tilt-top Table

Has either an oval top, 24 to 28 inches long by 20 to 24 inches wide, or circular one 24 to 30 inches in diameter. Oval top usually has convex molded edge and in center a copy in full colors of a contemporary genre painting (frequently a Landseer or Redgrave) framed by bands of shaped medallions done in gilt and enhanced by a pattern of irregular mother-of-pearl inlays.

The circular top has a central floral bouquet surrounded by a matching border in naturalistic colors, gilt and mother-of-pearl inlays. Top is hinged to a baluster-turned wooden pedestal. Circular base or rectangular one with incurved sides. Three painted iron feet, or four projecting wooden bracket feet, castered. Pedestal, base and feet decorated with gilt stenciling, matching that of the top. Chiefly of English provenance. *Ca. 1840–1865.* AA to B

256

256. Papier-mâché Work Table

General design and construction like preceding but has a rectangular workbox, about 18 inches long by 12 inches wide, in place of tilt-top. Box has a slightly overhanging lid with serpentine or scalloped edge and hinged top at rear decorated with either landscape panel or floral bouquet framed by gilt stenciling. Interior fitted for sewing aids. Sides of box have gilt-stenciled medallions. Pedestal baluster-turned; either circular or trilateral molded base; three low bun-like feet. Probably English provenance. Not as numerous as similar tilt-top tables. *Ca. 1840–1865.* AAA to BB

257

257. Lacquer Side Chair

Light, decorative chair with open concave back. Flat arched top rail surmounting flaring and rounded uprights; scroll-outlined, fret-pierced vertical splat supported by a shaped cross-rail. Back decorated with painted flowers and foliage, and gilt scrolls and mother-of-pearl inlays.

Upholstered rectangular seat, flaring, with serpentined front and conforming seat rail. Slender, angular cabriole front legs; rudimentary feet.

Legs and seat rail decorated to match back. Rear legs square, canted, plain.

Made in pairs or sets of six of beech, maple or other close-grained hardwoods finished in black lacquer with gilt and colored decoration enhanced by mother-of-pearl inlays. Some made in America but majority English or possibly French. More often found as single chairs today. Not numerous. *Ca. 1840–1855.* AA to AAA

258

258. Lacquer Armchair

Design of Louis XV substyle. Made of same material and similarly decorated as the preceding, it is about 42 inches tall by 24 inches wide. Back has a wide, serpentine, arched rounded top rail and cyma-curved uprights, decorated with gilt foliage scrolls, small painted flowers and mother-of-pearl inlays framing cartouche-shaped upholstered panel. Arms of elaborate open scroll-work, surmounted by broad rectangular arm pads.

Upholstered seat, rectangular, flaring, with straight front. Seat rails valanced. Front cabriole legs terminate in whorl or rudimentary feet. Rear legs plain, square, with backward cyma-curve. Open arms, seat rails and knees of cabriole legs decorated to match the back.

Beech, maple or other close-grained hardwood and finished in black lacquer with decoration of gilt scrolls,

sometimes combined with small painted flowers and
mother-of-pearl inlays. Probably English or French
provenance. Not numerous. *Ca. 1840–1855.* AAA to B

259

259. Lacquer Occasional Table

Oval or round top, 26 by 20 inches or 20 to 36 in
diameter; rounded or molded rim; gilt-decorated, with
floral bouquet in center done in naturalistic colors, or
inset black-and-white chess squares framed by floral
lunettes. Baluster-turned or tapering vase-shaped pedestal,
mounted on (1) tripod of cyma-curved, scroll-cut legs,
either uprolled or turned peg feet; (2) rectangular or
triangular plinth base, with concave sides and low feet;
(3) quatrefoil-shaped base with molded edges; projecting down-curved bracket feet, castered. With triangular base feet are turned and bun-shaped; with rectangular,
they are concave brackets, usually castered.

Maple, beech or other close-grained woods finished in black lacquer. Probably English origin. *Ca. 1840–1855.* AAA to BB

260

260. Lacquer Tilt-top Table

Construction and design similar to papier-mâché tilt-top table (*see No. 255*) but wood. Has circular top, 24 to 42 inches in diameter, with plain rounded edge or an ornate scalloped edge with units of design repeated eight to 12 times on its circumference. Decoration of top varies; may consist of central bouquet of flowers or of peacock perched on a curved tree-trunk surrounded by flowers and foliage in naturalistic colors. Rim ornamented by either a floral wreath or repeating stencil decoration in gilt.

Baluster-turned pedestal mounted on circular base, scrolled outline, supported by projecting cyma-curved feet. Pedestal, base and feet decorated with gilt stenciling in scroll-and-foliage motifs, sometimes enhanced by mother-of-pearl inlays. Total height from 27 to 30 inches.

Beech, maple or other close-grained hardwoods finished in black lacquer. Probably of English provenance. *Ca. 1840–1855.* B to BBB

261

261. Lacquer Cabinet Sideboard

Is 54 to 58 inches tall by 42 to 48 inches wide and 18 to 20 inches deep; has triple-arched and scrolled full-width pediment with shallow serpentine shelf at rear of rectangular top.

Top slightly overhanging with rounded or concave molded edge and rounded front corners. Carcase has solid sides, conforming front corners and is enclosed by a pair of nearly full-width doors. These have rectangular, slightly sunk panels; inner stile of right-hand one is fitted with an inset metal surround. Interior has one or two fixed shelves with rounded front edges. Plinth base has molded upper edge and rounded front corners.

Pediment, top, sides and door panels are decorated with floral bouquets and sprays, done in naturalistic colors and gold-stenciled rococo foliations. Doorframes and frieze have matching stenciling of gilt. Close-grained hardwood finished with black lacquer. Probably of English provenance. Unusual. *Ca. 1845–1855.* B to BBB

Section XVII

Cast-iron Furniture

USE OF IRON in place of wood by furniture craftsmen originated in the Latin countries of Europe, where iron and wood were combined in many handsome pieces. Later a good number of beds were made entirely of iron, indirect forerunners of the iron and brass beds produced in such quantities in America during the closing years of the nineteenth century and the first decade of the twentieth.

There is an important difference between the sixteenth-century pieces of Europe and those made here during the Victorian Period. With the European, only *wrought* iron was used, the work of blacksmiths, with each part formed individually according to the eye and skill of the smith. American iron furniture was constructed of *cast* parts; it was the work of iron founders, duplicated as many times as desired.

About 1830, cast-iron building units, columns, fronts and such architectural ornaments as grilles for doorways and balconies came into wide use, the best-known being those of New Orleans. From these to garden furniture was a logical step. France and England already had garden settees, chairs and tables of the more expensive wrought iron, which doubtless gave the American iron founders their inspiration.

One of the first manufacturers of cast-iron garden furniture was Robert Wood of Philadelphia, who published an impressive catalogue of his designs in the 1840's, promptly copied by other iron founders. By 1860 such furniture was being made by small local foundries in all sections, even as far west as California, since its weight deterred long-distance shipment. But thanks to Robert Wood's catalogue of designs, the patterns were more or less standard.

About 1855, cast-iron furniture for indoors appeared. Foliated hatracks, umbrella stands, cabriole-legged center tables, beds, mirror frames, fire screens and plant stands were made. Only the bed gained long-time acceptance.

Special Comments on Cast-iron Furniture

All pieces were in parts held together by iron bolts. Parts were cast in sand molds, by iron foundries. The patterns used to form the molds were of carved wood, which were impressed in the sand and then removed before the molten metal was poured in. The entire process was one that lent itself to mass production at low price. After a part had been cast and was cool, the two-part sand mold was opened and the casting removed, the casting tangs cut off and then cleaned of sand in a tumbling barrel.

The requisite parts for any piece were assembled and bolted together. Ordinary iron bolts with countersunk heads were used. Garden furniture was given an annual coat of paint to prevent rusting. Pieces for indoor use were painted more carefully, black with gilding or in colors simulating either rosewood or black walnut. Since they were designed as a substitute for the more costly pieces of the Louis XV substyle, their form and decorative details were of the same rococo type.

Patterns found in garden settees, chairs and tables, in order of popularity, are: grape, lily of the valley, fern and scroll.

Since cast-iron is brittle enough to break more readily than is generally realized, pieces of such furniture should be handled carefully. In buying a piece it is wise to look it over well for repairs, such as broken pieces that have been welded into place. Traces of such work can be seen on the reverse of a part so mended. Obviously a piece with several welding patches is not as desirable as one that did not require such repairs and should be priced accordingly.

About ten years ago, cast-iron furniture making was revived. It is now made mostly in the grape pattern, by foundries in Alabama and Ohio, as new furniture. Sometimes, for ease in handling, aluminum alloy is used in place of iron.

GARDEN FURNITURE

262. Grape Pattern Chair

Chair is about 30 inches tall and has a concave, nearly semicircular flaring back with a pierced stylized design composed of bunches of grapes, leaves and tendrils. Circular seat, about 20 inches in diameter, latticed in a geometric motif, has deep pierced skirt of grape, leaf and tendril design matching that of back. Three leaf-form scrolled legs, terminating in conforming projecting feet and braced by a triform rod stretcher. One of the most popular designs and fairly plentiful. *Ca. 1845–1870.* AAA to B

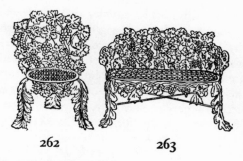

262   263

263. Grape Pattern Settee

Matching settee is about 30 inches tall by 44 inches long with slightly arched back and ends which curve forward to form downswept arms. Rectangular latticed seat; legs braced by an X-shaped stretcher. *Ca. 1845–1870.* AAA to BB

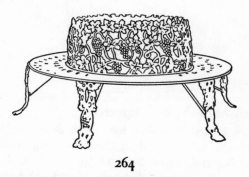

264

264. Grape Pattern Round-a-Tree Settee

Adjustable for a tree trunk six to 32 inches in diameter. Slightly sloping circular back about 16 inches tall, made in concave sections with a pierced design of grapes, leaves and scrolled tendrils. The circular seat, made in corresponding sections, is latticed in geometric motif and supported by six equally spaced scrolled legs in grape-leaf-and-tendril pattern with projecting leaf-shaped feet; legs braced by plain sloping bar brackets.

May also have been made in other designs matching other pieces of garden furniture. Is the scarcest of all pieces of cast-iron garden furniture. *Ca. 1845–1870.* BBB to C

265

265. Lily-of-the-Valley Armchair

Has an arched horseshoe back with downswept arms pierced in a balancing design of flowering lily-of-the-valley stalks and leaves. Straight front legs, with small hoof feet; rear legs in leaf design, canted. Also made in same design as a settee, about 60 inches long. *Ca. 1845–1870.* AAA to B

266

266. Fern Pattern Settee

Slightly arched back pierced in a balancing fern design supported by intertwining stems. Ends curved forward to form downswept arms joined to arched, trestle-like supports, done in matching fern design but with less piercing. Rectangular seat latticed in an arabesque motif; bowed front.

Settee about 32 inches tall, four feet to five feet eight inches long. Matching armchair also found in this pattern. Not as numerous as the grape pattern. *Ca. 1845–1870.* B to BB

267. Scroll Pattern Settee

Has triple-arch, pierced back of bold interlacing scrolls in balancing pattern framing central pendent bunch of grapes. Ends curve forward and form full-height arms. Rectangular seat has rounded ends, is latticed in geometric motif and has deep pierced skirt of valancing cyma-curved scrolls flanking central leafage cartouche. Four scroll-outlined, slightly concave legs, with grape-

and-leafage medallions at upper ends. Rudimentary scrolled feet, X-shaped rod stretcher.

267

Settee is about 34 inches tall by four feet long and has matching armchair. Design reflects Louis XV substyle. Not numerous. *Ca. 1860–1870.* B to BB

268. Garden Pedestal Table

Designed for use with foregoing chairs and settee. There is some variation in details of design, but all include circular top, pedestal shaft, shaped base. Table is 28 to 32 inches in diameter and about 28 inches tall. Circular top is finely pierced and has a scalloped rim. Design of top may be (1) allover arabesque geometric or scrolled or (2) central medallion surrounded by signs of the Zodiac or by scrolls. Supporting shaft is either three-sided, knopped, and shell-molded or baluster-shaped. Trilateral molded base with low projecting feet, or circular one.

An undamaged example is unusual. Generally found with small parts of top missing or repaired by welding. *Ca. 1845–1870.* AAA to BB

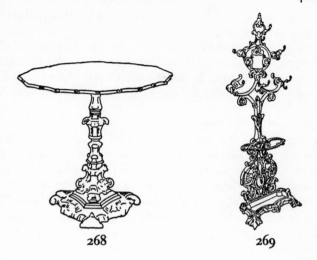

268   269

HOUSE FURNITURE

269. Hatrack

Six to seven feet tall with top of open balancing leafage scrolls to which are attached seven cyma-curved garment hooks and small cartouche-shaped mirror. Pilaster-like short shaft above larger cartouche-shaped plinth of ornate intertwining and balanced pierced scrolls. At bottom of shaft a projecting, scroll-formed loop for holding umbrellas and canes. Rectangular base with serpentine front and scrolled front feet; a conforming drip pan made of sheet iron. Maximum width 26 to 34 inches, depth eight to 12 inches.

Details of design vary. May reflect Gothic or Louis XV substyles. Some examples simple, others ornate, but all have top equipped with garment hooks and umbrella loop and drip pan.

Cast iron painted black with gilding, dark green, or brown to simulate black walnut. Examples painted white or some light color have been refinished. Not as numerous as garden chairs and settees. *Ca. 1850–1870.* AAA to B

Wall Mirror Hatrack

Scroll-designed frame about 36 to 42 inches wide, by 26 to 32 inches tall. Attached to frame and flanking mirror are six to eight cyma-curved, bracket-like garment hooks. Generally placed on a hall wall near entrance, usually with table beneath. Cast iron painted black with gilding, or brown to simulate black walnut. Not as numerous as preceding hatrack. *Ca. 1850–1870.* A to AA

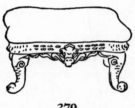

270

270. Upholstered Footstool

Upholstery-covered, slightly overhanging wooden top, about 12 inches long by eight inches deep, sometimes slightly outrounded corners. Conforming cast-iron base with scrolled and pierced valanced skirt. Four short cabriole legs with scrolled knees; rudimentary or whorl feet. From six to eight inches tall. Painted black with gilding, or brown to simulate black walnut or rosewood. Made by Clark Brothers of Boston or other iron founders specializing in iron furniture. *Ca. 1850–1865.* A to AA

Center Table with Marble Top

Has same design as rosewood Marble-top Center Table (*see No. 118*), being produced as less expensive and more durable substitute. Marble top is cartouche-shaped or oval, with concave molded edge; rests on cast-iron frame of conforming shape. Scrolled and pierced valanced skirt and four incurved cabriole legs with ornately scrolled knees; rudimentary feet, castered. Legs are braced by cyma-curved X-shaped stretcher with leafage medallion at center. Frame made in sections and bolted together. Painted to simulate black walnut or rosewood. Made by Clark Brothers, Boston. *Ca. 1850–1860.* B to BB

271

271. Cast-iron Bed

Identical headboard and footboard, 34 to 38 inches tall; elaborately scrolled openwork enclosed by a shaped frame which extends to floor forming either short cabriole or straight legs. Openwork is balancing C-shaped, S-shaped and cyma-curved scrolls that frequently surround large centered lyres or circular medallions. Headboard and footboard are connected by scrolled openwork sidepieces, generally with valanced lower edges. Bed is six feet four inches long by three feet six inches wide. Originally equipped with either longitudinal or cross slats of wood. Painted black with gilding, dark green, or brown to simulate rosewood or black walnut. A forerunner of iron and brass beds in vogue at close of nineteenth century. Not numerous. *Ca. 1845–1880 or later.* B to BB

272

272. Patriotic Mirror Frame

Designed for oval glass. About 14 inches tall by 10 inches wide, surmounted by a spread-eagle finial on cresting of balanced openwork (C-shaped scrolls with leafage embellishments). This frames a circular portrait medallion of General William T. Sherman. At bottom of concave molded frame is a pendent Stars and Stripes shield, flanked by laurel sprays supporting furled flags. Both eagle and portrait medallion gilded; shield and flags painted red, white and blue; rest of frame black, scrolls touched with gilt. Design commemorates General Sherman's early military victories. Similar mirror frames with portrait medallion of other public citizens occasionally found.

Made of cast iron; probably Pennsylvania origin. Interesting rather than rare. Bears patent date of 1862 on back. *Ca. 1860–1876.* A to AA

Pole Fire Screen

Rectangular glazed frame about 16 inches tall by 10 inches wide; contains a decorative needlework panel. Surmounted by openwork scrolled cresting; edged by narrow band of pierced leafage; at bottom, branching openwork leafage scrolls.

Frame is supported by an adjustable rod, about an inch in diameter, which slides up and down within the pedestal base and is secured by a decorative thumbscrew.

Pedestal base is a columnar shaft surmounting the figure of a little girl in contemporary dress. She stands on a molded socle with concave base of raised leafage supported by projecting scrolled feet, placed diagonally.

Painted black with gilding, or brown to simulate either rosewood or black walnut. Not numerous. *Ca. 1860–1875.* AA to AAA.

273. Conservatory Plant Stand

Central rodlike shaft about five feet tall, surmounted by a ribbed hemispherical bowl with convex, slightly overhanging conforming rim. Shaft supports two adjust-

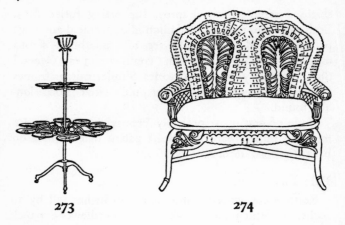

273   274

able, circular dish-like rests for potted plants supported by radial braces trimmed with open-work scrolls. Upper shelf has eight rests, lower one 10 that are slightly larger.

Four low-arched cabriole legs. Rudimentary feet, castered. Plain cast iron. *Ca. 1865–1880.* AAA to B

Wirework Plant Stand

Rectangular traylike top, 30 to 36 inches long by 16 to 18 inches wide; bowed or straight ends, low latticed gallery. Sometimes has slightly smaller secondary top, raised above it about 10 inches by extensions of the rod-like legs.

Legs are about three quarters of an inch in diameter, straight; often flanked on all four sides by large, triangular openwork brackets decorated with spiral wire scrolls. Legs are braced near floor by a combination box and X-shaped stretcher. Iron wire painted black, details

touched with gilt; dark green; brown. *Ca. 1850–1880.*
A to AA

274. Wicker Garden Settee

Is about 46 inches tall by 40 inches wide. Back has
either a balancing openwork scrolled cresting or a serpentine, arched and boldly rolled continuous one, downswept in cyma-curves to form slightly recessed arms. This
frames a double chair back, formed of balancing C-shaped
and S-shaped scrolls or balancing branching scrolls in
two balloon-shaped units surrounded by basket-woven
bands.

Space beneath arms filled by conforming scrolls of
geometric latticing. Cane seat is rectangular with rounded
ends, slightly bowed front. It may be plain or have a
valanced skirt done of basket weaving flanked by cyma-
curved scrolls. Four slender round legs—front ones
cabriole, rear plain but slightly canted—braced by
X-shaped stretcher. Legs and stretcher wrapped with
lengths of narrow split reed or rattan. Made of reed,
willow or peeled rattan, finish natural or painted. Generally has removable cushion. May be accompanied by
matching armchair. Seldom found in perfect condition.
Ca. 1850–1880. B to BB

SECTION XVIII

Handles

WITH Victorian pieces, as with earlier furniture, nothing enhances the appearance so much as proper handles. Yet they are among the decorative details most apt to disappear through two or more generations of use or misguided efforts to "modernize" a piece by replacing the original ones with others of later design.

Therefore, as a guide to selecting proper replacements for a piece which lacks the fittings it started out with, the principal kinds and designs of handles and keyhole escutcheons are described and the substyle in which they were used identified.

Replacements, especially of leaf-carved wooden handles, mushroom-turned knobs, and brass pendent-ring or bail handles, are available; sometimes a furniture repairer has sets of the other designs, salvaged from pieces that did not merit extensive repairs. Proper handles therefore can usually be found if one is willing to take the trouble to look for them.

Original handles on Victorian pieces were of two sorts — wooden and brass.

WOODEN HANDLES

275. Mushroom-turned Knob

Shaped like a mushroom button, and attached by a screw inserted at the rear. From an inch in diameter for

275

small interior drawers or a desk or secretary, to two and a half inches in diameter and projecting about an inch for a full-size drawer.

Maple, black walnut, rosewood or mahogany, used on pieces of the Transitional, Gothic and Spool-turned sub-styles as well as those of the Cottage type.

276

276. Rosette Knob

So turned that projecting knob is surrounded by a bead-molded rosette. All of one piece of wood. The knob itself is about an inch in diameter, has a beaded rim and projects about an inch. Rosette about two and a half inches in diameter, with double or triple beaded rim. Is attached like the preceding.

Mahogany, rosewood, black walnut or maple ebonized; used on pieces of the Louis XV, Renaissance and, occasionally, Louis XVI substyles.

277

277. Leaf-carved Handle

Design is of two leaves (usually grape) flanking a pendent plum, pear or small bunch of grapes. Lower edge has finger grip cut out behind the face. Varies in width from three to seven inches. Attached by screws from rear.

Most frequently black walnut or maple but also rosewood or mahogany. Used mostly on pieces of the Renaissance and Louis XV substyles.

278. Carved Looped Strap Handle

Realistically carved to resemble projecting semicircular loop of leather strap with buckle, punched holes and restraining loop. From six to eight inches long. Central loop is open at the rear and about three inches across. Attached at rear by screws. Black walnut; used on pieces of the Renaissance substyle.

278   **279**

279. Metal Keyhole Surround

Made of brass or cast iron. When inset, serves as a protecting internal rim for the shaped keyhole cut in drawer front or door stile. About an inch high and half as wide.

Used on pieces of Transitional, Gothic, Spool-turned sub-styles as well as many of the Cottage type.

280. Wooden Keyhole Rosette

Circular, from one to two inches in diameter. Single or double beaded rim, slightly raised, frames keyhole.

Mahogany, rosewood, black walnut or maple stained or ebonized. Used with various styles of handles on pieces of the Louis XV, Renaissance and Louis XVI substyles.

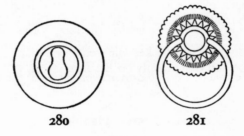

280   281

BRASS HANDLES

281. Pendent-ring Handle

Made of cast and stamped brass, bright finish or oxidized or nickel-plated. Has a pendent ring about an inch and a half in diameter hanging from plain round post, and has either a square chased plate placed diagonally or a circular one with scalloped rim and plain bead molding surrounding a conventionalized wreath. Plate is either an inch and a quarter square or an inch and a half in diameter. Keyhole escutcheon matches the plate of handle in shape and design.

Used only on Eastlake pieces.

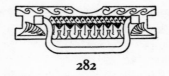

282

282. Shaped Bail Handle

Like the preceding, made of bright, oxidized or nickel-plated cast and stamped brass. Has angular or curved bail retained by two plain circular posts and a rectangular-shaped plate with a variety of chased designs. Complete handle from three and a half to four and a half inches wide.

Used with a smaller keyhole escutcheon matching plate in shape and design, only on Eastlake pieces.

283

283. Pendent Pear-shaped Knob

Combination of brass and wood. The pendent pear-shaped knob is of turned wood and is about an inch and a half in diameter. It is pierced by a metal rod and held in place by small acorn-shaped brass nut which also serves as decorative finial. Upper end of rod swivel-joined to post, so that knob hangs pendent. Post passes through a flaring and projecting rosette about an inch and a half in diameter with geometric chased decoration. Keyhole escutcheon is a flat rosette with design matching the plate of the handle.

Used only on Eastlake pieces of better quality.

Section **XIX**

Woods Used

THE Victorian Period is often considered the era of rosewood and black walnut. Certainly they were the two favored woods for good to fine furniture. But there were twelve others consistently used by cabinetmakers, custom shops and factories.

Among these were butternut, ash, maple and oak — from which complete pieces were made. Of the softwoods, pine held the lead and was the material for much of the painted Cottage furniture.

Since some knowledge of the different woods used during this period can be useful in placing a piece as to its substyle and kinds, the characteristics of all fourteen woods are briefly summarized:

Ash

A heavy wood of great strength; grain and texture similar to oak. Finished color a light cream. Used for Mid-Victorian bedroom sets with black walnut trim.

Basswood

A light, straight-grained softwood. In unfinished state, acquires a brownish-yellow tone with age. Chiefly used for interior parts.

Birch (Yellow)

Very hard; close-fibered as maple, but with more pattern of grain. Takes high polish. Finished color ranges from light brown to amber. Sometimes found with curly grain and used decoratively for table tops, skirts and drawer fronts of all-birch pieces. Some turned parts of chairs are of birch. Chiefly used by country cabinetmakers and small factories.

Butternut

Hard and close-grained, it takes excellent polish. Color when finished is very light brown. Also called "white walnut," but finer in texture. (Both trees are of same botanical family.) Used by cabinetmakers and early factories of the Middle West until about 1865.

Cherry

Very hard and close-grained with visible but not pronounced pattern. Sometimes finely flaked when quartersawed. Takes high polish. Reddish-brown color when finished, which approaches that of mahogany. Wide boards often have a yellowish streak of sapwood at one side. Sometimes found with curly grain, less pronounced than that of maple. Used for some of the later pieces of the Eastlake substyle of the better grade. Also used by country cabinetmakers for pieces of the Transitional substyle.

Chestnut

Medium hardwood with large pores; distinct pattern of grain. Somewhat resembles oak. Takes good polish.

Warm, mellow brownish yellow when finished. Used by factories for popular-priced beds and bedroom sets in the Eastlake substyle.

Mahogany

Tropical wood of great strength, hardness and firm texture, with a variety of grain and figures depending on location in tree and method of sawing. Takes high polish. Color varies from deep reddish brown to red with brown undertone, according to the finishing.

Used by cabinetmakers and cabinet shops for furniture of the Transitional, Gothic, and Louis XV substyles. Was replaced as top quality cabinetwood by rosewood shortly after 1840. Crotch-grain veneer, used for the decorative quality of its markings, comes from crotch of the two main branches. Veneering of entire pieces prevailed during the Transitional substyle.

Maple

Very hard, close-grained, with distinct fineness of fiber and pores. Takes a high polish. Color when finished varies from light brownish yellow to a rich amber. There are three varieties — straight-grained, curly and bird's-eye. The straight-grained has even texture without distinctive markings, except for a fine flaking when so sawed as to present a cross section cut of the annual growth rings. Curly markings vary from random twists to those that alternate so regularly as to be described as "tiger-striped." Bird's-eye markings consist of small, closely placed, knotlike whorls. Straight-grained maple was used for simpler pieces in all the substyles, especially spool-turned beds and turned spindle-back chairs.

Curly maple and bird's-eye maple were used decoratively for gallery pieces and desk interiors. Was not used for entire pieces, except as veneer for late factory-made bureaus and other case pieces.

Oak

Very strong hardwood with visible pores and distinct pattern of grain that can be intensified by quarter-sawing. Takes high polish. Was used for some late random pieces in the Eastlake substyle, made locally.

Pine (Southern Hard)

Strong, relatively hard with a pronounced grain of alternating clear and pitch wood, it takes a fine polish. Finished, it is a light brown with reddish pitch stripes. Used for occasional pieces locally made from Virginia south and west to Kentucky. Used for some Lazy Susan tables and hunt boards.

Pine (White)

Sometimes called "pumpkin pine." A straight-grained softwood available in wide knot-free boards. Finished, color can vary from a warm yellow to a light amber. Widely used for backboards, drawersides, backs and bottoms of case pieces, for unseen structural parts, tops of simple tables and headboards of four-post beds. Used in large quantities for Cottage bedroom sets by factories.

Cupboards and other simple country pieces were made of pine; was standard wood for Windsor chair and Boston rocker seats, for seats of painted benches and painted chairs. Also used for gilded mirror frames and was the base wood for mahogany and rosewood veneered pieces.

Rosewood

Very hard brittle, fine-grained wood. Takes a high polish. Of a red-purplish color when finished. Sometimes has streaks that are a deep old ivory in color. Comes from forests of Brazil. When freshly cut, logs have an odor much like that of roses, hence the name. Much elaborate furniture of rosewood was made during first twenty-five years of the Victorian period, such as the laminated pieces by Belter.

Satinwood

Hard fine-grained dense wood, quarter-sawed to accentuate the fire of its grain, which is often very curly. Takes high polish, satiny and lustrous, light honey-yellow when finished. Used for interiors of fine desks and secretaries and also for custom-made bedroom sets trimmed with rosewood carvings and moldings.

Walnut

Strong hardwood of fine texture and handsome grain. Sometimes has pleasing curly grain. Color finished warm reddish brown to chocolate brown known as "black walnut." This tone was achieved by treating it with a stain or acid wash before varnishing. Black walnut was used throughout Victorian Period for all types of furniture, especially after 1850, by both cabinetmakers and factories.

Suggested Books on American Victorian Furniture

American Antique Furniture, Edgar G. Miller, Jr.
* *Art Decoration Applied to Furniture*, Harriet Prescott Spofford
* *A Day at the New York Crystal Palace and How to Make the Most of It*, William Carey Richards
Decorative Art of Victoria's Era, Frances Lichten
* *Dickinson's Comprehensive Pictures of the Great Exhibition of 1851* (The London Crystal Palace Exposition)
The Encyclopedia of Furniture, Joseph Aronson
Field Guide to Early American Furniture, Thomas H. Ormsbee
* *Illustrated Catalogue of the Centennial Exposition*, Philadelphia, Thomas Bentley
How to Know American Antiques, Alice Winchester
* *Hints on Household Taste in Furniture, Upholstery and Other Details*, Charles Lock Eastlake
Victoria Royal, Rita Wellman
Victorian Furniture, Ruth and Larry Freeman
Victorian, the Cinderella of Antiques, Carl W. Drepperd
* *The World of Science, Art and Industry in the New York Exhibition* (Crystal Palace), Benjamin Silliman, Jr., and Charles P. Goodrich

* Out of print; consult Public Library reference books.